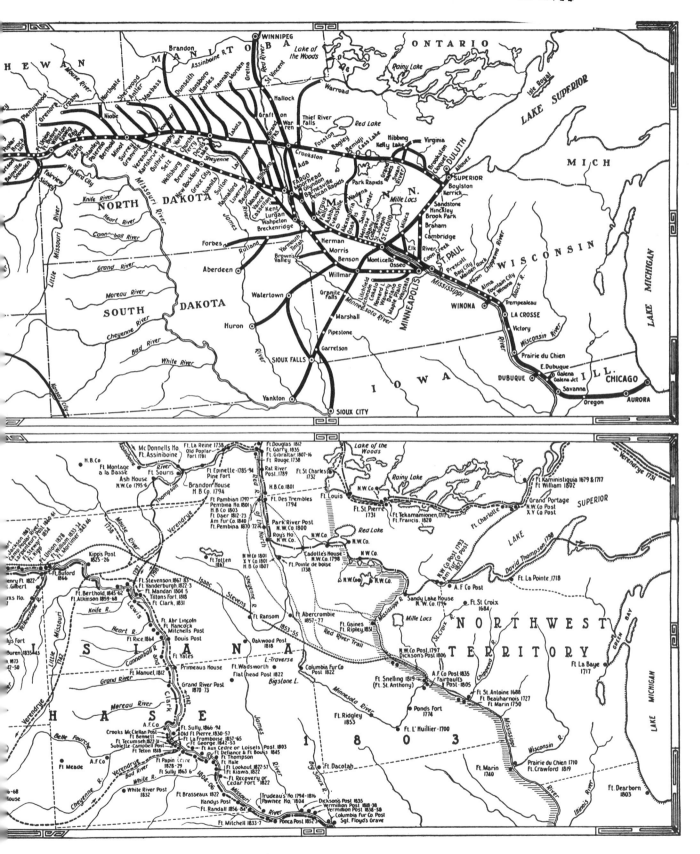

Charles R. Wood
Dorothy May Wood

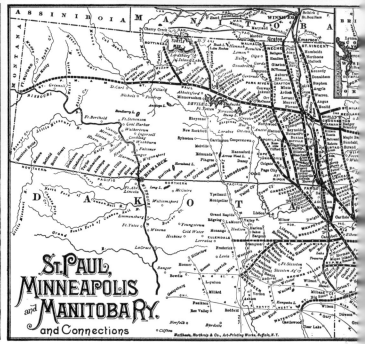

THE GREAT NORTHERN RAILWAY

A Pictorial Study by Charles & Dorothy Wood

Published by Pacific Fast Mail

Great Northern train on Loop near Scenic, Washington

© 1979
Pacific Fast Mail
Edmonds, Washington
All Rights Reserved
Library of Congress #77-91780

Book design/cover illustration "The Empire Builder" Mike Pearsall
Illustrations Mike Pearsall/Howard Fogg

Printed by Evergreen Press, Vancouver, Canada
Typography by K&H Printers, Everett, WA

Dedication

To the hill crews of the Great Northern and Burlington Northern

Charles R. Wood
Seattle, Washington 1978

Acknowledgements

The authors wish to thank the following people who gave their time and effort, and most importantly their material. They are:

From the railroad John Budd, Pat Stafford, Kim Forman, Pete Volkert, Walt Grecula, Charles Rasmussen, Bob Smith, Tom Hoff, Stan Thorsen, Bill Race, James Norvell, Jim Frederickson and Arnold Sundquist.

Dr. George Fischer, Ed Traficante, Wayne Olsen, Phillip C. Johnson, Dick Harris, Wally Swanson, W. R. McGee, Mallory Hope Ferrell, Harold K. Vollrath, Charles Felstead, Dr. Phil Hastings, W. R. Wilkinson,

Stan Styles, Bob Oestreich, Casey Adams, Myron Gilbertson, Claude Witt, Paul Woolgar, Mrs. Lee Pickett, Mrs. Joe F. Gaynor, Charles G. Nelson, The Strandrud family, Walt Thayer, Vic Olson, Ed Mueller, John Coleman, Dale Suit, Sid Goodrich, Harry Searles, Howard Durfy, Fred Spurrell, Walt Mendenhall, Gordon Rogers, Martin Erickson, Phil Kohl. Jim Vyverberg, Warren Wing, Joe Williamson, James S. Harker, Stanley H. Gray, Howard Fogg, W.C. Whittaker

Bob Morton, U. S. Forest Service, Bev Russell, Seattle Times. Charlie Martin, Stan Townsend and

Ken Middleton, Fraternal Order of Empire Builders.

Oregon Historical Society.
Tom Ward, Army Corps of Engineers. Ed Nolan, Archivist, Museum of History & Industry. Edwin L. Rothfuss and Betsy Graft, Glacier Park Natural History Association.

Washington State Dept. of Commerce. The Everett Herald. The Wenatchee Daily World. Coffins Old West Gallery.

J. Foster Adams photos, courtesy Carl Ulrich, Mid-Continent Ry. Museum and Wisconsin State Historical Society. Miner Enterprises, Inc.

John Ritchie, President, Northwest Railfan Group, Minnesota Historical Society, British Columbia Provincial Archives, Vancouver Public Library, Everett Public Library, Okanogan Historical Society. Seattle Public Library, Spokane Valley Historical Society, Eastern Washington State Historical Society and Trans Union Corp.

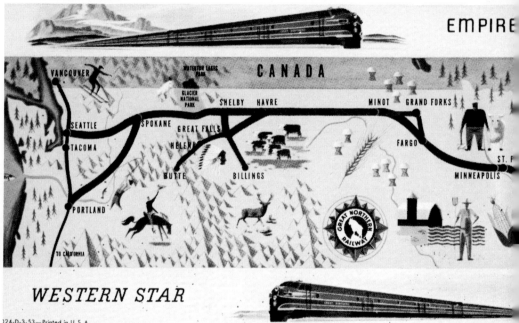

EMPIRE

WESTERN STAR

024-D-3-53—Printed in U. S. A.

Table of Contents

I The Great Adventure 12

II Glacier National Park and the Great Northern Railway 72

III Conquering the Cascades 128

IV More than Mountains 250

V Oriental Limited/Empire Builder 290

VI Steam: from Prairie to Tidewater...374

VII Omaha Orange, Cascade Green and Big Sky Blue . . . the Diesels.......................466

Appendix 544

Roster of Motive Power 548

Bibliography...556

Index..558

Presidents of the Great Northern

James J. Hill
1890-1907

Louis W. Hill, Sr.
1907-1912, 1914-1919

Carl R. Gray
1912-1914

Ralph Budd
1919-1931

William P. Kenney
1932-1939

Frank J. Gavin
1939-1951

John M. Budd
1951-1970

Foreword

Although Great Northern Railway was not officially established until September 18, 1889, its genesis began years earlier in the hopes and dreams of its founder, James J. Hill.

He was a man of remarkable qualities, whose vision was matched by deeds. Hill's dramatic venture into railroading and his achievements in building this nation's northernmost transcontinental line earned for him the accolade of Empire Builder. In an era when the industry's fortunes were often capricious, Great Northern, guided by Mr. Hill's enlightened managerial talents and spurred by his tireless energy, laid an enduring steel trail across northern rivers, plains and mountains to the Pacific Coast.

Mr. Hill was unswerving in his dedication to the goal of developing the resources of the area his railroad served. Unlike other lines that had been built west of the Mississippi, Great Northern, neither sought nor received subsidies or large grants of land but acquired state grants with the purchase of predecessor lines in Minnesota.

In 1878 Mr. Hill acquired the St. Paul and Pacific and the First Division, St. Paul and Pacific. He reorganized these properties in 1879 as the St. Paul, Minneapolis and Manitoba Railway Company. Neither that line nor its successor, Great Northern, was ever in receivership—a fate that overtook many other railroads in the Northwest.

Hill's main premise was that Great Northern could not prosper unless its territory prospered. That concept successfully guided GN throughout its 81-year history.

Great Northern literally settled much of the territory it traversed, villages and towns springing up at points where the railway built depots and established engine and train facilities. Its agents in Europe provided a steady stream of immigrants seeking opportunities to own land and make a better life for their families by tilling the rich soils of the northern plains. Immigrants also helped push GN rails westward and many first and second generation offspring of these pioneers found permanent employment with the company.

Under the travel slogan it developed, "See America First," the railway attracted passengers from the densely populated areas of the nation to the fine vacation lands within its territory. Great Northern became synonymous with excellent passenger trains. The Oriental Limited and its successor, the Empire Builder, enjoyed international renown. The railway maintained the highest level of train service possible long after passenger trains had begun incurring staggering deficits.

Great Northern was quick to apply the advances of technology to its operations. It was a leader in the adoption of diesel locomotives and in the early use of electronic computers. When it built Gavin Yard at Minot, N.D., there was no electronic classification yard in the nation more modern. In the 1920's, the Cascade Tunnel, longest rail bore in the western hemisphere and an engineering marvel, was built to improve the main line crossing of the Cascade Mountains.

When Mr. Hill retired from the railway in 1912 he said: "Most men who have really lived have had, in some shape, their great adventure. This railway is mine." Others also found their own great adventure with Great Northern; thousands of dedicated, loyal employees spent their working careers in the service of the company.

Great Northern ceased to exist when it became a component of Burlington Northern, a new and exciting transportation venture, on March 2, 1970. But the GN heritage endures because of the historic and sound role it played in the settlement and development of the Northwest.

(J. M. Budd)

On September 8, 1887 the track laying crew laid seven miles
of track between Havre and Fort Assiniboine. The band of the
20th Infantry serenaded the track laying crews as they
approached the Fort. Built in 1878, Fort Assiniboine was to
have been the first of a line of forts along the Canadian
border, but was the only one completed.

Great Northern Railway

1. THE GREAT ADVENTURE

James J. Hill referred to the Great Northern as "my great adventure." Surely it must have been so, for his life was a great adventure and the Great Northern occupied the greatest share of that life, which began September 16, 1838 in a log cabin in Rockwood, Ontario (about 40 miles west of Toronto) and ended nearly 78 years later on May 29, 1916. He died in his 38 room mansion on Summit Avenue, located along the highest of the terraced bluffs in St. Paul that overlook the Mississippi River. The son of a poor Canadian farming couple, he went to work at the age of 14 as a clerk in a village store to help support his mother after the death of his father, continuing his education evenings and Sundays.

In 1856, at the age of 18, Hill left Canada for the east coast of the United States. He sought to work passage aboard a ship bound for the Orient, where he hoped to establish a trading business. Perhaps, like many others, Hill was inspired by Asa Whitney, a New York City merchant who had made his fortune in China in the 1840's. Whitney was also one of the first influential advocates of a transcontinental railroad, which he envisioned not merely as a steel band to tie the continent together, but more as an overland route to expedite and enlarge trade with the Orient. While Whitney's plan for a transcontinental railroad had not been adopted, he generated considerable interest in the increasingly profitable trade with the Orient.

Running out of funds in Syracuse, New York, and failing to find either passage to the Orient or work in the East, Hill headed for St. Paul by packet boat, intending to reach the Pacific Coast of Canada. He arrived in St. Paul on July 21, 1856, just 16 days after the last Red River ox cart brigade (the only transportation west) had departed. So he was forced, still without funds, to spend the winter in the expensive frontier town.

The first white man to visit the site of St. Paul had been Father Hennepin, who arrived by canoe in 1680. He was one of three men sent by Robert Cavalier Sieur de la Salle to explore the upper Mississippi River, and he was captured by the Sioux near the mouth of the St. Croix.

With his captors Father Hennepin also reached the Falls of St. Anthony, which bars further navigation up the Mississippi River. He named them for his patron saint, St. Anthony of Padua. He was rescued shortly thereafter by a French fur trader, Daniel Greysolon DuLuth. Others followed. Jonathan Carver of Connecticut explored the region for the King of England in 1766-1767, acquiring title to an immense tract of land by treaty with the Indians, but the Revolutionary War brought an end to his plans to establish a colony there. He also explored the Minnesota River, a stream some 475 miles long arising out of Big Stone Lake in South Dakota.

In 1805, following the Louisiana Purchase, Lieut. Zebulon Pike concluded treaties with the Sioux for the land upon which Fort Snelling was to be built while exploring the adjacent territory at the behest of the U.S. Government. In 1819, soldiers paddling up river by keel boats established the fort on the north bank of the Minnesota River at its juncture with the Mississippi. The fort served as an outpost of the United States authority. In 1825, Mendota, just south of the sites of the Twin Cities, was settled by the American Fur Company with Henry Hastings Sibley as Factor. The Government sent a party of thirty under Henry R. Schoolcraft, an Indian agent at Sault Ste. Marie, to track the source of the Mississippi in 1832. Three hundred years after the discovery of the "Father of Waters", its origin was found at Lake Itasca. Joseph N. Nicolet explored Minnesota in 1836 and was sent on a second trip by the U.S. to map the area.

In 1837 a Swiss watchmaker named Perry, turned away by the soldiers at Fort Snelling, traveled downstream a few miles to the site of St. Paul (a popular camping place for the Sioux) to settle. The co-founding father was Pierre Parrant, a colorful if somewhat unsavory character known as Pig's Eye, who made and sold liquor to the soldiers and Indians, and bestowed his name on the infant community. It was still known as Pig's Eye Landing when Fathers Galtier and Ravous, in 1841, established the log Chapel of St. Paul, giving the city a more acceptable name. For several years St. Paul remained scarcely more than a collection of crude buildings along the levee, the lowest of four terraces upon which the city was built. Steamboats from the lower Mississippi unloaded their cargo and took on the furs and the few agricultural commodities which were grown by the early settlers. By 1853, the population of St. Paul was still predominantly Indian. The only way to reach the upper terraces from the levee was by a series of steps carved into the steep bluffs. With its strategic location at the head of navigation on the Mississippi, however, St. Paul was destined to grow, and it became second in importance only to St. Louis in the fur trade.

The village of St. Anthony on the east bank of the Falls was settled in 1845. The first claim had been staked by a lumberman, Franklin Steele, in 1838. He completed a water driven sawmill in 1847. Logs floated downstream from the heavily forested upper Mississippi to the Falls, where water power was used to saw them into boards. The west side of the Falls was settled in the early 1850's, with a wooden suspension bridge connecting the two sides. By the 1860's the power from the Falls was being used on a large scale, and the early flour mills were established.

In 1850, part of the Fort Snelling military reservation was opened to settlement and Col. John J. Stevens built his house on the site of the later Great Northern station. In 1854, he surveyed and outlined the city of Minneapolis. (The name is a combination of the Sioux and Greek words for water and city.) The smaller community grew towards St. Anthony and was connected to it by a bridge in 1855. The two cities were united in 1872, and by the following year Minneapolis had encompassed all settlements on both sides of the Falls. Although the Falls descended 82 feet within the center of the city, the broad plateau high above the River at the Falls was nearly level with the surrounding country, and the site was a much easier and less expensive one on which to build a city than that of St. Paul.

Until 1848, when Wisconsin became a state, Minnesota was a part of the Wisconsin Territory. Now Congress redefined the borders and established the Territory of Minnesota—extending west to the Missouri and White Rivers in the Dakotas and north to Canada—with St. Paul as its capital. Except for Fort Snelling, the land was held largely by the Indians. The entire territory had a population of about 5,000 whites, and St. Paul, its largest city, boasted about 840 souls. Settlers for the new territory began arriving in numbers in 1849, their numbers increasing each year. When the new Governor, Alexander Ramsey, arrived from Pennsylvania, he could find no place to stay in St. Paul and had to lodge his family in nearby Mendota with Henry Sibley.

During the mid 19th Century, settlers came largely from Germany, Sweden, Norway, Denmark and Holland. They also came from the poor, rocky soil of New England. All came with a common dream— to build their farms on the fertile soil of the new land. Like the fur traders before them, they initially came by the Great Lakes and rivers. They came down the Ohio to the Mississippi and turned north. The first settlers (up to 1850) preferred to clear the land from the forests rather than move out on the treeless prairies; for the forests provided them with fuel and with the material for their homes and fences. Water and game were abundant. The soil was well drained and easily tilled, unlike the prairie soil with its heavy sod and matted roots. Further, they suspected that soil which grew no trees must be poor soil. But they soon realized the fertility of the prairie soil. It was so rich that the crops were too abundant to be harvested with the hand implements they possessed. With the coming of the railroads and the availability of new agricultural machinery—McCormick's reaper, Marsh's harvester, Appleby's self-knotting binder and steel toothed cultivator, and the John Deere plow to handle the special problems of the prairie soil—settlers moved quickly out onto the grasslands west of the Mississippi.

In North Dakota, South Dakota, Minnesota and up into Canada, they planted the spring wheat. They could not be as certain of a cool, moist fall as the region further south. The freeze came earlier in the winter and the low temperatures without snow killed the winter wheat. They plowed in the winter, and the insects buried in the ground were brought to the surface and killed by the winter cold. They planted in the spring. The rain fell in the spring and early summer, and the hot dry weather of late summer ripened the wheat. Some of the crop was taken to St. Paul for shipment down the Mississippi and some was milled into flour at St. Anthony and sent east. Flour from the spring wheat was considered less desirable than that of winter wheat until 1878, when the first complete roller mill in the U.S. was completed at Minneapolis. The new process made possible better flour from the spring wheat than from the winter wheat and made Minneapolis the flour capital of the world.

Settlers moved into the Red River Valley in the late 1850's. The valley is actually two prairies, one on either side of the Red River of the North, each about 25 miles wide and extending about 300 miles from Wahpeton to Winnipeg. The valley lies in the bed of an ancient lake, formed during the Ice Age and dammed by glacial ice to the north. About the size of Lake Superior, Lake Agassiz drained as the northern ice melted and left the fertile valley. The Red

River of the North is formed by the joining of the Bois de Sioux and Ottertail Rivers at Wahpeton. It flows north across the border into Lake Winnipeg and hence by streams drains into Hudson's Bay. About two thirds of its 500 mile length is navigable.

The first permanent settlement in the Red River Valley was begun with the construction of Pembina House by the Northwest Company in the Spring of 1801. Hudson's Bay Company erected a fort nearby in the fall of the same year, and the XY Company built a fort shortly after. In 1811 Lord Selkirk of Scotland, investing heavily in the Hudson's Bay Company, acquired land for a colony in the Red River Valley. The first settlers, arriving the following year, established the colony on the present site of Winnipeg, while those arriving later moved south to build at Pembina, resulting in violence between the colonists and the Northwest Company. By 1821 the Hudson's Bay Company, having eliminated or absorbed its competition, became the sole possessor of the Red River Valley, claiming the land east and west of the juncture of the rivers at Wahpeton. The northern boundary of the Louisiana Purchase, in dispute for fifteen years, had been established at the 49th Parallel by an International Boundary conference in 1818. A survey of the boundary between Lake Superior and the Red River by Major Stephen H. Long of the U.S. in 1823 revealed the fact that all but one of the 60 houses in Pembina were on the American side of the border.

All goods imported to or furs exported from the valley traveled the long difficult route through the Canadian wilderness to Hudson's Bay. This route was open only about two months of the year, and it was apparent to the traders that it would be much easier to freight goods via the settlements on the Mississippi. Pack animals were too expensive for most to own, and wheels seemed the only way to cover the overland route. In 1844, six carts of furs traveled from Pembina to Mendota. While not a financial success, this venture proved that the trip was possible; and in spite of every effort on the part of Hudson's Bay Company to stop them, regular wagon trains soon ran from Pembina and St. Joseph to Mendota and St. Paul—a distance of some 450 miles requiring 30 to 40 days. The route was shortened considerably by the advent of steam boats on the Red River in the 1860's. The two wheeled cart, used mainly by the Bois Brules (mixed bloods) was a crude box fastened on

cross members and an axle, costing about $15 to build. It could carry from 600 to 1,000 pounds. Drawn by horses or oxen, these carts were usually good for three round trips. The Pembina buggy, a lighter, more maneuverable vehicle than the cart, had spoked wheels instead of solid, but the wheels of both vehicles were unlubricated and the noise was ear splitting. They were silenced only by the coming of the railroad.

The first practical railroad locomotive had been demonstrated in 1830. In only a decade, track mileage had increased from 23 miles to 2,818 miles, and the railroad had become the most desired form of transportation in the United States. Every city, town and village vied to offer every possible inducement to attract the railroads, and new settlements sprang up as the rails advanced. As early as 1847, a pioneer scientist of the Northwest, Professor Increase A. Lapham, had proposed and mapped two railroad routes in Minnesota, one to begin on the shores of Lake Superior near Duluth and the other to begin at St. Paul. The two routes would meet near what is now Fergus Falls on the Red River (Ottertail). In 1850, James M. Goodhue proposed in his Minnesota Pioneer that a railroad be built following an old Indian trail from the Red River to the mouth of the Columbia. Exploration of a northern rail route from St. Paul to the

Pacific Northwest was completed by the Governor of the Washington Territory, Isaac I. Stevens, in 1855.

When James J. Hill reached St. Paul in July, 1856, there were still no rails in Minnesota, although a number of charters had been granted, starting in 1853. Nor were there rails over the nearly 2,000 miles from St. Paul to the Pacific Coast—still held by fierce Indian tribes. Only one railroad from the East had reached the Mississippi—at Galena, Illinois. In the summer months, steamboats moved daily between St. Paul and Galena. In addition, about a dozen boats shuttled between St. Paul and the other settlements lower on the Mississippi. St. Paul was now a city of 4,000 to 5,000, and the entire Territory of Minnesota contained about 100,000 whites—concentrated largely along the rivers. The overland routes—difficult, limited, and time consuming in seasonable weather—were nearly impassable in the winter. Rails were vital to open up and settle the country not adjacent to navigable waters; and by 1858, when Minnesota became a state, there were some twenty railroads chartered, many with generous land grants to aid in their financing.

On May 22, 1857 the Minnesota Legislature chartered the Minnesota and Pacific Railway Company to build from Stillwater on the St. Croix River to St. Paul, to St. Anthony, to Breckenridge—with a branch line via St. Cloud to St. Vincent. Due to the panic of 1857, it was impossible to sell the company's bonds, and the state accepted $600,000 worth of first mortgage bonds as security for a loan of $600,000 worth of state railroad bonds. In 1860, with 62-½ miles of completed roadbed between St. Paul and St. Cloud, the company defaulted on all bond interest and sold the property to the State of Minnesota for $1,000. The property, returned to the company in 1861, was again forfeited. The newly chartered St. Paul and Pacific Railroad received these rights from the legislature in 1862, and completed the line between St. Paul and St. Anthony—the first ten miles of railroad in the state.

The first run of the St. Paul and Pacific, June 28, 1862, carried many notables on board the wooden coaches, including the Governor of the State. Built in Paterson, New Jersey, the little American type locomotive—the first locomotive in Minnesota—had traveled via rail to La Crosse, Wisconsin and thence by river barge to St. Paul. The little wood burner, named for the chief engineer of the Minnesota and Pacific, William Crooks, had arrived in St. Paul September 9, 1861, but was not put into service until the arrival of the passenger cars on the morning of the inaugural run.

The story of railroad building in Minnesota is one of booms, over confidence and reckless financing. A fortune was to be gained by title to the land grants, and many were willing to build the track, if they could raise enough money, to obtain the land. Often the roads were built with only a paper business for years to come. State and local bonds issued to promote building were discounted for the immediate profit of promoters and construction companies.

The history of the St. Paul and Pacific was also a story of legislative corruption and corporate fraud. Its predecessor, the Minnesota and Pacific, had been under the control of Russel Sage, a robber baron from Troy, New York, and his hand-picked group. They caused the Minnesota Legislature to hand over vast land grants and bond issues. By the use of dummy construction companies and other devices, they managed to pocket the money and bankrupt the road in five years. Then, in order to eliminate the debt, but keep the land grant, they coldly reorganized into two new companies. The first was the St.

Paul and Pacific, chartered in 1862. The second was the First Division of the St. Paul and Pacific, organized in February, 1864 — with special permission of the Minnesota Legislature — by holders of special preferred stock in the SP&P. This group contracted with E.B. Litchfield of Brooklyn, New York, owner of 8,500 shares of this stock, to take over the best part of the SP&P, with all its rights and grants, in order to build the line from St. Anthony to Breckenridge and from St. Paul to Sauk Rapids. The world seemed full of Litchfields. Egbert S. Litchfield was a partner of Hill's in handling the freight for the SP&P. His two half brothers, E.C. and E.D. Litchfield, were also holders of the special stock, and it was the Litchfields who constructed the line from St. Paul to Sauk Rapids. Because of financial difficulties, it took five years to complete this 60 mile stretch. Iron rails were used instead of steel, and they were of about fifteen different designs.

All of the Litchfields were in sympathy with or under the control of the Northern Pacific. They transferred all of their interest and rights in the First Division to Edwin D. Litchfield, who in turn sold them to the NP in 1870. The NP had already acquired the SP&P and paid for the capital stock of the First Division with $1,500,000 in SP&P bonds and $500,000 in cash. Although separate companies for the sake of appearance, the Board of Directors for the NP, the SP&P, and the First Division were now identical and in 1871 they prepared to reap the harvest. The latter two companies issued $15,000,000 in bonds — in addition to the $13,100,000 issued during the past six years — to construct the lines from St. Cloud to St. Vincent and from Sauk Rapids to Brainerd, headquarters of the NP. The reputation of the SP&P was so bad that they found no takers on this side of the Atlantic; but they disposed of most of the bonds to Dutch bankers in Amsterdam. Financial looting again plunged the lines into collapse a year later with little construction completed; and the Dutch bond holders applied for a receiver. Jesse P. Farley of

Dubuque, Iowa was appointed the receiver for the SP&P and the General Manager of the First Division with orders to get the railroad out of difficulties and to complete the lines. In three years he was able to raise only $100,000 through debentures and to complete the road from East St. Cloud to Melrose and from Barnesville to Crookston. In addition, the NP went bankrupt in the Panic of 1873. Unable to fulfill the terms of its purchase agreement with Litchfield, it was compelled to return the capital stock to him. Reorganization of all the properties seemed the only solution, that is if anyone could unsnarl the legal and financial tangles involved and raise the money to complete the road.

One man at least was interested—James J. Hill, an ambitious, talkative, shrewd, hard working dreamer who was a little ahead of everyone else. He had the vision to see not what was at the moment, but the potential. He turned the accident of being stranded in St. Paul into an opportunity, because he saw St. Paul not as a hamlet, but as a crossroad of western trade. He was always the student; and he had a fantastic memory. He read everything—history, engineering, science, art, geology and finance—cataloguing what he read in his mind.

During his first nine years in St. Paul he was employed by four different firms. His first job was as a shipping clerk, receiving and discharging freight for J.W. Bass & Co., agents for the Dubuque and St. Paul Packet Company's line of Mississippi River steamboats. He was a night watchman aboard a steamboat wintering in St. Paul; he was an agent for McCormick's reaper; he was a river pilot (although unofficially); and all the while he studied steamboat construction and operation. He handled the first shipment of Minnesota wheat in 1857; and he cut the first stencil for barrels of Minnesota brand flour.

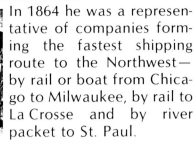

In 1864 he was a representative of companies forming the fastest shipping route to the Northwest—by rail or boat from Chicago to Milwaukee, by rail to La Crosse and by river packet to St. Paul.

In 1865, he went into business on his own as the representative of the Northwest Packet Company, a large river concern connecting with railroads at the lower river points. Gradually he brought all of the important carriers of freight into his fold as he became agent for Dunleith Packet Lines, Chicago & Northwestern, Milwaukee & Prairie du Chien and Illinois Central. In the spring of 1866 he became an agent for the St. Paul and Pacific. He built a warehouse to receive river freight by enlarging the station, giving preference to customers of the railway. Freight came in on the same level as the car tracks, so that it did not need to be rehandled, saving shippers from 6 cents to a dollar a ton drayage. In 1867 he formed his first partnership, J.J. Hill & Co., a wood, coal, and commission firm. The name was changed two years later to Hill, Griggs & Co. and they held the fuel contract with the SP&P.

He was also an agent for the Red River buyers, and in 1870 he went into partnership to build and operate a steamboat on the Red River of North. By the following year he had a through line for passengers and freight to Winnipeg. In 1872 he joined with Norman Kittson in the Red River Transportation Company with the secret connivance of Hudson's Bay Company.

Hill was gaining influence and prestige in St. Paul, and through his diversity of interests, he had his fingertips on the pulse of the growing Northwest. In his almost computer-like mind he was forming a detailed outline of where transportation was needed, its potential growth and profits, and the size of the system that would be required.

He knew that rails must someday replace the steamboats, and he also knew that whoever owned the St. Paul and Pacific would possess two and a half million acres of the richest agricultural land in the midwest.

Across the border in Winnipeg, there was another man with an interest in the St. Paul and Pacific—Donald A. Smith, a member of the Canadian Parliament. His constituents in Manitoba desperately needed a lifeline to the Atlantic and trade with Britain. The CPR was dead for the near future, but a rail line from Selkirk to the border would give them what they needed if the American line out of St. Paul could somehow be revived. In 1873 on his way to Ottawa via St. Paul, he stopped to see an old friend from the Hudson's Bay Company, Norman Kittson. Could he find out the situation regarding this railroad? If the price was right, he might be able to raise the money to buy and complete the road to the border. Perhaps the Dutch could be persuaded to finish it. He really didn't care who owned it, if it could be completed to the border.

Kittson, well-to-do and in his sixties, was not personally interested; but he brought the matter to Hill. Now Hill knew where he would turn for financial help in acquiring his railroad. Smith was not only influential politically; he was wealthy in his own right. He was also one of the largest stockholders and chief officers of the Bank of Montreal and the Chief Commissioner of the Hudson's Bay Company. Hill did his homework well and had the answers for Smith on his next trip through St. Paul in 1874. There were various classes of bonds covering nine different issues with a face value of $18,000,000, but some with a market value of only five cents on the dollar. They were secured by a land grant on the unfinished sections of the road. The grant was worth about two to three million dollars, which was about what it would cost to complete the road. There was about 500 miles of completed road, and, finally, the Dutch wanted no further part in it.

If they could buy the bonds cheap, form a new company, and force foreclosure, the new company could buy the bankrupt road for a song, complete it, and sell the land to make a profit. There was a hitch however. As a result of the fraud perpetrated by Russel Sage and his group, the Minnesota Legislature had passed a law making land grants non-transferable to a new company after a foreclosure. This had to be revoked. With the aid of political friends this was accomplished in March, 1876 with new legislation allowing a company sold under foreclosure to reorganize and keep the land.

In the two year interval Hill had studied every detail of the railroad until he knew more about it than those who were running it. In 1876 Johan Carp, representing the Dutch bond holders, arrived from Holland to look over the railroad. Farley, the receiver of the defunct company, introduced him to Hill and Kittson.

There is controversy over the role that Farley played in the proceedings, whether his close association with Hill and Kittson was used to pump him for information or whether he was in collusion with them to keep the value of the property down for cheap sale. One thing is certain, John S. Kennedy, agent for the Dutch bond holders who had recommended Farley as receiver, became a large stockholder in the railroad and a multimillionaire with Hill and his associates. In the negotiations Farley was pessimistic about the future of the road and persuaded Carp that it was time to sell the bonds.

At this point George Stephen, a cousin of Donald Smith, entered the picture. He was a conservative, polished member of the Montreal business establishment and President of the Bank of Montreal. He knew little of the Northwest, and was lukewarm to the idea of a railroad. Because of his cousin's enthusiasm for the project, however, he met with him and Hill in January, 1877, and after viewing Hill's facts and figures, he became very interested. He had a mathematical mind and the statistics aroused the gambler in him. It would be a tremendous exploit if they could carry it off — it would ruin him if they could not. Although the next few years took a terrible toll on him, bringing him near to a breakdown, he couldn't resist the adventure. He was totally involved.

Hill was the most confident of the group, believing that once a man set his mind to something it was half done. He immediately composed a letter to the Dutch bond holders that was a feeler rather than an offer. He wanted to get an idea of what they would settle for, and while he had determined the value of the road alone at $12,216,718 and the land grant at an additional $6,585,205, he wanted them to think it worthless. Without cash he didn't dare risk acceptance of his offer of $3,500,000, so a proviso was added that the cash would not be paid until the property was unencumbered and a clear title could be issued. It was an impossible condition and, as expected, the Dutch refused.

He then went to New York to try to persuade Litchfield to sell his stock and thus avoid a legal battle. Edwin Litchfield wasn't interested at any price. He was trying to reach an agreement with the Dutch to prevent foreclosure and take control himself. The Dutch had accepted the Litchfield's plan of reorganization for the SP&P; but in August, 1875 the NP had been sold at foreclosure and reorganized by a committee of bond holders, leaving the Litchfields with no capital backing to finance

more bonds. Without credit they were unable to pay the dividends and the Dutch withdrew from the agreement.

In May another letter was sent to the bond holders offering from eleven to eighty cents on the dollar for the various issues, stipulating a sixty to ninety day notice to raise the funds if the offer were accepted. In September the Dutch agreed to the deal if Stephen could raise the money. The partners agreed to share risks and profits equally. The enterprise was divided into five shares with the fifth share to be used by Stephen to negotiate the loan. He had expected to raise the money in London; but he was unable to convince the bankers of the soundness of the investment. He returned home without the funds at Christmas, and it was a gloomy group that met. Four years of planning seemed to have gone for nothing.

Stephen now decided to deal directly with the Dutch committee's New York agent, John S. Kennedy. They met in January, 1878, and the partners offered to buy the bonds at the previously agreed price, but on credit with $100,000 down and the balance within six months after the foreclosure and issuance of clear title. Until then the bonds would remain in escrow, with the holders receiving 7% interest on the purchase price. The balance of payment could be made in cash or in 6% gold bonds of the new company with a $250 bonus of preferred stock for each $1,000

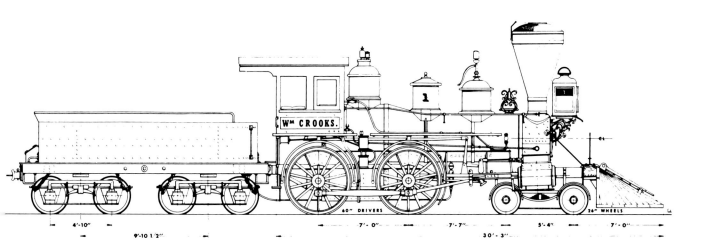

bond. The purchasers would get immediate possession of the property and would furnish the money to extend the lines and save the land grants. Kennedy firmly recommended that the Dutch accept the proposal, and by now they were ready to accept any price. The purchase was concluded February 24, 1878, and Kennedy was brought into the syndicate at that time. Many of the Dutch took the bonds rather than the cash, which proved to be a wise decision. They were pleased—they had sold cheaply, but the road would have netted them nothing if it hadn't been put in working order.

The road had been purchased for $5,540,000 or about twenty-five cents on the dollar. There was no time to celebrate —there were formidable problems ahead. The new owners had to raise money immediately—$100,000 to pay the deposit to the bond holders; $280,000 to pay the line's debts; $140,000 to pay the half yearly dividends; $500,000 to purchase the Litchfield stock if he would sell, and $1,000,000 to complete the road. In addition the NP was making waves, the Minnesota Legislature had passed a law limiting the time for railway construction, and the new owners of the railway were encountering difficulties in obtaining the lease of the Pembina Branch. There was ample justification for the nervousness suffered by Stephen and Kittson.

Smith and Stephen personally borrowed money from the Bank of Montreal (a bank under their care), turning over every asset they had to secure a $280,000 loan to pay the debts. Kittson and Hill also mortgaged everything they owned to obtain a line of credit. To raise construction money Farley was sent to obtain a court order permitting him to issue receiver's debentures. The hearings dragged on perilously close to the time limit, and Hill went before the judge. The judge was impressed and signed, but with reluctance.

With Stephen handling the financing, Hill now concentrated on building the road. The uncompleted line from Sauk Rapids to Brainerd had been forfeited by default under the new law the previous year. Now two sections of the line would have to be completed by the end of 1878 or the company would lose the land grants and franchises. The thirty-five miles from Melrose to Sauk Center was completed twenty-four hours ahead of its August deadline. The thirty-three miles further to Alexandria was well ahead of its December schedule, and in addition the gap between Crookston and St. Vincent was in operation by November 11.

Stephen had negotiated with MacKenzie in Ottawa for a ten year lease of the Pembina Branch, but Conservative opposition in Parliament threw out MacKenzie's bill. MacKenzie then allowed the St. Paul running rights on the branch, but the contractors in possession of the road charged the

Minneapolis and St. Anthony in 1857, a few months after the arrival of James J. Hill in 1856. St. Paul at this time had a population of between 4,000 and 5,000 and was the territorial capital of Minnesota.

22

SP&P confiscatory rates. Then a new Government was formed, which modified the agreement to allow use of the line only until completion of the Canadian Pacific Railroad. It was better than nothing.

In regard to the NP—a coded message had reached Kennedy & Company in New York in October, 1877 to the effect that the NP was negotiating with the Canadian Government for exclusive control of the line from St. Vincent to Fort Garry (Winnipeg) and promising to build a line from their road to St. Vincent. Directors of the NP were also attempting to elect their friends to the Minnesota Legislature in order to have a forfeiture declared on the SP&P line from Crookston to St. Vincent. If they had been successful, it would have ruined the SP&P, and the partners would have been battling two governments and the most powerful railroad system in the Northwest. The NP Directors now continued to harass by threatening to build a line parallel to the SP&P. Hill responded by threatening to cancel the agreement by which the NP used the SP&P tracks and to boost the fees for these running rights and the use of the SP&P terminal in St. Paul. He also threatened to survey a line to Yellowstone Park and ask Congress for one half of the NP land grant to the Rockies. The NP withdrew—out-bluffed.

Litchfield was handled by a squeeze play. The strategy was to keep him worried. Suit was filed against him and his brother in Minnesota for appropriating railway construction funds to their own use. Litchfield sold in January, 1879, removing an obstacle to foreclosure.

Foreclosure was granted in March, 1879, and the St. Paul, Minneapolis and Manitoba was formed in May with Stephen as President and Hill as General Manager. In June the new company bought the foreclosed property for $6,780,000 in receiver's debentures and bonds and floated a $16,000,000 bond issue to pay off the Dutch. The largest share of the land grant was sold for $13,068,887, and $15,000,000 in stock was created. Each partner received

57,646 shares which in three years was worth over $8,000,000. Additional issues of stocks and bonds in 1882 and 1883 netted them each another $11,000,000 profit. The road was a rolling gold mine. Its earnings increased from $1,000,000 to nearly $3,000,000 in the first year. Even with heavy expenditures for property improvements and new construction, a dividend of $975,000 was paid to the stockholders in 1882. In that year Hill was elevated to the presidency of the road, and for the 25 years that he was in that position and the five years that he served as Chairman of the Board he received no salary, maintaining that the growth in his investment was sufficient compensation. In view of the above figures, one can understand why.

The partners were all Canadians of Scottish ancestry—shrewd, willing to take risks, and dedicated to the work ethic. The Scots comprised only one fifteenth of the population of Canada, but by their adherence to their work, save, and study creed, they had gained control of the fur trade and of the major educational and financial institutions of the country, and maintained a powerful influence in the government as well. It was men of this ilk that parlayed a catastrophe into a railroad and transformed a dream into an empire.

When the Manitoba was organized in 1879, there were some 560 miles of completed road, all in Minnesota. The company proceeded at once to finish the St. Vincent extension from Alexandria to Barnesville, and to extend the Fisher's Landing spur west of Crookston to Grand Forks in the Dakota Territory. They also purchased a line from Morris (on the line to Breckenridge) to Brown's Valley on the Minnesota/Dakota border, and under a separate organization built the line between Barnesville and Moorhead, putting 695 miles into operation by the end of 1880.

Capital stock of the St. Paul and Duluth Railroad Company, running from St. Paul to the head of Lake Superior, was purchased in order to obtain the vital link with the Great Lakes. Under the charter of the Minneapolis and St. Cloud Railroad Company, a 66-½ mile connection between St. Cloud and Hinckley on the St. Paul and Duluth was built and put into operation by December 1882. In addition, large tracts of land were acquired on Lake Superior for terminals, elevators, warehouses and docks.

Under the auspices of the Manitoba, the Minneapolis Union Railway Company built the famous stone arch bridge in Minneapolis, and opened passenger stations on each side of the river, constructing four main tracks between St. Paul and Minneapolis to handle the business of the Manitoba and its railway tenants.

Colonizing agents of the Manitoba were busy in Europe promoting land sales in the lush Red River Valley. The cheap railroad land and the free government land lured immigrants by the tens of thousands each year. They flocked to Minnesota and began to push further out into the Dakotas. With the growth of business and population, plans were laid not only for further extensions in Minnesota, but for the penetration of the line into (North) Dakota; and by the end of 1885 there were 1,470 miles under operation. Through purchase and construction the line had been pushed west from Grand Forks to Devil's Lake (N.D.) with branches north and south to serve as feeders to the main line. Now the decision, considered by many to be sheer folly, was made to extend the line into Montana and west to Puget Sound.

In 1886, the Montana Central Railway Company was incorporated in Montana, supposedly by independent interests, to run a line from Great Falls to Helena and Butte. In truth the company was directly affiliated with James J. Hill and the Manitoba. The Montana Central would be the connecting link with the westward moving Manitoba, providing it with access to the rich mining country around Helena and Butte. And the Manitoba was moving westward rapidly. In the same year it reached the Mouse River, over 100 miles west of Devil's Lake, and Minot was founded.

Minot became a vast staging area in late 1886 and early 1887 as construction materials, wagons, horses and men arrived in preparation for the work that would commence when the prairie had firmed after the spring thaw.

The original main line, paralleling the Red River of the North as far as Grand Forks and then turning due west via Devil's Lake to Minot, met its goal — to go west while providing service to as many communities as possible. As transcontinental traffic increased, however, a faster, more direct route via Fargo and Bedford to Minot was built. This line, known as the Fargo-Minot Cut-off or the Surrey Cut-off, was completed in 1911, and was the longest stretch of tangent track on the Great Northern. Two hundred twenty-four miles long, it cut some thirty miles from the original route.

The General Railway Act of March 3, 1875, which granted access through public domain in the Territories of Dakota, Montana, and Washington, had cleared the way legally for the projected 555 mile line between Minot and Great Falls, 413 miles of which passed through Indian and military reservations. Construction records were broken as the Manitoba pushed westward from Minot in April, 1887, reaching Helena November 16. The 645 miles of track were completed on an average of three and one fourth miles each working day, with one all time record breaking day in August of eight miles. The line to Butte was completed in 1888.

In 1888, Hill also organized the Northern Steamship Company with a fleet of six 2,600 ton ships to transport grain across the Great Lakes from Superior to Buffalo, New York where he had built a three million bushel capacity circular steel elevator. In 1889, the completed line to Duluth and West Superior gave the Manitoba complete ownership of a road to the head of the Great Lakes, replacing the partial ownership through the St. Paul and Duluth. This was done in competition with Eastern interests and made the railroad independent of other Lake lines. In addition, lines were constructed from Willmar to Sioux Falls, from Benson to Watertown and Huron, and from Tinatah to Ellendale and Aberdeen, as the railroad grew and more feeder lines were necessary to keep the main line viable.

The country was growing too — four new states entered the Union within a few days of each other. North and South Dakota became the 39th and 40th states on November 2, 1889, followed by Montana on November 8 and Washington on November 11. Idaho became the 43rd state on July 3, 1890. The Manitoba had become too limited an entity for the vast transportation system developing; and for that reason, on Hill's 51st birthday, September 16, 1889, a new company was formed using the charter of the Minneapolis and St. Cloud Railroad Company. In February, 1890 the new company — the Great Northern — leased the properties of the Manitoba for 999 years. It was under the banner of the Great Northern that Jim Hill would pursue his great adventure west from Pacific Junction over the spine of the continent and the formidable Cascades to Puget Sound.

Overleaf: The name "Jas. J. Hill" appears on the sign above the windows of his warehouse on the St. Paul levee in 1865. To save drayage charges, it was so designed that the ships unloaded their cargo on the same level as the rails of the St. Paul & Pacific. Upper left: Hill at age 18, when he first arrived in St. Paul. Upper right: Hill in 1872 when he formed the partnership with Norman W. Kittson in the Red River Transportation Company.

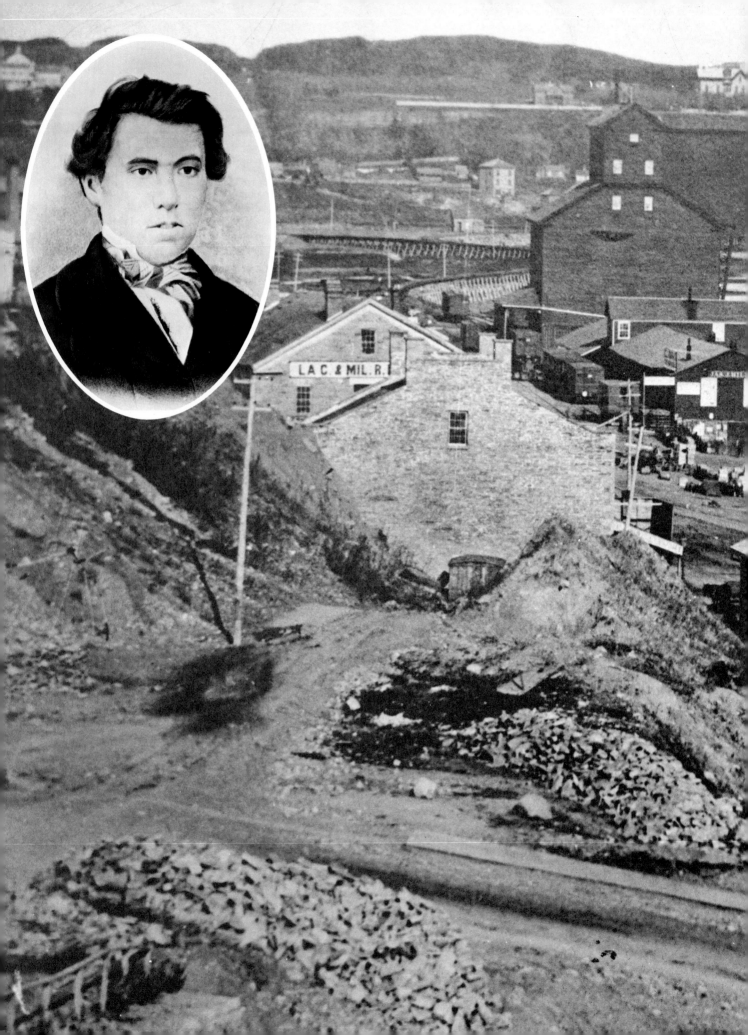

No. 1. FIRST DIVISION No. 1.
ST. PAUL & PACIFIC R. R.
TIME CARD.
Into Effect July 2nd, 1862.

ST. ANTHONY AND MINNEAPOLIS TRAINS.

LEAVE.	A. M.	ARRIVE.	A. M.	LEAVE.	P. M.	ARRIVE.	P. M.
St. Paul	8:00	St. Anthony	8:45	St. Anthony	12:20	St. Paul	1:00
St Anthony	8:50	St. Paul	9:40	St. Paul	3:45	St. Anthony	4:30
St. Paul	11:30	St. Anthony	12:15	St. Anthony	4:35	St. Paul	5:20

Extra trains will meet all Steamboats for the accommodation of Passengers living in St. Anthony.

Special trains will be run on Sunday and Evenings by special arrangement.

No Engines allowed on the road except on order of the Superintendent or Master Mechanic.

Irregular Trains slow on curves, and look out for Section men.

In case of doubt, follow the safe course.

SIGNALS

1.. A red flag by day—a red light by night, when swung upon the track; the absence of lights or flags at places where usually shown; and all signals given, are signals of danger.

On perceiving either, the Engineer must bring the Train to a dead stop; nor shall he receive any information from any person as to the cause of the signal, until the Train is brought to a stand.

2. A white flag or a white light indicates that the track is all right for Trains to pass.

3. One sound of the whistle is signal to apply brakes.
Two sounds of the whistle is signal to let go the brakes.
Three sounds of the whistle is signal to back the Train.
Four sounds of the whistle is signal for changing a switch.
Five or more rapid sounds of the whistle is the signal for the flag or signal-men who have been sent out to guard train, to come in.
A long continued sound of the whistle is signal for approaching a Station or Road Crossing.

4. One Stroke of the bell signifies stop.
Two strokes of the bell—go ahead.
Three strokes—back.

5. A lantern swung across the track is a signal for stopping. Raised and lowered perpendicularly—the signal for the Train to go ahead. Swung in a circle—for the Train to back.

6 One large white head-light on the front of the Engine, and a red light on the rear of the Train, must always be exhibited by all regular trains upon the road after dark.

7. A red flag by day or a red light by night, when placed upon the front of an Engine, indicates that the Engine or Train is to be followed by another, which is to be considered a part of the signal Train; and no Train will move out of sidings until the Train has passed.

8. Signal Cords shall be used on all Passenger Trains, and shall extend from the rear car to the whistle or signal bell of the engine

Officials of the St. Paul & Pacific gather with their guests at Breckenridge, Minnesota, October, 1871. Identified by number in the the group are: (1) Col. A. De Graff, who built most of the railway lines in Minnesota during this early period; (2) William B. Litchfield, president of the St. Paul & Pacific; (3) Col. William Crooks; (4) Mr. Willmar, who represented the Dutch bondholders of the road; (5) C.A.F. Morris, chief engineer at the time this picture was taken. The locomotive is the William Crooks, named after the first chief engineer of the road. Insets Above: left, Col. William Crooks—right, C.A.F. Morris.

Great Northern Railway

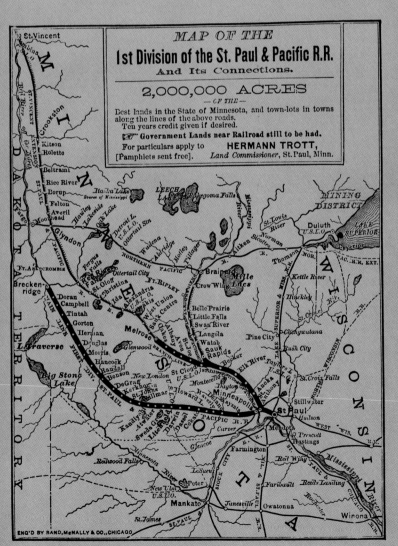

MAP OF THE
1st Division of the St. Paul & Pacific R.R.
And Its Connections.

2,000,000 ACRES
—OF THE—

Best lands in the State of Minnesota, and town-lots in towns along the lines of the above roads.

Ten years credit given if desired.

☞ Government Lands near Railroad still to be had.

For particulars apply to   HERMANN TROTT,
[Pamphlets sent free].   *Land Commissioner, St. Paul, Minn.*

ENG'D BY RAND, McNALLY & CO., CHICAGO.

THE FIRST DIVISION
—OF THE—

St. Paul & Pacific Railroad Co.

OFFERS FOR SALE

1,500,000 ACRES,

PRAIRIE, TIMBER, AND MEADOW LANDS,

At moderate prices and on 10 years credit, if desired.

ALSO,

Town Lots in Towns at Railroad Stations.

ON THE MAIN LINE,

Between Benson and Breckenridge, we also sell

Whole Sections, at **$6.00** per acre, on three and a half years time, free of interest, on condition that the purchaser breaks the whole section within a year from purchase.

GOVERNMENT LANDS

Still to be had under the Homestead and Tree Planting laws, along the lines of this Company. 240 acres can thus be secured, free of charge. The State of Minnesota pays a bounty of $2.00 each year for every acre of trees planted, and also $2.00 for every half mile of trees planted along public roads—both during the first ten years after plantation.

For particulars, address,

HERMANN TROTT,
Land Commissioner,

ST. PAUL, MINN.

EDW'D D. ATWATER,
Secretary.

Minneapolis' first railroad passenger station is shown in 1873. The railroad, the St. Paul and Pacific, ran from St. Paul to St. Anthony (Minneapolis) following essentially the same route followed today. The freight station in the center, is on the site of the present Burlington Northern freight station at Fourth Avenue North.

Great Northern Railway

The William Crooks, still locomotive No. 1 on the Great Northern roster, chuffs across the famous stone arch bridge across the Mississippi. The little American (4-4-0) type, built in Patterson, New Jersey, was a sister engine of the General, which won fame in Georgia during the Civil War.

—OF THE—

SAINT PAUL & PACIFIC RAILROAD.

WINTER TIME TABLE.

Taking effect Sunday, November the 16th, 1873.

MAIN LINE.

Miles from St. Paul.	STATIONS.	Going West.	Going East.
0	ST. PAUL.............	Le. 8.35 A.M	Ar. 2.00 P.M
11	MINNEAPOLIS...	9.25 "	1.20 "
25	WAYZATA..........	10.25 "	12.20 "
28	LONG LAKE......	10.37 "	12.06 P.M
33	MAPLE PLAIN..	10.54 "	11.49 A.M
40	DELANO	11.25 "	11.25 "
49	WAVERLY.........	11.55 "	10.48 "
54	HOWARD LAKE	12 12 P.M	10.31 "
57	SMITH LAKE.....	12.30 "	10.20 "
61	COKATO.............	12.45 "	10.00 "
67	DASSEL.............	1.07 "	9.38 "
72	DARWIN......... ...	1.30 "	9.20 "
78	LITCHFIELD......	2.12 "	8.58 "
86	SWEDE GROVE.	2.39 "	8.35 "
91	ATWATER	2.57 "	8.20 "
98	KANDIYOHI	3.21 "	7.57 "
104	WILLMAR.... Ar. Le.	Ar. 3.40 P.M Le. 8.00 A.M	Le. 7.40 A.M Ar. 5.10 P.M
118	KERKHOVEN.....	9;10 "	4.10 "
134	BENSON.............	10.30 "	2.55 "
150	HANCOCK...........	11.45 "	1.25 "
159	MORRIS.............	12.35 P.M	12.35 P.M
178	HERMAN..........	1.55 "	11.05 A.M
201	CAMPBELL........	3.35 "	9.20 "
217	BRECKENR'GE...	Ar. 4.30 P.M	Le. 8.15 A.M

Main Line Train remains over night each way at Willmar.

BRANCH LINE.

Miles from St. Paul.	STATIONS.	Going North.	Going South.
0	ST. PAUL.............	Le. 7.30 A.M	Ar. 1.30 P.M
10	ST. ANTH'NY JC.	8.05 "	1.00 "
27	ANOKA...............	8.55 "	12.10 P.M
34	ITASCA...............	9.20 "	11.50 A.M
39	ELK RIVER.......	9 50 "	11.25 "
48	BIG LAKE.........	10.35 "	10.40 "
56	BECKER	11.05 "	10.10 "
63	CLEAR LAKE....	11.40 "	9.45 "
75	ST. CLOUD.........	12.50 P.M	8.50 "
76	SAUK RAPIDS ...	1.10 "	8.00 "
82	ST. JOE.............	1.25 "	8.10 "
108	MELROSE...........	Ar. 3.25 P.M	Le. 6.00 A.M

ST. PAUL & DELANO TRAINS.

	STATIONS.	Going West.	Going East.
0	ST. PAUL	Le. 2.30 P.M	Ar. 10.25 A.M
10	MINNEAPOLIS...	3.35 "	9.35 "
25	WAYZATA...........	4.40 "	8.25 "
28	LONG LAKE........	4.55 "	8.05 "
33	MAPLE PLAIN...	5.20 "	7.40 "
40	DELANO	Ar. 5.50 P.M	Le. 7.00 A.M

MINNEAPOLIS ACCOMMODATION.

Leave St. Paul..8.35 A.M., 12.25, 2.30, & 5.30 P.M.
Arrive Minn'lis...9.25 A.M., 1.12, 3.27, & 6.12 P.M.
Leave Minn'lis...7.50 & 9.35 A.M., 1.20 & 4.15 P.M.
Arrive St. Paul..8.35 & 10.25 A.M., 2.00 & 5.05 P.M.

SUNDAYS ONLY.

Le. St. Paul, 9.00 A.M., Ar. Minn'polis, 9.42 A.M.
Le. Minn'polis, 4.30 P.M., Ar. St. Paul, 5.15 P.M.

J. H. RANDALL,
General Ticket Agent.

E. Q. SEWALL,
Superintendent.

THE FIRST DIVISION

—OF THE—

ST. PAUL & PACIFIC

RAILROAD.

WINTER TIME TABLE.

1873 and 1874.

Passengers must get their Baggage checked before it will be carried over the road, and on the arrival of the train at place of destination, must present the check and take possession of their Baggage.

The Company will not be responsible for the safety of any Baggage after its arrival at station for which it is checked, it being no part of the business of this Company to receive and store Baggage, unless a special contract is made to that effect.

E. Q. SEWALL,
Superintendent.

J. H. RANDALL,
Gen'l Ticket Agent.

Great Northern Railway

A disclaimer of responsibility for baggage after its arrival at the station is contained in the 1873/74 winter timetable of the SP&P. Above right: The Sanforth & Cooke American type 4-4-0 was one of six similar locomotives used on the SP&P in the 1870's. Right: Typical of SP&P boxcars built by Haskell & Barker in 1879, this particular car awaits restoration at the GN St. Paul shops in the 1920's as part of an historic train to be powered by the William Crooks.

Great Northern Railway

Great Northern Railway

Map of the St. Paul, Minneapolis and Manitoba and Connections.

MATTHEWS. NORTHRUP & CO,. ENGR'S & PRS., BUFFALO, N.Y.

34

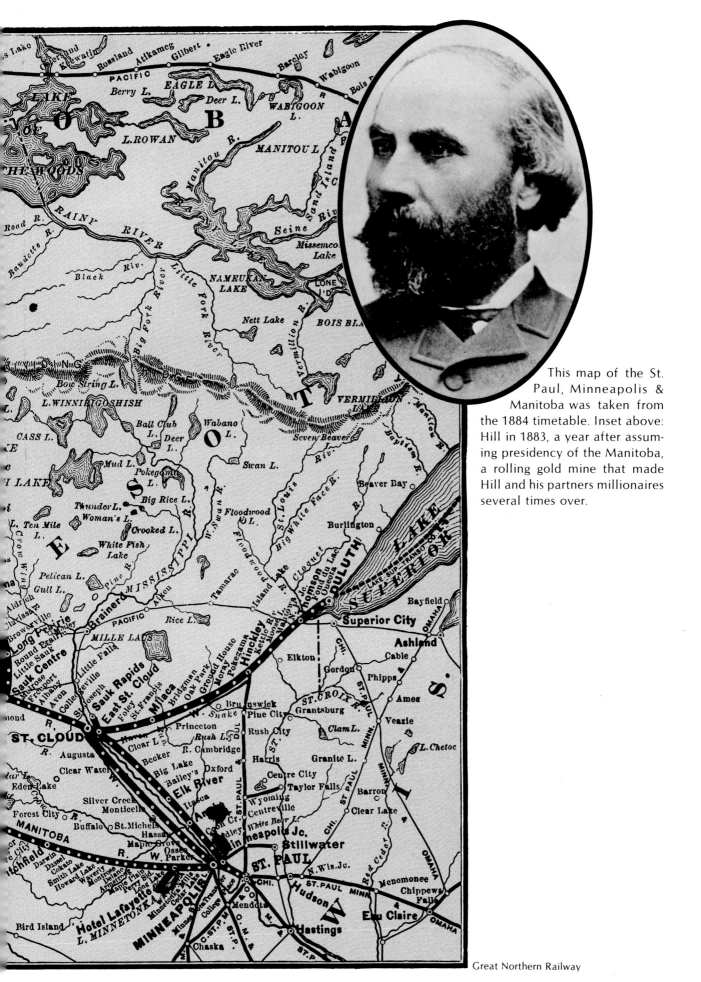

This map of the St. Paul, Minneapolis & Manitoba was taken from the 1884 timetable. Inset above: Hill in 1883, a year after assuming presidency of the Manitoba, a rolling gold mine that made Hill and his partners millionaires several times over.

Great Northern Railway

Martin Erickson

Burlington Northern

Immigrants, by the tens of thousands, were attracted by the offer of free government land or the low priced railroad land. When their few belongings were unloaded at some godforsaken spur, they found a small station, perhaps a grain elevator, and a pair of railroad tracks leading east and west as far as the eye could see. The primitive rutted roads led to widely separated sod huts and shanties, built by other sod busters like themselves. They were paralyzed by winter cold and bogged down by the quagmire of spring thaws. In summer, heat blistered the crops and dried the cracked surface of the ground as hard as concrete. The only form of communication was the railroad, and yet most of them stayed, and they made farms out of the dust, roads out of the ruts, and towns out of the crossroads.

Trade with the Orient and the timber of the Northwest were only two of the reasons that drew Jim Hill and the Great Northern west. On the high prairie of Montana and the Dakotas was virgin land, land that had never felt the bite of the plow, land for growing grain and raising cattle, land to fire the imagination of the immigrants who came to homestead and develop it. Along this road in north central Montana, close to the Missouri River — Fort Benton to the north, Great Falls to the south — the fields of grain seem to reach to infinity.

Great Northern Railway

In early 1887 the supply yard at Minot began to take on the appearance of a military supply depot as carloads of rail, ties, spikes and timbers were stock-piled for the impending push west. Left above: Little switchers like No. 192 worked night and day in twelve hour shifts as the material arrived. Left Below: Belkirk, the office car of Shepard-Winston & Company, general contractors for the extension, sets out on the prairie in September, 1887.

Great Northern Railway

During 1887, 16,406 carloads of material were forwarded out of Minot as the railhead advanced towards Great Falls and Helena. The construction records were remarkable when it is considered that there were no roads or other supply points to work from. Construction materials were brought to within a half mile of the railhead by material trains. Teams then took the ties and the timber for bridges ahead, while the rails were moved to the end of track by iron cars drawn by horses. The railroad ties, already in position to receive the rail, were hardly more than logs with one flat side, so that the rails would have a bearing surface when spiked down. Although the methods were primitive, and little grading was needed on the flat prairie, the whole operation was skillfully organized and supervised by Shepard-Winston & Company.

Great Northern Railway photos

Above: A group of railroad officials and civic dignitaries were taken
by special train to the site of the link-up between the Manitoba
and the Montana Central in late 1887 to celebrate the joining
of the two roads. Much of Montana — long accessible
only by steamboat and wagon — now had two major railroads, the
Northern Pacific and the Manitoba, offering direct
routes to eastern markets.

Left above: A train of the Montana Central, organized and built in
the interests of the Manitoba, pauses in a rocky canyon
near Helena in the late 1880's or early 1890's. Although the rails
were laid directly on the ties without the benefit of tie plates, it is
evident that the retaining walls were carefully built of hand cut
stones and were designed to last for decades.

Left below: Started during the mining boom of the 1850's, Libby
along the Kootenai River on the west side of the Rocky Mountains,
was one of the oldest towns in Montana. Long hampered by lack of
transportation to the outside world, Libby eagerly awaited the
coming of the railroad.

All photos Great Northern Railway

43

"Most men who have really
lived have had, in some shape,
their great adventure.
This railway is mine."

James J. Hill
"The Empire Builder"

"He has captured more territory with the coupling pin, and made it habitable for man than did Julius Caesar with the sword."

Ex-Senator John J. Wilson
Alaska-Yukon-Pacific Exposition of 1909

Hill made study and hard work take the place of the capital that he lacked. He seized upon every opportunity, set forth to meet every challenge, and believed that anything could be accomplished once a man set his mind to it. His presence was commanding and he spoke with a fierce infectious enthusiasm, whether addressing a meeting of farmers, officiating at a last spike ceremony, dedicating a depot or meeting with his executives. With his son Louis, he promoted diversified farming, rotation of crops, raising of swine and cattle, irrigation, conservation and replanting of forests, for they believed that as the country and the people served by the Great Northern grew and prospered, so too would the Great Northern.

All photos Great Northern Railway

At right: During part of a thirty day period of sub-zero weather, two carloads of coal were stuck between Mondak and Sherwood, Montana. Farmers, in desperate need of fuel, drove teams to the site, and here on February 2, 1907, over 500 teams are lined up waiting for the coal. Allowing 200 to 300 lbs. per person, the conductor parcelled it out in sacks, which the teams returned to the scales for weighing. Snow had packed and frozen so hard that teams could drive over fences, outbuildings, and all to get close to the railroad tracks. This was part of the country that the Great Northern agents had described as "invigorating in the winter".

Above: The steamboat S.S. Benton works its way up the Missouri River in the 1870's. In 1887 James J. Hill neatly laid the tracks of the Manitoba in an arc around Fort Benton, at the head of navigation on the Missouri, when the city fathers denied his demand for a free right-of-way through the town. Delivery of goods by steamboat from St. Louis some 2,000 miles away, depended much upon the depth of water in the Missouri — high water generally being from mid-May to mid-September. Once the goods were landed at Fort Benton, there still remained the problem of overland transportation, with freight charges as high as $100 per ton. With the completion of the railroad, Fort Benton — almost overnight — ceased to be a river port. As Hill had forseen, the railroad had written finis to the river traffic.

As the railroad moved west, a continuous flow of immigrants moved into the territory almost as soon as the tracks had been laid, and grain elevators, coal docks, warehouses and freight stations were built to handle the increasing flow of traffic to both new markets in the west and the expanding markets in the east.

Upper photo Great Northern Railway
Lower photo Walt Grecula

NEW G. N. GRAIN ELEVATORS, SUPERIOR, WIS.

Great Northern Railway

Walt Grecula

RESIDENCE OF J. J. HILL, ST. PAUL, MINN.

Hill built his $200,000 mansion on Summit Avenue in St. Paul in 1889. It was built to last with an iron framework, walls of uncut brownstone and a slate roof. It contained 38 rooms, not including 18 bathrooms, had 35 fireplaces, a ventilating system and electric lights. A forced air furnace, laundry and kitchen were in the basement. Three sets of hand carved doors were at the entry of the main hall which was 100 feet long. Also on the main floor were a library with a gold ceiling and an art gallery with a two and one half story pipe organ built in. A hand carved stairway with stained glass windows on the landing led to the second floor bedrooms. Servants' quarters were on the third floor, and a theatre and storage occupied the fourth floor and attic. Wall panelling was either hand carved or leather. Rich tapestries, Persian carpets and fine porcelain were personally selected by Hill. His art gallery contained the works of Corot, Delacroix, Rousseau, Monet and Renoir. The home is now controlled by the Archdiocese of St. Paul, and only hints remain of its former glory.

Hill's private yacht, the Wacouta, was used to entertain many prominent people. The exact dates of his ownership are not known, but in his later years, he gave personal attention to planning fishing trips in Canadian waters.

Great Northern Railway

A Great Northern passenger train pauses at Cokato, Minnesota about 1900. Cokato, on the main line to Breckenridge, was one of a score of small rural towns built up and served by the railroad. Locomotive No. 127, a 4-4-0 (American type) was built by the Schenectady Locomotive Works in 1882 and was scrapped in 1916.

Below: Not all of the horses were iron. Between Great Falls and Lewistown, prior to the building of a branch line in 1912, service was provided by Great Northern stage. Carrying passengers, GN Express and the U.S. Mail, the stage covered 120 miles in 18 hours. Horses were changed every nine miles, and the service was not a great deal slower than that provided by mixed service on other branches.

Great Northern Railway

⸙ EASTERN MINNESOTA ⸙ RAILWAY

The Eastern Railway Company of Minnesota, first known as the Lake Superior & Southwestern, was incorporated in 1887 for the avowed purpose of securing the number of railroads necessary for construction of a Union Station in Superior. The Eastern was partly operational by October, 1888, and by the autumn of 1889, had become the Great Northern's link between St. Paul or St. Cloud and Lake Superior. By 1890, the road, financed by the GN, owned 70 miles of track running northeast from Hinckley to Superior, and had invested nearly $2,000,000 in terminal facilities (yards, coal docks, grain elevators and a 20 stall roundhouse) at Superior, and $500,000 for similar facilities in Duluth. At this time, the Northern Steamship Company, a subsidiary of the Eastern, began direct service from both cities to Buffalo, New York with six freighters. Motive power for the Eastern was supplied mainly by little Moguls, such as No. 204 shown at right. By 1900, there were 60 Moguls in service, along with 5 Americans (such as No. 101 above) and 89 switchers of 0-6-0 wheel arrangement.

Photos collection of Wayne C. Olsen.

In 1912, Train No. 34 pauses, just south of Superior, at Boylston Jct. where the line from the Iron Range joins the line from St. Cloud/St. Paul.

Wayne Olsen collection

Dock No. 1 at Superior, built in 1886-87-88, at a cost of $320,000, measured 1,800' by 264', with 18' of water in the slip. The Northern Steamship Company's "North Star" loads beside Great Northern Elevator A, built on the crib front, sand filled dock at an additional cost of $440,000.

Whaleback No. 107 from Buffalo loads grain from GN Elevator A. Named for the unusual rounded shape of their hulls above the waterline, whalebacks were in vogue for some years on the Great Lakes, but lost favor after they proved to be too unstable in rough seas.

Early 1890 photos
Wayne C. Olsen collection

Left: Structures such as this graceful wooden trestle crossing the Kettle River near Sandstone, about 50 miles from Superior, in the late 1890's, were replaced as soon as funds for improvements became available. Although simple and economical to build, they were fragile when heavy loadings were imposed, prone to burn from locomotive ashes and a headache to maintain at any time.

✦Early days on the Iron Range✦

James J. Hill at the urging of his two eldest sons — James N. and Louis W. Hill — purchased the Duluth, Superior and Western in 1897 and the Duluth, Mississippi & Northern in 1898. In the former he acquired an ore dock and a shortline railroad, while in the latter he acquired a logging railroad with access to Hibbing, Minnesota and thousands of acres in St. Louis and Itasca Counties, that were part of the Mesabi Iron Range, the richest deposit of high grade ore in the U.S. This investment would return millions of dollars each year in direct revenue to the railroad. Above, No. 221 heads a little passenger train at Virginia, Minnesota in 1910.

Great Northern Railway

Left, is one of the early wooden ore cars of the GN, and below, Engine No. 1978, a Mallet compound built by Baldwin in 1910, hauls an ore train in northern Minnesota. This M-2 class locomotive, with the odd 2-6-8-0 wheel arrangement, survived in part until mid-1945. The boiler was used to build a heavy Mikado type. Although these steam engines, as well as the wooden ore cars and passenger trains have long ago disappeared from the scene, the low profile (.4%) main line from Kelly Lake to the docks at Allouez, engineered by John F. Stevens, remains. Over this line, ore trains now move the lower grade taconite pellets in blocks of 200 cars or more — 15,000 tons.

reat Northern Railway

Wayne C. Olsen collection

Top: A track construction train of the GN, near Superior about 1900, has a primitive conveyor system alongside to carry the ties forward to the railhead.

Below: All but 300' of the 1,200' long steel and wood trestle over the Nemadji River on the Belt Line branch of the Great Northern (between Saunders and Allouez), collapsed under the weight of a 40 car ore train, on May 11, 1899, killing the engineer. The coroner's jury did not fix responsibility for the accident, although it was believed at the time that, since the locomotive and cars fell simultaneously and in "even alignment" along the full length of the collapse, the 98' high trestle suffered from a "general and uniform weakness" along its entire length and was simply over-loaded by the enormous and highly concentrated weight of the ore train.

Bigger and bigger power was needed as tonnage grew yearly by astronomical proportions, and the Iron Range became the heaviest tonnage district on the GN. A huge locomotive for its day, No. 2000, on the Iron Range at Kelly Lake in 1909, was the prototype of the unusual but successful 2-6-8-0 wheel arrangement. It was constructed from two locomotives, with the lead engine from a Mogul and the rear engine from a Consolidation.

Below: A recently rebuilt 2-8-8-0, No. 2013, is posed on the Mesabi Division in 1941. At one time, twenty five of these engines were the mainstay of ore operation on the Iron Range. Left: In 1925, one of these, Engine No. 2020 with C. W. Lee at the throttle, established a record by moving 12,500 tons (160 loads) from Gunn to Allouez (101 miles) in 4 hours and 54 minutes.

Wayne C. Olsen Collection

Paul A. Woolgar

Iron ore from the docks at Duluth, Two Harbors and Superior is moved across the Great Lakes to ports on Lake Michigan and Lake Erie by the famous iron ore boats. The season usually starts about the first of March, when the lake ice begins to break-up, and continues until about the first of December. At Allouez Bay, Wisconsin, outbound boats have been caught in the ice and could be prisoners for days or even weeks.

Right: In November, 1928 the Edward J. Berwind was one of several ore boats caught in a severe storm on Lake Superior. Even with her tanks flooded, to get the ship as low in the water as possible, the inclinometer was soon showing rolls as heavy as 40-45 degrees. Fortunately, the thousands of tons of iron ore, loaded at the Great Northern docks, had frozen into a compacted mass that effectively prevented any shifting of the ore cargo, and thus loaded, the Berwind was able to ride out the storm and make port. Five other ships were not so fortunate, as their cargo shifted and they went down.

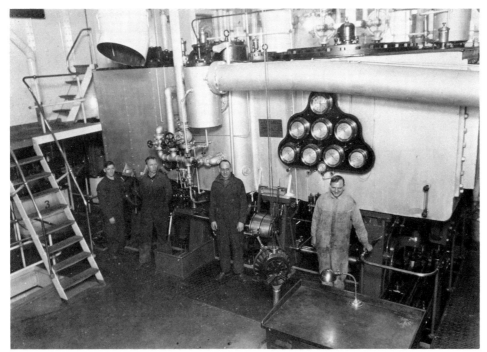

In the engine room of one of the ore boats that used "triple expansion" steam engines, steam pressure was usually around 180 lbs. per square inch. The superheated steam moved from the high pressure 20-24" cylinders to the medium pressure cylinders that measured 30-40" in diameter, and lastly into the low pressure cylinders of 42-50" in diameter. At slow speeds of 90 to 120 revolutions per minute, the engines developed from 3,000 to 6,000 horsepower. The reciprocating and rotating masses of the engines were so large that if the rpm's were increased, the engines threatened to tear themselves to pieces.

Walt Grecula

Walt Grecula

Ed Mueller Collection

In 1937 near Hibbing, Minnesota on the Mesabi Iron Range, miles of track circled hundreds of feet down into the Mahoning huge open pit mine — once the largest in the world. From here the ore cars were assembled and cut into trains at nearby Kelly Lake. From Kelly Lake articulateds, 2-10-2's and heavy Mikes moved 10 to 16 thousand ton ore trains to the docks at Allouez.

Upper left: At Scranton Mine (also near Hibbing) a Scranton Company switcher is ready to take a cut of GN cars up out of the mine to an interchange yard in 1944.

Lower left: A Scranton Company switcher eases a four car cut of ore cars down into the open pit mine at Hibbing, Minnesota — the heart of the Mesabi Iron Range.

Northcote
Hallock
Kennedy
Donaldson
Stephen
Argyle
Warren
Angus
Euclid
Salol
Roseau
Badger
Greenbush
Strathcona
Middle River
Holt
Thief River Falls
St. Hilaire
Beaudette
Rainy
Rainy
Lake
International Falls
River
Kelliher
Grand Falls
Red Lake
Vermilion Lake
Ely
Mallory
Fisher
Wylie
CROOKSTON
Red Lake Falls
Tilden Jc.
Mentor
Erskine
McIntosh
Fosston
Lengby
Bagley
Shevlin
Solway
BEMIDJI
CASS LAKE
GRAND RAPIDS
CHISHOLM
HIBBING
VIRGINIA
Buhl
Mahoning
Kelly Lake
Nashwauk
Bovey
Coleraine
Gunn
Schley
Bena
Allen Jc.
Hillsboro
Grandin
Argusville
Climax
Beltrami
Lockhart
Ada
Borup
Felton
Glyndon
Shelly
Halstad
Perley
FARGO
MOORHEAD
Leech Lake
WALKER
Akeley
Nevis
Park Rapids
Leech L.
Deer River
Cohasset
Warba
Swan River
Mississippi
Lynwood
Goodland
Casco
Baden
BROOKSTON
CLOQUET
Carlton
DULUTH
SUPERIOR
Casselton
Davenport
Downer
Baker
BARNESVILLE
Rothsay
Carlisle
Pelican Rapids
FERGUS FALLS
Menahga
Sebeka
WADENA
Hewitt
Bertha
Eagle Bend
Browerville
Long Prairie
SAUK CENTER
Brainerd
Mille Lacs
Wawina
Floodwood
BROOK PARK
Boylston
Foxboro
Holyoke
Kerrick
Bruno
Askov
Sandstone
Hinckley
Wolverton
Kent
WAHPETON
BRECKENRIDGE
Campbell
Dalton
Ashby
Melby
EVANSVILLE
Alexandria
YARMOUTH
Tintah
Melrose
Freeport
Albany
Avon
Collegeville
SAUK RAPIDS
Foley
Oak Park
Foreston
MILACA
Book
Ogilvie
Mora
Henriette
Grasston
Braham
Stanchfield
Grandy
Cambridge
Isanti
Bethel
Cedar
COON CREEK
Fairmount
Norcross
Herman
Donnelly
Elbow Lake
Osakis
Hancock
Cold Springs
Roscoe
Princeton
Big Lake
ELK RIVER
Anoka
St. Croix R.
BROWNS VALLEY
Beardsley
Graceville
Chokio
MORRIS
Paynesville
BENSON
ST. CLOUD
Clearwater
Monticello
Albertville
Osseo
Robbinsdale
ST. PAUL
Turtle
Stockholm
South Shore
LaBolt
Albee
Nassau
Bellingham
Louisburg
Appleton
Holloway
Danvers
Kerkhoven
Pennock
WILLMAR
Kandiyohi
Atwater
Grove City
Litchfield
Dassel
Cokato
Howard Lake
Delano
Lester Prairie
Mound
WAYZATA
HOPKINS
MINNEAPOLIS
Minnetonka
Hudson
Chippewa Falls
Eau Claire
Raymond
Clara City
Maynard
GRANITE FALLS
Hanley Falls
Cottonwood
MARSHALL
HUTCHINSON
Mississippi
Thomas
Hayti
Lake Norden
Arlington
Wentworth
Russell
Florence
Ruthton
Holland
PIPESTONE
Jasper
GARRETSON
Manley
Hills
Mankato
Lake Crystal
Owatonna
Dodge Center
WINONA
Trevi
Heron Lake
Worthington
Albert Lea
Blue Earth
Taopi
LA CROSSE
SIOUX FALLS
Lennox
Alvord
Doon
Sheldon
Algona
Manly
Viborg
Irene
Volin
YANKTON
Sioux Center
Maurice
Struble
Merrill
Hinton
Mason City
Oelwein
Clarion
I O W A
M I N N E S O T A
W I S
N. P.
M. ST. P. & S. S. M.
ST. P. & P.
C. & N. W.
C. ST. P. M. & O.
C. B. & Q.
CHI. RK. ID. & P.
C. R. I. & P.
C. G. W.
D. W. & P.
ST. P.
I. C.

In northern Minnesota and Wisconsin, freezing weather can be expected any time from November to April. Iron ore compacts easily, and when frozen in the ore cars into a solid mass, it is impossible to dump into the ore pockets on the ore docks until it is thawed and loosened by steaming. Before the construction of stationary steaming plants, steam locomotives were used to supply the steam to the classification yard. It was then distributed by pipes laid under the tracks, and inserted into the cars by flexible hoses. Above: a group of old Mikados are utilized as ore steamers in the Superior yard, while below, long lines of ore cars at Allouez wait to have the ore loosened before moving in cuts to the ore dock.

Wayne C. Olsen collection

Left, the GN high-line leaves the Duluth Union Depot, now a national monument, with the "Gopher", southbound on the elevated trestle in the late 1930's. Above, destined for the scrap line, steam powered Rotary X1501 waits in the yards at Duluth for a call to duty that will never come again. About 50 miles northwest of Duluth is Brookston, the junction point of the main line going west towards Bemidji and Crookston with the tracks leading north to Kelly Lake and Hibbing. Here in August, 1955, a Mike assigned to duty on the Iron Range, trails **an a**uxiliary water car.

Wayne C. Olsen collection

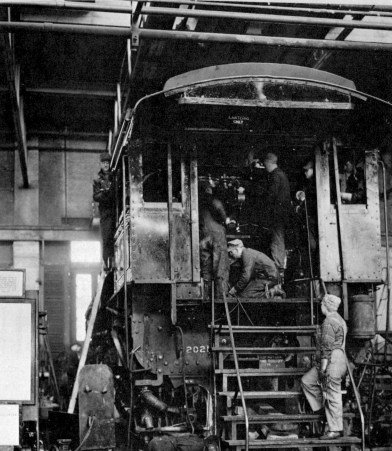

At right heavy switcher No. 837 pushes a cut of ore cars out onto GN Ore Dock No. 1 at Allouez. At one time the GN had four ore docks, but following World War II Dock No. 3, a timber dock dating back to the early 1900's, was dismantled for economic and safety reasons. The three remaining docks, largely concrete and steel, still comprise the largest ore dock installation in the world. Left, the backshops at Superior, shown during World War II, (note woman worker) were capable of handling everything from heavy locomotive repairs and rebuilding to new locomotive construction. Mallet No. 2021 is in for heavy repairs, and a hardstand, mounted on its own small flanged wheels, is pushed up to the back of the cab. A narrow shelf with a raised edge, just below the white stencilled "Lanterns Only" sign above the doorway, was mainly for the use of the head end brakeman, who rode the cab with the engineer and fireman.

Wayne C. Olsen collection

Casey Adams

Above: A westbound freight, under a huge canopy of exhaust smoke, works out onto Gassman Coulee Bridge, west of Minot. For the next 80 miles, the rails climb gradually towards the plateau of the Missouri River — called Plateau du Coteau du Missouri, by early geographers. The highland starts about the center of the state and runs diagonally towards the northwest corner of North Dakota.

Above Left: GN locomotive 113 and train No. 1 wait at Barnesville, Minnesota in 1898. In 1885 to 1896, Barnesville, very close to Fargo, North Dakota, was headquarters of the old Northern Division of the St. Paul & Pacific. The little 4-4-0 gleams from pilot to tender, reflecting the care that it has received. These were the days when a locomotive was a very personal thing to her crew, and when the engine was in for repairs, the crew laid off until it was ready to go back into service. The depot and hotel were destroyed by a fire in 1904, and no record exists of what happened to the beautiful little American type No. 113.

A GN Express Co. horse drawn wagon prominently displays one of the most famous corporate symbols in America. The Rocky Mountain Goat was adopted as the GN trademark just prior to World War I.

Past Blackfoot, Fort Browning, Triple Divide, Spotted Robe, Glacier, Bison and Rising Wolf, the Builder has been steadily climbing towards the summit of the Great Northern main across the Rockies. The exhaust from the stack of the big boilered 4-8-4 roars its defiance at the sky in measured beats, four to each revolution of the 80" drivers of 2588, now slowed to a bare 30 miles per hour. The flanges shrill and squeal on the curves as the Builder continues to fight its way across the backbone of the Continental Divide, April 1941.

W. R. McGee

2. GLACIER NATIONAL PARK AND THE GREAT NORTHERN

Since 1887, when the Great Northern joined rails with the Montana Central at Great Falls, it had been consolidating its gains in Montana. It now had direct access both to the rich mining area of Helena and to Butte, a thriving city of 20,000 with the richest copper mines in the U.S. At Great Falls, one of the largest ore smelters in the world was being built, in addition to a huge hydro-electric plant to supply more power to Butte. The carloadings between Butte, Helena and Great Falls were rising every day. The railroad was paying for itself as it went along, not only by serving areas that had lacked transportation, but by helping to bring immigrants to the vast prairies, whose farms and newly built towns would soon create more traffic for the road.

By 1890, the newly organized Great Northern was ready to push west again from Pacific Junction (near Havre). The immediate objective was to get across the Rocky Mountains, down into the Flathead Valley and Kalispell. The long range objective was to get to tidewater on Puget Sound — 819 miles away.

Simultaneously, although this was not part of the plan, the GN would also materially assist in the creation of Glacier National Park.

The locating work of the route west had been completed in 1889 and 1890 by John F. Stevens and C.F.B. Haskell, locating engineers under the direction of E.H. Beckler, Chief Engineer of the Pacific Extension of the GN. The extension in Montana, also known as the Assiniboine Line, was chosen over alternate routes further south. These others, explored by Major Rogers in 1887, included one known as the Dearborn Line, which was located near Helena at the junction of the Dearborn and Missouri Rivers. Both the Dearborn and the Assiniboine locations would have entered Spokane, but by different routes. That the Dearborn Line would have parallelled the existing Northern Pacific for some distance was definitely not to the liking of James J. Hill, who preferred that the GN create its own towns and business rather than share them with another road.

The selected Assiniboine route aimed directly at Marias Pass and also at the area which was to become Glacier National Park. This is not to say that the route was selected because of the possibility of a National Park right on the main line. The primary consideration, of course, was a crossing of the Continental Divide with manageable grades. However, the choice would prove to be a fortunate circumstance both for the Great Northern and for the creation of the park itself.

There is considerable evidence that the existence of Marias Pass was fairly well known, almost back to the time of the Lewis and Clark Expedition of 1804-1806. Explorer David Thompson reported in 1810 that white traders, accompanied by Indians, had crossed the Mountains by a "wide defile of easy passage" eastward of

Flathead (at that time Selish) Lake. Maps dated 1859, in the possession of the Oregon Historical Society, clearly show Marias Pass, and it is marked as such. In 1864, the Montana Territorial Legislature passed an act to incorporate the Fort Benton & Kootenai Road Company, which would build a wagon road from Fort Benton (where the Marias River joins the Missouri) through Marias Pass. It was to intersect the Hell Gate and Kootenai Wagon Road near Columbia Falls on the west side of the Rockies; but the road was never built because of Indian trouble. The Blackfeet, jealous of their territory, posted sentinels in the pass to prevent its use by others. Even the Flathead Indian tribes to the west, more friendly to the white man, avoided Marias Pass because of their fear of the warlike Blackfeet. Until the Blackfeet were quelled in 1870, few explorers, hunters, or visitors entered the area. Thus, while the existence of the pass was known earlier, it remained for John F. Stevens to relocate the pass and to determine its suitability as a route for the railroad. This he did, reaching the pass December 11, 1889, and very nearly freezing to death in the process.

Even after it was clear that Marias Pass was the best route across the Rockies into the Flathead Valley, a great deal of locating work was still necessary. The pass had to be surveyed from the the west side to the summit, and the railroad had to determine the best route out of the Flathead Valley to some point where it could follow the Kootenai River to the Montana/Idaho border.

To accomplish these tasks, in December, 1889, Mr. C.F.B. Haskell, on orders from Mr. Beckler, was sent into the Flathead Valley, via the NP to Helena and Missoula, and thence by stage and team to Demersville at the north end of Flathead Lake. Established in 1887, Demersville flourished until it was by-passed by the railroad, which opted for a site some 4-1/2 miles to the north, where Kalispell was established in 1891. Some time following this, the town

literally packed up and moved to Kalispell.

Mr. Haskell's first assignment was to explore the western approaches to Marias Pass. Proceeding up the pass — by horse and on foot — he was to take barometric readings as he went, also noting the character of the soil and the country generally. The goal was to build the road with a maximum grade of 2.2% coming down the pass. Once off the summit, he was to determine a location along the Middle Fork of the Flathead not to exceed a grade of 1%.

With two men and supplies, Mr. Haskell left Demersville for the second time on the 29th of January, 1890. He hoped for an easier trip than the one to the summit of Marias Pass on January 5th, but according to Haskell's journal, this terrible trip took 52 days. They had to carry everything on their backs; and with only one blanket apiece, they encountered snow six feet deep and temperatures as low as 44 degrees below zero. They staggered back into Demersville, in a near state of collapse, on the twenty first of March. They had done their locating work well, however, and the reports were forwarded to Mr. Beckler.

On the second trip, Mr. Haskell explored the country west of Kalispell to the Kootenai River, locating Haskell Pass, which would take the railroad over the Cabinet Range of the Rocky Mountains into the valley of the Fisher River, and located the railroad to the juncture of the Kootenai and Fisher Rivers. Because of the 1.5% grades, the Haskell Pass route was abandoned in 1902, nearly ten years after the railroad was completed, and the main line was relocated through Columbia Falls, fifteen miles north of Kalispell. By swinging northwest along the base of the Whitefish Range and along the west shore of Whitefish Lake (at the head of Flathead Valley), the grade could be reduced to less than .3%. Accordingly, the railroad relocated northwest into the valley of the Tobacco River beyond Whitefish, then making a huge loop that came within 8 miles of the Canadian border at Eureka, Montana, swung southwest again to pick up the Kootenai River at Rexford, close to its juncture with the Tobacco River. Following the Kootenai down river some 42 miles, the railroad picked up its original location at Jennings. Kalispell remained on the important branch line that terminates at Somers on Flathead Lake.

In May of 1890, Mr. Haskell left Demersville by boat for Ravalli, then took the NP to Missoula, and from there went north and west along the Clark Fork of the Columbia to Kootenai, Idaho on the north shore of Pend Oreille Lake. From there he continued north to Bonners Ferry to begin the exploration and location of the railroad along the Kootenai River. The Kootenai, a natural route out of Northwestern Montana, had been used for many years by explorers, fur traders and hunters. It would have been navigable for nearly 500 miles but for the high, thundering Kootenai Falls between Libby and Troy that effectively prevented the Kootenai from being used as a major artery of transportation. Navigating as far as the Falls in a bark canoe, and covering 30 miles above the Falls on foot, Haskell completed the location of the Great Northern from Marias Pass to Bonners Ferry, a distance of nearly 235 miles.

After crossing hundreds of miles of flat and rolling prairie, from the Minnesota/Dakota border to Pacific Junction, the Great Northern rails surmounted a low plateau that extends southward from the Sweet Grass Hills — three lonely buttes looming out of a sea of prairie grass. Here, at what would later be the town of Galata, the first glimpse was had of the magnificent peaks of the Continental Divide, still nearly 100 miles away.

With two notable exceptions, construction of the railroad west from Pacific Junction up to the park itself was fairly simple — typical prairie construction of grade, fill, culvert, and ditch the right-of-way. Sixty miles from the summit, however, a 1,200 foot long 180 foot high trestle had to be built to span Cut Bank Creek, which flows out of Glacier Park. Forty-five miles beyond Cut Bank, an 800 foot long 214 foot high trestle was constructed over Two Medicine Creek, which required 45 days to complete and consumed three quarters of a million board feet of timber. Both of these huge structures were designed by Mr. Beckler, with Two Medicine becoming the highest trestle on the Great Northern.

Construction of the railroad through Marias Pass proceeded simultaneously from both east and west. On the east side, supplies from Havre advanced with the railroad. Material for the west side of the pass was brought in to Ravalli on the NP and then hauled some 30 miles by wagon to Flathead Lake, where the supplies were taken by steamboat to Demersville. Demersville served as the material yard for construction both east and west of the Flathead Valley — west towards Haskell Pass and east towards Marias Pass. Two crossings of the Flathead River were necessary, and the huge bridge at Coram (six miles east of Columbia Falls) is one of the most spectacular sights in the Rockies. Although there were 54 miles, much of it heavy mountain construction, between Coram and the summit, only five short tunnels were built along the entire distance. The longest tunnel was 780 feet long, the shortest 180 feet and the total length of all five tunnels only 1,600 feet. This was fortunate because all drilling work was done by hand with the material hauled out by cart.

Many writers had attracted national attention to the Glacier area. As far back as 1883, Lieutenant John T. Van Orsdale, who had been making reconnaissance trips into the park area since 1873, wrote in the Fort Benton River Press, "I sincerely hope that the publicity now being given to that portion of (Northwestern) Montana will result in drawing attention to the scenery that surpasses anything in Montana or adjacent territories. A great benefit would result to Montana if this section could be set aside as a national park".

Another writer deeply impressed by the magnificence of this alpine wilderness, which rises so abruptly from the rolling prairie on the east side of the Rockies, was James Willard Schultz. His articles attracted the interest of the editor of the popular Forest and Stream magazine, George Bird Grinnell. The two men visited the area in 1885, camping, hunting and exploring in the vicinity of St. Mary Lake; and Grinnell, like Schultz, fell in love with the area, vowing to return.

In 1887, a number of travelers came to the east side of the Glacier Park area. Arriving in Helena on the NP, they took a stage to Fort Benton on the Missouri River, and then by horse and trail wagon proceeded to the Blackfeet Agency at Badger Creek, on the eastern boundary of the Rockies. Among these travelers was George Bird Grinnell; and during this trip he explored and named the glaciers at the head of Swiftcurrent and Grinnell Valleys. Returning to Glacier every year for many years, he became an authority on the park, the wildlife, and the Blackfeet Indians as well, tracing their history, culture, and traditions. He earned the respect and admiration of the Blackfeet, who adopted him as a member of the tribe, giving him the name Pinut-u-ye-is-tism-o-kan, or the "Fisher Cap"

The U.S. Government, at the specific request of the Blackfeet, appointed Grinnell to negotiate with them for the acquisition of the area east of the Continental Divide. The purchase was made in 1891. Later known as the father of the movement to establish Glacier National Park, Grinnell wrote many articles to attract national attention to the region. One of his most famous, "Crown of the Continent", appearing in Century Magazine in 1901, is now regarded as having been a significant influence on the ultimate establishment of the park in 1910.

By 1892, trains of the Great Northern

were moving through Marias Pass, across the Flathead Valley to Kalispell, and then over Haskell Pass into the Valley of the Fisher River. They followed the Fisher river north to its confluence with the Kootenai River at Jennings, turned west again to follow the Kootenai through northwestern Montana, and passed out of Montana at its lowest point (1820 feet) into Bonners Ferry, Idaho. At this time, Henry L. Stimson, who later became Secretary of War, ranged over much of the east side of the park area, exploring and hunting with Dr. James of New York and "Indian Billy", a Blackfoot guide. He climbed the east side of Chief Mountain, long regarded by the Blackfeet as menacing and an area to be avoided. He also discovered and explored the mountain which was later named for him, Mt. Stimson.

With the completion of the railroad, and with access to it from nearby Kalispell and Belton, people began to settle in the vicinity of Lake McDonald. In the late 1870's, Duncan McDonald was freighting supplies to Canada by following the North Fork of the Flathead (which joins the Middle Fork between Columbia Falls and Belton) over an old trail that went north into Canada. Finding this trail blocked by unfriendly Indians, he took a more easterly route swinging north into the next paralleling valley. Near what is now Apgar, he carved his name on a tree; and later arrivals settling in the area named the nearby lake after him.

Milo P. Apgar, for whom the village and west entrance to the park is now named, homesteaded at the southern edge of Lake McDonald with Charles Howe, and the two of them built cabins for the visitors who came now in increasing numbers. Mr. Howe was the first to sight Avalanche Lake from Mount Brown in 1894, and his description and enthusiasm for the surrounding peaks, lakes, and valleys encouraged Dr. Lyman B. Sperry from the University of Minnesota to explore the Avalanche Lake Basin and later to climb and walk upon Sperry Glacier. It was here, near Apgar, a short time later, that Charles Russell built his summer

home, "Bull Head Lodge", and did much of his painting.

At the site of the present Lake McDonald Hotel, George Snyder built a simple two story frame structure, and visitors to his hotel arrived at the GN's Belton Station. They were then ferried across the Middle Fork of the Flathead River by rowboat and loaded into the buckboard wagons of Ed Dow's stage line to be bounced and jounced over the rough primitive road, previously cut through the heavy timber by settlers, to the foot of the lake. Here the visitors embarked on Snyder's small steam launch for the ten mile trip up the lake to his hotel. In 1897, a bridge built by Jack Wise across the Middle Fork of the Flathead allowed the stages to run all the way from the Belton Depot to the foot of the lake. John Lewis purchased the Snyder property, and during the winter of 1913/1914, he built the 65 room Lewis Hotel (now the Lake McDonald Hotel). The hotel was sold to the National Park Service in 1930 and operated by the GN.

Further exploration in 1896 by Dr. Sperry convinced him of the feasibility of building a trail into the area east of Lake McDonald, which in its present state was virtually inaccessible. He proposed bringing University of Minnesota students into the area during the summer to build the trail under his supervision, if the Great Northern would provide the necessary transportation and supplies. He presented his plan to James J. Hill, who accepted the proposal. During the summers of 1902 and 1903, trails were completed to the east side of Gunsight Pass and to Sperry Glacier. These trails, as engineered by Dr. Sperry, are still in use today; although they were later rebuilt by the Park Service.

Dr. Sperry also discussed with James J. Hill the enormous potential for developing tourism in the park over the rails of the Great Northern. The Northern Pacific had been promoting tours to Yellowstone for years and had built a branch line from Livingston to Gardiner to serve Yellowstone directly. Yet here, right on the front doorstep of the Great Northern, was a tourist potential to match that of Yellowstone; and the Great Northern could serve the area directly from its main line. With both an east (Glacier Park Station) and west (Belton Station) entrance, there was no need to build a branch line.

As exploration continued deeper into the hidden reaches of the park, it also was becoming more and more apparent that here was a magnificent mountain wilderness so unique that it deserved and needed federal protection and policies to guide the tourist developments that were taking form. On the other side of the border, the Canadian Parliament had set aside Waterton Lakes Park in 1895, naming it for Charles Waterton, the naturalist, who made a botanical survey in the Canadian Rockies in the early part of the nineteenth century. He is credited with being the first white man to visit the park's principal lake, Waterton Lake.

Covering roughly 1,600 square miles, the Glacier-Waterton Lake area (now the Waterton-Glacier International Peace Park) is geologically inseparable. Formed millions of years ago by the wrinkling of the earth's crust, it rose from what had been a part of a huge inland sea. When the sea water drained away from the uplifted and broken rock crust, it exposed the solidified sediment of the sea bottom, thousands of feet thick. Under continual strain for millions of additional years, the western part of the earth's broken crust gradually slid up and over the eastern part, until a 300 mile long section had moved some 33 miles east on both sides of the U.S./Canadian border. This gigantic overthrust — the Lewis Overthrust of Glacier — capped very young rock with stratas of old rock estimated to be more than a billion years old. This capping of young rock with old resulted in the layering effect of the different strata of argillites, sandstone, limestone and shale in shades of yellow, red, gray and green, one atop the other.

The sculpturing of the mountains began a million years ago during the Pleistocene Epoch, a time of advancing and receding glaciation. As the glaciers advanced through the V shaped valleys, the grinding action of millions of tons of hard glacial ice deepened the valleys and changed them to U shapes. Crests between the valleys were reduced in thickness, and the peaks became saw-toothed and sharpened. Moving glaciers carried the exfoliated rock along, and as they receded, deposited the scaled rock, forming the cirques and amphitheaters that today hold many of the beautiful small lakes of the park. Other valleys, dammed by the morainal debris left by retreating glaciers, form many of the larger lakes that are fed by the glaciers and melting snow. The deep valleys, the beautiful lakes, rushing streams, plunging waterfalls, alpine mea-

dows, the hanging valleys left by glaciers at higher elevations, the steep cliffs and vertical escarpments, were formed by a process still going on (although on a much smaller scale).

On December 11, 1907 Senator T. H. Carter of Montana introduced a bill in Congress to establish Glacier National Park. Sent back to Carter for rewriting, the revised bill was again submitted February 24, 1908. Approved and amended by the Committee on Public Lands, it passed the Senate and was sent to the House on May 16th, where Congressman Charles N. Pray of Montana guided it through the House Committee on Public Lands. Returned to the House for a vote, no action was taken and the bill died. Introduced by Senator Carter for the third time June 26, 1909, the bill passed the Senate and lay in the Public Lands Committee until it was reported out by Senator Dixon of Montana on January 25, 1910. Passed by the Senate on February 9th, it was again sent to the House where it was approved with amendments which the Senate objected to. Agreement was reached on the amendments to the bill by a Senate and House conference committee and on May 11, 1910, President Taft signed the bill creating Glacier National Park. It was not, however, until August 22, 1914 that Congress accepted exclusive jurisdiction over the park from the State of Montana.

Not everyone was in favor of a national park in the area. There were those who felt that the government should not concern itself with recreation; and some groups around Kalispell opposed the park on the grounds that the GN was promoting the park to block other railroads from entering the area. What they failed to realize was that there was no other pass north of Marias suitable for a railroad. Cut Bank (Pitamakan) Pass, at an elevation of over 7,000 feet, surrounded by vertical cliffs and plagued by deep snow, would not have been considered by an engineer in his right mind.

It was true that the Great Northern exerted considerable leadership in promoting legislation for Glacier National Park, and also had a commercial interest in the creation of the park, but Louis W. Hill, then President of the GN, loved the park for itself. Along with its other sponsors, he hoped to create a public recreation area for Montana that would attract visitors and be a source of income for the sparsely settled state, as well as for the GN. Louis W. Hill not only devoted his own energies, he deeply involved nearly every department of the GN to help develop the park. With the passage of the bill, opposition quickly simmered down, and the people of Kalispell, so close to this magnificent area, shared in the benefits derived from the heavy summer tourist business.

On August 8, 1910, Major William R. Logan, commissioned by the Secretary of the Interior as Superintendent of Road and Trail Construction, came to the park with his clerk, Henry W. Hutchings. In the fall, with headquarters in tents at Apgar, six rangers were assigned to Major Logan to patrol the entire park boundary. Patrolling the million acre park was a difficult and lonely task. There were only two serviceable trails, one between Lake McDonald and St. Mary Lake via Gunsight Pass, and the other from McDonald Creek Valley to Many Glacier over Swiftcurrent Pass at an elevation of 7,186 feet. With the coming of winter, the rangers retreated to Fort Belknap, returning to Apgar in the spring to begin work on the new park headquarters at Fish Creek. They also extended the telephone line system, rebuilt the road between Lake McDonald and Belton, and started construction on a road from Apgar to Fish Creek. Major Logan had received his appointment as the first Superintendent of Glacier National Park on April 1, 1911, and during the summer he rented Apgar's cabins on Lake McDonald for their quarters.

Funds available to the park for road and trail construction were very limited. The GN stepped into the breach with its own funds to build the roads and trails necessary for supply and transportation of visitors. In 1911, the GN began construction of the road from East Glacier to Many Glacier, the predecessor of the Blackfeet Highway. At this time also, the GN began work on the magnificent visitor accommodations at St. Mary Lake, Many Glacier, Belton, Two Medicine, and East Glacier.

During 1910/1911, the GN relocated much of its main line in the pass between the summit and Essex, a small town some 18 miles below the summit at the foot of the 14 miles of 1.8% grade eastbound. This was done to reduce the curves. At the same time the section was double tracked. Later, the road was partially double tracked another 42 miles to Columbia Falls. There was always snow in Essex during the winter, and two work gangs continuously shoveled snow by hand onto flatcars for dumping into Bear Creek. Seven (helper) engine crews were stationed at Essex, and the little town possessed not one but three water tanks to replenish the big Mallets and 2-10-2's that served as pusher engines on the grade. Known as Walton for a number of years after 1926, Essex remained a sizable railroad center until the 1940's, when the diesels began to take over on "Walton Hill".

The park crew spent the winter of 1912 at the newly constructed Belton Chalet.

The number of park rangers had been increased to sixteen, but patrolling the lengthy borders of the park was still a rugged job. During the winter, one ranger froze to death between cabins on the east side of the park, another was buried in a snowslide for 24 hours, finally digging his way out unaided, and a third

ranger broke his hip in a fall down a snow bank and alone made his way back to his cabin in two days. Work continued at Fish Creek, so the winters of 1913 and 1914 were also spent at the Belton Chalet. By the summer of 1914 the Fish Creek Headquarters was able to quarter personnel all year.

The GN was rapidly completing the accommodations in various areas of the park. The construction of these camps, cabins, chalets, and hotels was a tremendous undertaking, accomplished under the most difficult conditions. The 155 room Glacier Park Hotel at East Glacier, completed in 1913, was similar in architecture to Old Faithful Inn at Yellowstone. The lobby of the magnificent rustic wooden structure is supported by pillars of Douglas Fir over 800 years old, 40 feet high, and up to 40 inches in diameter. The logs were brought in by the trainload from Western Washington, and the Blackfeet, awed by the size of the timbers, called it the "Big Tree Lodge". Located on the shores of Swiftcurrent Lake, Many Glacier Hotel, even larger than Glacier Park Hotel, was opened in 1915. With the completion of the major portion of the GN hotels in the park as well as the many private hotels and cabins on Lake McDonald, lodging was available for as many visitors as the railroad could bring.

Although there still was no road across

the park itself, a thousand miles of trails lay within the park boundaries. All concessions for transportation, as well as for accommodations in the park, were now under Federal control. Besides the boats on the lakes, this transportation consisted largely of the pack and saddle horses. The GN had backed an early day packer, W.J. Hilligoss, who set up a line of tent camps at East Glacier, Two Medicine, Cut Bank Creek, St. Mary Lake, Gunsight Lake, and near the Sperry Chalets. These facilities could service either saddle trips across the park or shorter trips within the park. In 1915, a combine of small pack and saddle concessionaires under W.F. Noffsinger began to operate under a contract with the National Park Service. At one time, The Park Saddle Horse Company, the largest saddle horse outfit of its kind in the world, owned over 1,000 head of horses and served over 10,000 park visitors a year.

In 1917, the Park Service, having already outgrown its Fish Creek Headquarters, moved to new quarters on the site of the present Headquarters at Apgar. The site was purchased by Steven T. Mather, then Director of the National Park Service, with his own funds from Edwin E. Snyder. In the same

year, the Glacier Park Hotel Company, a subsidiary of the GN incorporated in Minnesota in 1914, signed a 21 year contract with the Department of the Interior. Employees for the hotels and chalets, during the June to September season, were drawn from college student applicants across the country. These summer positions in the park were eagerly sought after and highly prized. The last in the GN chain of hotels was the Swiss type Prince of Wales Hotel, opened in Waterton Lakes National Park in 1927.

In the first stages of the development of the park, the GN began an extensive advertising and promotional campaign to attract visitors. Louis W. Hill is credited with the slogan "See America First", which began to appear about 1914 as a part of the rectangular Great Northern herald. At the same time, the words "Glacier National Park" appeared on the bottom edge of the herald. In 1921 the herald was redesigned. The first of the famous round heralds appeared with a white Rocky Mountain Goat in the center against a background of sawtoothed peaks. The slogans "See America First" and "Glacier National Park" appeared around the perimeter of the herald. With Rocky Mountain goats abounding in the park, particularly around the Sperry Chalets, the design was nothing short of inspiration, serving to identify the park and the Great Northern as one. The design became world famous, although over the years it was modified by dropping the slogans and putting the goat in profile.

The GN promoted the park and its beautiful facilities, operated by the Glacier Park Hotel Company, in many different ways. Timetables always mentioned the park on the covers and featured ads promoting the park, its tours, and its facilities. On-line and off-line newspapers carried advertising both during the summer months and before the start of the tourist season. Writers and editors were invited to view the park and to sample the accommodations as part of a continuing publicity campaign. Feature articles and color advertisements appeared in many nationally circulated magazines, including the National Geographic. A wealth of material was free for the asking — just a note to the passenger department of the Great Northern would bring back a flood of pamphlets, many in color, on the park, the Glacier Park Limited, the Oriental Limited and the Empire Builder. At a nominal cost, the same department would send books about the park and the Blackfeet Indians by such famous authors as Mary Roberts Rinehart, Grace Flandreau and James Willard Schultz, as well as prints of paintings by Winold Reiss and W.L. Kinn.

W.R. Mills, advertising agent for the GN, and H.A. Noble, manager of the Glacier Park Hotel Company, sought permission in August, 1925 to place locomotive bells at the summits of Swiftcurrent, Logan, Siyeh, Gunsight, Cut Bank, and Stoney Indian passes and at Grinnell Glacier. The Director of the National Park Service, not favoring the idea, delayed decision on the request until September, 1926, at which time the bells were placed at Swiftcurrent, Piegan, and Siyeh passes. In 1929, a fourth bell was placed on Mt. Henry. The bells, following a Swiss tradition, were beautifully toned and continued to delight visitors until 1943, when they were donated to a World War II scrap metal drive.

In 1926, James Willard Schultz, who had done so much to establish and promote the park, convinced the Great Northern in St. Paul that the names chosen for the stations and hamlets through the pass were completely out of character with the names in the park. As a result Highgate became Singleshot, Fielding — Blacktail, and Java — Nimrod. Sidings and passing tracks were also renamed — Bison, Grizzly, and Silvertip. Thus the emphasis began to shift from James J. Hill's Oriental and English themes to a new Western mood. Playing cards featuring Blackfeet Indians were sold on the trains and in ticket offices. At East Glacier, during the summer season, Blackfeet in full tribal regalia met the trains of the Great Northern during their 15 minute stops. Other Indians, similarly attired, were employed to lend atmosphere to commercial facilities; and tourists were encouraged to pose with their Indian "friends".

In August, 1930 Two Medicine Chalet was set aside for President Hoover and his party, and became the "Summer White House". President Hoover was an ardent fisherman, and Upper Two Medicine Lake, one of the best fishing spots in the park, was set aside for his use. Thousands of less prominent people visited the park and returned each year to spend their vacations. Even in the era of great national depression, travel to the parks soared.

The Department of the Interior proclaimed 1934 as "Travel America Year — Travel to your National Parks", a slogan not far removed from the "See America First" motto coined by the Great Northern some years before. In the 1930's the Great Northern sponsored a series of Monday evening radio shows called The Empire Builder programs. Broadcast over the NBC network, these shows covered virtually every major city in the USA and were timed to reach tourists before the start of the summer season. One of these shows featured the Empire Builder speeding along the southern boundary of Glacier National Park.

Ernie Pyle, famous war correspondent of World War II, arrived for a hiking trip through the park in 1939. Then a traveling columnist for the Scripps-Howard newspapers, he wrote a series of articles describing Glacier as "number one...least trammeled, most beautiful and most awesome of all the parks".

These articles received national attention, and the Great Northern published a folder containing the log of Ernie Pyle's trip and descriptions of the hiking trails in Glacier Park.

In 1940, the Department of the Interior repeated its theme of 1934. The GN boosted the program with three new 16mm color movies of the park made the year before by William S. Yale, a GN employee. These films, along with two similar films made in 1938, were shown throughout the country, with all equipment provided by the GN free of charge. The only requirement was that the films had to be shown either by Mr. Yale or by a traffic representative of the Great Northern.

A variety of all expense tours of the park were sold via the GN. These ranged from an overnight stop to trips of a week or more covering the park area by bus, boat, horseback, and hiking. During the summer season, from June 15 to September 15, every passenger train of the GN served Glacier National Park with the exception of the later, streamlined Empire Builder, whose fast schedule did not permit lengthy stops at East Glacier and Belton. The

Builder's place was filled by the Western Star and its predecessor, the Oriental Limited of the late 1940's. At one time, during the 1920's the Glacier Park Limited ran as the secondary train to the Oriental Limited, with both trains serving the park during the summer season. Special convention trains to the park were promoted; and until the 1940's, there was service between Cody, Wyoming (Yellowstone Park) and Glacier over the Burlington and Great Northern via Billings and Great Falls.

As the number of good highways and freeways increased, the number of visitors coming via the railroad declined steadily. Coming from Kalispell, the first private automobile had entered the park in 1911 via the west entrance. The road ended about five miles below Belton Depot. From this point the car was driven along the tracks of the Great Northern to Belton and thence into the park itself. The first automobile to enter the park on the east side came over the new road to Many Glacier in August, 1913, with Louis W. Hill and his party as passengers. Travel by car along the southern edge of the park, between Belton and East Glacier over Marias Pass, was not possible until 1930, when a section of U.S. Hwy 2 (Theodore Roosevelt Highway) was built paralleling the railroad for most of the distance. The Great Northern, however, had offered an early form of "Piggyback" service between Belton and East Glacier, transporting cars over Marias Pass on railroad flatcars.

The Going-to-the-Sun road, allowing automobile travel from east to west through the park over the Continental Divide, was dedicated at ceremonies in July, 1933. Engineers for the Bureau of Public Roads began reconnaissance for this road in 1916; a preliminary survey being made in 1917-1918. Construction was begun in 1921, and by 1924, a road was complete on the east side to Sun Point and on the west side as far as Logan Creek. The remaining gap, between Sun Point and Logan Creek, was originally surveyed with an 8% grade over the summit of Logan Pass. Not satis-fied with the original survey, the Bureau of Public Roads ordered Frank A. Kittridge and his crews to conduct a second survey. The new route drastically reduced the grade to 5-1/2%. Construction contracts were awarded, and the road was completed in early 1933. It is still in use today, although travel is not permitted over the pass after sundown, and cars pulling trailers of 19' or over are not allowed due to some very tight switchbacks on the west side. Going-to-the-Sun road offers the traveler a breathtaking panorama of the park. From Lake McDonald, Avalanche Creek, and Mt. Cannon the road moves upgrade above glacier-carved McDonald Valley, and climbs steeply past Heavens Peak and along the Weeping Wall, where water drains continuously across the road from melting snow and ice above. It then passes along a man-made ledge to the summit of Logan Pass, elevation 6,654 feet. On the east side of the pass, the road skirts along the northern side of St. Mary Lake. About seven miles before reaching the east entrance of the park, at the Narrows, the yellow limestone rock on each side of the road clearly marks the under lake crossing of the Lewis Overthrust. The limestone is the lowest strata of rock that was lifted up and pushed out over the plains when Glacier was formed millions of years ago. Once beyond the eastern boundary of the park, there is an abrupt transition from mountains to high barren plains. There are few places where the mountains begin and end so abruptly without lesser ranges intervening between the plains and the mountains. Coming from the east, the effect is startling.

The facilities in Glacier Park were closed during World War II and did not reopen until the 1946 season. Because of physical deterioration of the structures during the long period when they were not in use, Cut Bank, St. Mary, and Going-to-the-Sun Chalets were razed. Later, cabin camps with stores and coffee shops were added at Swiftcurrent and Rising Sun.

In 1951, a bombshell of sorts was

dropped by the executive officers of the GN when they indicated to the press that the Great Northern was losing interest in the operation of its extensive facilities in the park. After conversations with the Park Service and Senator Mike Mansfield of Montana, the Hungry Horse News of Kalispell printed the story and it was picked up by the St. Paul Dispatch.

The Public Relations Department of the GN, on July 20, 1951, issued this statement, quoting from an earlier release by the Glacier Park Hotel Company. "Conditions have changed materially since we entered the park operation in 1913. At that time and for years thereafter the railway was the only means of reaching the park and it was felt that construction and operation of the hotels by us was necessary. The necessity for our operating the property has ceased to be of urgent importance. Travel habits have changed due to the automobile. For example in 1950 Glacier Park was visited by 485,000 persons of whom 9,000 arrived by train, while in 1925 only 40,000 visited the park but of these 12,500 arrived by train. Glacier National Park continues to be important to the Great Northern and will be in the future. This is the only railway serving the park and of course its trains will continue to take people to and from there irrespective of who operates the tourist facilities. The park is being operated for the benefit of the large volume of vacationists and we feel quite certain that arrangements will be made to continue operation of facilities in the park next year."

Arrangements were made to continue operation of the facilities in the park, and they remained in force until December 30, 1960 when the properties were sold to Glacier Park Incorporated. Through 1966, the new company invested three million dollars renovating and modernizing facilities in the park as part of the "Mission 66" program, in cooperation with the National Park Service.

Today visitors to the park top the 1,000,000 mark annually, but the park is served by Amtrak rather than by the GN. The visitors arriving by train comprise but a small percentage of what they once did; and Glacier Park Company Incorporated has geared itself to the tourist arriving by automobile. The incomparable scenery of Glacier, however, still awaits the visitor. Its trails and historic buildings stand as monuments to all those in the past who labored so hard to create and develop Glacier National Park. James J. Hill, Louis W. Hill and the Great Northern Railroad place high among them.

Great Northern Railway

John F. Stevens, Chief Engineer of the Great Northern,
points to Marias Pass leading through the Rocky Mountains. To honor
him for his discovery of the pass in December, 1889, the
Great Northern erected this statute close by the tracks at Summit,
Montana in 1925. In the same year, Stevens was awarded the
John Fritz Medal for engineering achievement.

Above: Were it not for the falls of the Kootenai, some 11 miles west of Libby, the river would be continuously navigable for 500 miles.

Right: In August, 1903 a grading team works on a hillside cut near Fortine as the new GN main via Whitefish was being built.

Glacier Natural History Assn.

Philip C. Johnson

The Empire Builder of 1968 crosses the 1,200′ long trestle over
Cut Bank Creek, flowing out of the east side of the park.

After slowing to catch orders for movement down Marias
Pass in double track territory, No. 27, with bell ringing, drifts
past Summit station in 1939. During the winter months,
Summit often was inaccessible, except by rail, and the station
also provided living quarters for the operators. At an
elevation of 5,213′, Summit is the highest point on the main
line, located right on the Continental Divide — the waters of
Summit Creek flow to the east, those of Bear Creek to the west.

Above: A brand new train of F-3's and refrigerator cars poses on Two Medicine Bridge — 210' above the North Fork of Two Medicine River — just outside the east entrance to Glacier National Park. Above left: The original Two Medicine Bridge in 1891 was a wooden structure that consumed three quarters of a million board feet of timber. At 214' it was the highest trestle on the GN.

Above George Bird Grinnell is regarded as the father of the movement to establish Glacier National Park. Above right: Blackfeet Indians pose for their picture near Glacier Park Hotel in 1915. The Blackfeet, once regarded one of the most warlike tribes in the Northwest, were greatly feared not only by white men, but by neighboring tribes as well. It was from land largely under their control that Glacier Park was formed.

National Park Service

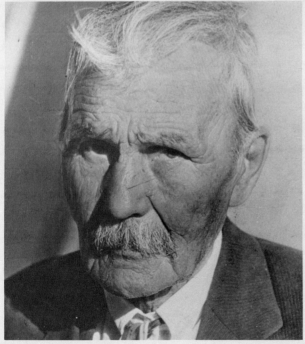

Left: Duncan McDonald, freighting
supplies to Canada in the late
1870's, carved his name on a tree by
the shore of the lake which now
bears his name — Lake McDonald.

National Park Service

The Apgar cabin, at the foot of Lake McDonald in 1893, stands on the present site of the village of Apgar near the west entrance to the park. The original Belton Bridge over the Middle Fork of the Flathead, connecting Belton and Apgar, was built in 1897.

Left: Dr. Lyman B. Sperry of the University of Minnesota, with the agreement of James J. Hill, used college students to build the trails to Gunsight Pass and Sperry Glacier during the summers of 1902 and 1903.
Below: The Sperry party at Avalanche Lake.

Travel in the park was often as colorful as the scenery.

Initially, travel in the park was possible only by hiking and pack horse. By the early 1900's, boats were in service on both Lake McDonald and St. Mary Lake, and by 1914 buses were put into service by White Motor Company as the "Glacier Park Transportation Company". Although modern transportation now provides easy access to the park, there are still over 1,000 miles of trails, making Glacier the greatest hiking park in the United States.

All photos National Park Service

Red Eagle, Little Chief and Citadel Mountains
are in the background across from St. Mary Lake.

A brand new class P-2 Mountain type leads the Oriental
Limited of 1923 past Red Eagle along the southern boundary of Glacier.

McCartyville, a railroad construction town located about five miles west of the summit of Marias Pass, was at one time considered the toughest town in the state of Montana.

Right: Frank Liebig, a forest ranger appointed to the park area in 1902 — armed with a saw, a double-bitted ax, a rifle and a box of ammunition — patrolled alone the entire area from Belton to Canada, across the Rockies to the prairie and down to the foot of St. Mary Lake.

Claude Witt

Essex, 27 miles upgrade from Belton, has been a helper station from the time the line was built through Marias Pass. It appears above as it looked in the early 1920's. At that time and through the 1930's, it had about 400 residents and 8 passenger trains a day.

National Park Service

eft above is the original two story frame Snyder otel on Lake McDonald in 1896. A small steam unch provided transportation from Apgar to the otel located 10 miles up the lake. Left is the Lake 1cDonald Hotel, built during the winter of 1913/14 ear the site of the Snyder Hotel.

Louis W. Hill, shown at Glacier National Park in 1910-1911, as president of the GN, devoted considerable energy to the establishment of the park as a tourist center for all to enjoy. Under his leadership, virtually every department of the GN became involved in this mammoth effort. Although there were no roads, and the sources of supply for the material to build the hotels and chalets planned were far removed from the site, Many Glacier Hotel and Granite Park Chalets were opened to receive the first visitors by 1915. That the park happened to be on the main line of the GN was a happy circumstance. Visitor usage rose from a mere 4,000 in 1911, to nearly 750,000 by 1959.

The magnificent 155 room lodge at East Glacier was completed in 1913. At an elevation of 4,800', snow still lays heavy around the depot platform in April, and the lodge is not officially opened for guests until mid-June. The logs for the 40' pillars in the lobby were Douglas Fir, over 800 years old, brought in from Washington State. Indians in full tribal regalia were employed to lend atmosphere, and a Blackfeet greets guests at the main entrance to the lodge in 1915.

National Park Service photos

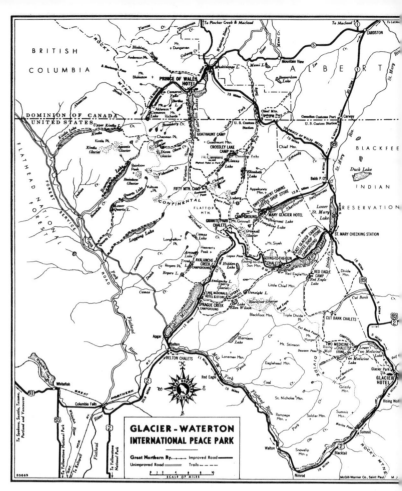

Heading up the east slope of the Continental Divide, Going-to-the-Sun Highway, above the shore of St. Mary Lake, passes under Deadhorse Point, a dangerous area of crumbling rock. Just beyond, at Sun Point, were the Going-to-the-Sun Chalets. Closed during World War II, they were never reopened, but were razed because of their deteriorated physical condition and the cost to repair them.

National Park Serv

Great Northern Railway

The Prince of Wales Hotel, built in 1927 at Waterton Lake, completed the system of hotels and chalets built by the Great Northern. They were operated and managed by the Glacier Park Hotel Company, a wholly owned GN subsidiary.

Many Glacier Hotel, built in 1915 by the Great Northern Railway on the shore of Swiftcurrent Lake, looks across at Grinnell Point and Mount Gould.

103

The Glacier Park Limited, behind a new Mountain type, winds down Marias Pass not far from Essex in 1923. During this period one of the hostlers at Essex was always accompanied by his dog while moving engines around the small yard. To the right is Pullman conductor O. E. Moats and his famous five handed railroad watch with which he kept track of the three time zones between St. Paul and Seattle. Conductor Moats was a veteran of many years service on the GN on both the Glacier Park Limited and the Oriental Limited.

National Park Service

Charles R. Wood

Essex in the 1970's remains a key link in the movements up and down Marias Pass. The heaviest grade eastbound begins here, and helpers are cut in to assist eastward movements. Essex station is open 24 hours a day, and three operators plus a relief operator work the three shifts around the clock.

Izaak Walton Hotel at Essex was built by the Great Northern not long after U.S. Hwy 2 was completed across Marias Pass. Now owned by Sid and Millie Goodrich, it is a haven for ski fans in the winter and rail fans year around.

Charles R. Wood

Charles R. Wood

U.S. Hwy 2 crosses the summit of Marias Pass. The railroad station is located behind the white buildings to the left.

In the fall of 1926 the Glacier Park Hotel Company, with permission from the Park Service, placed locomotive bells on Piegan, Swiftcurrent and Siyeh Passes. The use of the beautifully toned bells, ringing loud and clear in the mountain air for those who crossed the passes, was based on an old Swiss tradition. Shown is the bell at Piegan Pass, now removed.

National Park Service

Glacier Park station, located scarcely a stones
throw from Glacier Park Lodge, shows little activity on this
June 9, the day before the opening of the lodge for
the 1976 season.

National Park Service

Above: In the winter of 1923 a new 2-10-2 type built by
Baldwin takes a tonnage test train out of Belton. Left: On the
big curve at Blacktail, another 2-10-2 pauses on its way down
the pass with a westward drag freight.

During the spring of 1940 and 1941, photographer and N.P. conductor, W.R. McGee paced the Empire Builder through Glacier National Park, taking the series of photos reproduced on the following pages...

Left: On a fill high above the Middle Fork of the Flathead River, the Empire Builder of 1940 is on the gauntlet track just west of Nimrod. In the disastrous flood of 1964, almost this entire stretch of track was washed out, leaving nothing but a gaping hole that took tens of thousands of yards of material to fill.

Below: Two hours and seventy miles west of Shelby, No. 1, The Builder, stops at Glacier Park Station to take on water. It is April, 1940, and although Glacier Park Lodge is not yet open to receive summer visitors and guests, the water plug is open the full year around.

Left: A quarter mile east of Rising Wolf, the Empire Builder nears the summit of Marias Pass and the Continental Divide in the spring of 1941.
Left below: The silvered smokebox of 2588 reflects the early afternoon sunlight as the engine rounds another curve just west of Rising Wolf. Both 2588 and 2586 were assigned to the Empire Builder between Havre and Whitefish, crossing the First and Second Subdivisions of the Kalispell Division.
Below: Near Pinnacle, its battle with the 1% westbound grades won, the big Northern has stopped working steam, and the Builder rolls easily downgrade towards Belton.

Burned trees in the background notwithstanding, the scenery surrounding this
stretch of track along the Middle Fork of the Flathead River on the southern
boundary of Glacier is so outstanding, that the westbound Empire Builder schedule
has always been set so that it can be seen in the daylight. Glacial silt turns the
water a grayish green, the deeper pools taking on a darker hue. Here near Belton
the track is only a few feet above the river level as the water cascades in froth and
foam over the rock formations. U.S. Highway 2 parallels the track on a slightly
higher grade, making it somewhat less prone to washout in times
of flood and high water.

W. R. McGee

At Hidden Lake, Train No. 435 with engine 2059, one of the huge R-2's built at Hillyard, on the point, drifts downgrade towards Red Eagle and Belton with retainers on the cars turned up. In the 7 miles between Blacktail and Nimrod, all freight trains were required to use twenty minutes descending the heavy grade, as they were also in the 7 miles between Summit and Blacktail. In both cases the car retainers were turned up to assist in holding back the trains. Inspection and a running air test were required before leaving Summit. In the days before dynamic braking, descending a steep grade was far more difficult than climbing the grade, for once on the descent, it was impossible for the engine brakes alone to hold the train back.

Seattle Tin

One of the first 2 unit FT type freighters was put into service on the GN in 1941 on Walton Hill, the 1.8% helper grade over Marias Pass. Later in the fall of 1941, a 4 unit FT type freighter was also put in service on the hill, and these early diesels performed invaluable service for the GN during the war years.

The late afternoon sun reflects off the sides of the cars and F units of the Builder as it eases across the Flathead River viaduct at Coram, Montana. The coordinated color scheme is almost a perfect match on the cars and engine units, and it is not difficult to see why the Builder of the 1950's was regarded by many as the most beautiful train in thè world.

Philip C. Johnson

W. R. McGee

No. 3, the Western Star, drifts downgrade along the southern boundary
of Glacier Park, near Hidden Lake, in 1952. Diesels 355 A-B-C and D are P-3's,
delivered to the railroad in 1947. Equipped with steam heat boilers, they are
longer than the freight service F-3's, and with a higher gear ratio —
considerably faster. Much of the track on the Second Subdivision was double
track, and all of it was equipped with automatic block signals. With crossovers
and interlocking plants at Summit, Blacktail, Singleshot, Nimrod, Walton,
Columbia Falls and Half Moon, both passenger and extra movements could be
run against or around the current of traffic to expedite movements.

Above: The Empire Builder of the late 1950's rolls through the gently rolling terrain of the Blackfeet Indian Reservation, a few miles east of Glacier National Park. This train represented the zenith of the Builder, with three domes for coach passengers, and the Great Dome further back for Pullman passengers.

Upper right: An upper quadrant signal beckons "clear" as the westbound Builder whines down Marias Pass in the late fall of 1957. The view from the cab of a covered wagon type diesel — in this case an F-7 — is superb. The serenity of the pass, on this October afternoon, is deceiving. In the winter, snow slides often thunder down across both tracks of the main, and further down the pass, the flooding waters of the Flathead River — more than once — have left nothing but rails and ties suspended above huge washouts.

Lower right: Business car A-28, with the unusual drum head GN herald on the observation railing, is spotted at East Glacier in July, 1951. The official car for the president of the Great Northern, A-28, was equipped with mechanical air conditioning, train radio and other suitable appliances. As of 1965, the GN had 12 business cars, in essence, mobile offices that could be taken anywhere on the vast system.

Dr. Philip R. Hastings

Philip C. Johnson

The Builder of 1968 rolls around a curve east of Belton that was washed out in the 1964 flood. In the foreground, bulldozer tracks are still clearly visible four years after the flood.

Philip C. Johnson

C. M. Rasmussen collection 3 photos

June, 1964 was a month long to be remembered by the Great Northern. The trouble started during June 6, 7, and 8, when over eight inches of rain was dumped on a large area of the Continental Divide. For a distance of nearly 75 miles along the Great Northern transcontinental main line bordering Glacier National Park — from Two Medicine to Belton and nearly to Columbia Falls — the rampaging flood waters of the Middle Fork of the Flathead tore at the railroad. With irresistable force, the swirling muddy water ripped out huge chunks of embankments, scoured bridge footings, and flooded tunnels, plugging them with debris. Snowshed footings and side walls were undermined, and thousands of cubic yards of fill and embankment material tumbled into the waters of the Flathead like a sand castle hit by the waters of an incoming tide. A freight, moving upgrade from Essex, stalled when a stock car in the middle of the train sagged on the undermined tracks and derailed. The air brakes promptly set in emergency, and a brakeman, crawling between cars, was able to uncouple the derailed stock car at both ends. The pusher engines took one half of the train back to Essex, while the lead engines pulled the rest of the train out of immediate danger. Three work trains and a force of over 300 men with 30 bulldozers, four 1½ yard shovels, and numerous other pieces of equipment, replaced culverts, a million yards of fill material, six miles of signal and communication line and many miles of rail. Three weeks and $3,000,000 later, the railroad was moving again. On June 29, Mr. C. M. Rasmussen, then General Manager of Lines West, prepares to help drive the last spike to re-open the railroad. Another three weeks of cleanup and detail work were still necessary to stabilize and settle the record setting repair job.

47. Brown's Glacier Park and Observation Car, at National Park

Oriental Limited crossing the Rocky Mountains.

GREAT NORTHERN RAILWAY'S STREAMLINED *Empire Builder*

ALONG THE BORDER OF GLACIER NATIONAL PARK IN MONTANA   8B-H389

Through the years the GN conducted a massive advertising and public relations program promoting the park and the facilities operated by the Great Northern's wholly owned subsidiary — the Glacier Park Hotel Company. Examples of some of the literature, cards and brochures distributed by the GN during the half century it was active in the park concessions are reproduced on these pages.

126

Glacier National Park
WATERTON LAKES PARK

. "America's most Sublime Wilderness, Lying partly
. in the United States in Northwest Montana and ·
. partly in the Lower Canadian Rockies"

GREAT NORTHERN RAILWAY

Tourist use of the park rose from a mere 4,000 in 1911 to over three quarters of a million annually in the years that the Great Northern was most active in promoting Glacier National Park.

On the highest level of the switchbacks, a passenger train, with two engines leading and one pushing, makes its way to the summit. On the next level a little Mogul type chuffs upgrade, and in the foreground one of the biggest mountain engines that Jim Hill could buy — a twelve wheeled type — comes upgrade past the water tank with a passenger car. While the track has neither tie plates nor inner guard rails, heavy rail braces are spiked to the outside of about every fifth tie, to reinforce the rails and prevent any spreading.

3. CONQUERING THE CASCADES

Troy, Montana, the western terminus of the Kalispell Division is the point of change between Pacific and Mountain Time Zones. Leaving Troy on the south bank of the Kootenai, as the river begins its bend northwest, the GN continues westbound on the Spokane Division. Passing through Yakt, the most westerly station on the route in Montana, the railroad crosses into the heavily forested 50 mile wide Idaho Panhandle at Leonia. The depot platform straddles the border, with the east end in Montana and the west in Idaho. Following the Kootenai, the line reaches Bonners Ferry, once the junction point with a GN branch north to Creston, B.C. and an outfitting point for the gold and silver miners headed there. At Bonners Ferry the railroad leaves the Kootenai and swings southwest for 33 miles to Sand Point on the north shore of Lake Pend Oreille. For a distance of 29 miles the road follows the western arm of the lake and the Pend Oreille River which flows out of it through Priest River and Albany Falls into Newport, Washington. At Newport the Pend Oreille River turns due north to eventually join the Columbia across the Canadian border, and the railroad turns south for Spokane. From Scotia to Chattaroy the line passes through the Little Spokane River Valley.

At Dean, just outside of Spokane, A GN branch (built under the charters of the Spokane Falls & Northern and the Nelson & Fort Shepherd Railroads) reaches north and east through Marcus, Washington to Nelson, B.C. A right-of-way to build a branch north and west of Marcus through the Grandby area and then down the Kettle River Valley to Republic, Washington, was granted to the Washington & Great

THE WILD WENATCHEE—IN TUMWATER CANYON

Northern Railway in June, 1901. This road, built to bring out the many minerals being found in the Danville area, was in operation by the spring of 1902. As part of the agreement, the GN was required to construct the custom buildings at Danville and Laurier. In 1905 the line was extended from Curlew on the west branch to Ferry, and by 1907 it ran via Molson and Chesaw to Oroville in the Okanogan Valley. While the "ore train every twenty minutes" visualized by James J. Hill failed to materialize, the well-built road still operates in 1976 from Spokane to Kettle Falls to Republic. The main line continues on through the railroad yard at Hillyard into Spokane, where James J. Hill had convinced the citizens of the merits of donating to the GN a right-of-way through the city.

With the locating work in Montana completed, John F. Stevens and C.F.B. Haskell, his assistant, were sent to Washington State to locate the railroad from Spokane to Puget Sound. Leaving Bonners Ferry on June 3, 1890, Mr. Haskell proceeded to Spokane Falls (as Spokane was then known), arriving on June 8th. Spokane (first settled in 1872) still showed the effects of the disastrous fire that — ten months earlier — had destroyed 32 blocks in the heart of the city. He liked the area, describing it as the only decent country since leaving Minneapolis, and felt that Spokane had a great future.

Coming down the Columbia — "the greatest river" he had ever seen — he arrived at Waterville, about seven miles from the river on June 25th. Instead of continuing to the Cascades, he was ordered to return cross-country via horseback to Spokane

Falls. Leaving Waterville on the 28th of June, he arrived that night at Coulee City, and described it as "a miserable little town about six weeks old". Coulee City was located at the only possible crossing in Grand Coulee — an old bed of the Columbia, 100 miles long and in some places up to 5 miles wide and 1,000 feet deep. The NP was building a line through Coulee City, and the town was a beehive of activity. Traveling through Wilbur and Davenport, he reached Spokane Falls on the 5th of July, little impressed with the hot, dry rocky Big Bend country, comparing it unfavorably even with South Dakota, for which he had no great admiration.

Back in Waterville on the 18th of July, he left for Moses Lake, then west to the Columbia, Ellensburg and up Snoqualmie Pass. He also visited Seattle and Tacoma on Puget Sound, returning via the NP and Stampede Pass to Ellensburg, from there by stage to Waterville and by horseback to Spokane. On September 12, 1890, he returned to Waterville to meet with Stevens and Beckler.

While Haskell had been kept busy in the Big Bend country for most of the summer, Stevens had been exploring the whole Cascade range between Stampede Pass and the Canadian border, searching for a suitable pass through the Cascades. The decision of where to cross the Cascades would be the main determination in the decision as to where to cross the Columbia. On a trip up Wenatchee Lake, Mr. Stevens had discovered a creek flowing into the lake from the south that turned abruptly west into the high country. On a previous trip along the summit he had observed a low gap in the main range, and believed that the creek could flow nowhere but into this gap. Time did not permit further exploration as he had to return to his headquarters in Waterville. He then dispatched Mr. Haskell to Wenatchee Lake with orders to follow the creek to all of its heads. Haskell left Waterville on the 15th of September via Orando on the Columbia, then up the Wenatchee River to the creek near Wenat-chee Lake. At the head of the creek (Nason Creek), Mr. Haskell found the pass, and carved "Stevens Pass" on a cedar tree before continuing west to the Skykomish River. There was no indication that the pass had been previously known — the trail had to be cut all the way through the heavy timber and almost impenetrable brush. On a later trip John F. Stevens and Mr. E.H. Beckler confirmed the pass as the most suitable crossing for the GN.

Work parties remained in the mountains until driven out by the snow, and then continued working through the winter of 1891 on the prairie east of Wenatchee. In February they went down the Columbia to Moses Coulee, and then returned to Wenatchee to work their way toward the summit as the snow line would permit. By June 5th, still camped at Stevens Pass, the preliminary work had been completed and the locating work begun. The locating continued through the summer and fall of 1891.

As the line moved through Spokane, heavy bridge work was required crossing and recrossing the Spokane River, which arises out of Lake Coeur d' Alene and flows through the heart of the city. Five bridges in all cross the river. West of the station, the third bridge crosses from Havermale Island to the south shore of the river; the fourth, and largest bridge, crosses directly over the Falls and the fifth crosses the river as it turns north at the outskirt of the city.

The track turns from the Spokane River at Lyons to travel the one hundred and forty miles to the Columbia. From the highest point (two thousand three hundred twenty feet) at Bluestem, the line begins its descent into the Big Bend country, named for the Big Bend of the Columbia River. Ideal wheat country, it encompasses approximately seven thousand square miles.

The stop at Soap Lake (according to the 1916 GN timetable) allowed passengers to benefit from "a medical lake efficacious in the treatment of rheumatism and ailments of the stomach" — the lake deriving its name from "its cleansing effect on the innards of mankind".

Leaving the Big Bend country at Ephrata, the track heads west and descends, by a horseshoe curve, the sheer walls of Crater Coulee. Still descending, the track follows the east bank of the Columbia northward. From the station at Columbia River a GN branch reaches northeast up Moses Coulee to Mansfield, Washington. The main line continues to Rock Island, through the tunnel; and just north of the station it crosses to the west bank of the Columbia over a 906′ long steel bridge 70′ above high water.

Near the confluence of the Columbia and Wenatchee Rivers, the rails arrive at Wenatchee, "The Apple Capitol of the World" and the junction point between the Spokane and Cascade Divisions. Dr. Jewett brought the first apple trees into the Wenatchee Valley in 1873 by packhorse and brought water to them by digging ditches. With the coming of the railroad, homesteaders irrigated them by means of water wheels set on floats in the Columbia. In 1903, a high line canal was built from Peshastin to distribute water from the Wenatchee River.

Following the Wenatchee River, the line turned northwest to Cashmere and began the ascent up the east slope of the Cascades. Some 20 miles west of the Columbia, the line reached Leavenworth at the head of the Wenatchee River Valley. The tracks, still following the Wenatchee River, then turned north into the Tumwater (Talking Water) Canyon; and the railroad climbed along a 10 mile twisting course between the sheer, yet heavily forested, canyon walls. Emerging from the Tumwater Canyon at Chiwaukum, the line proceeded westward through a deep gap in the mountains, up Nason Creek Canyon with its nearly perpendicular cliffs, to Berne and across the summit to Wellington. From Wellington the tracks descended the west slope of the Cascades along the north wall of the Tye River Canyon. The line ran through Embro, Martin's Creek Tunnel, and Scenic, ending in Skykomish, a western terminus of the Cascade Division. At Skykomish the Beckler and Tye Rivers

unite to form the south fork of the Skykomish River. The tracks continue west, bridging both the Skykomish and Miller Rivers, to reach Index at the confluence of the north and south forks of the Skykomish. From the shadow of Mt. Index, the railroad proceeds west through Goldbar and Sultan, where it leaves the Skykomish, to Monroe and Snohomish. It then follows the Snohomish River into Everett.

The Cascades, a relatively young range of mountains, extend some 700 miles from Canada to northern California. Stevens Pass lies on the southern boundary of the vast primitive area known as the North Cascades, the largest alpine wilderness in the contiguous United States. From the Canadian border to Snoqualmie Pass, some 30 miles south of Stevens Pass, there are 288 peaks between 7,000 and 9,000 feet high. There are over 500 glaciers, covering an area of nearly 100 square miles — three times the glacier area of the rest of the 50 states, excluding Alaska. The Cascades form the demarcation line between two distinct climatic zones, with Ponderosa Pine, mixed conifers and grasslands on the dry continental eastern slopes, and heavy stands of giant Douglas Fir on the wet, temperate west side. On the east side, the air is much drier and the temperatures more extreme, falling below zero degrees for long periods during much of the winter. While rain can be heavy and continuous from October to April on the west side, snow is not encountered often below the 1,000′ level. Even at the higher altitudes, temperatures can climb above freezing, making the snow extremely heavy and unstable.

Earlier surveys, using the technology of the 1880's, had deemed the Cascades nearly impossible to cross. For this reason the NP had located its original line via the Columbia River Gorge to Portland, Oregon, and then north to the Puget Sound country, a detour of nearly 200 miles. It was through this formidable country that the GN had decided to poke its rails to gain access to the heavy and extremely valuable stands of timber on the west side of the Cascades, then largely being transported by the pioneering NP and large fleets of lumber schooners operating along the coast. Additional heavy duty, high capacity overland transportation also was needed badly to serve the entire Pacific Northwest, which was growing rapidly.

At the time Chief Engineer E.H. Beckler decided to cross the Cascades via Stevens Pass, it was known that this route would eventually require a summit tunnel about 2-½ miles long if the line was to be of a permanent nature. Construction of a tunnel through nearly solid granite, however, would require several years to complete, and with the GN locating engineers under heavy pressure to complete the transcontinental line, time was of the essence. Surveys had indicated that a temporary switchback arrangement, almost identical to that used by the NP prior to the completion of Stampede Tunnel, could be used to cross the summit in short order.

The line had been surveyed up the Tumwater Canyon to what would later be called Cascade Tunnel Station, at an elevation of 3,382', without exceeding a 2.2% grade. The survey up the west slope from Skykomish to Wellington, at 3,136', also was done without exceeding a 2.2% grade. Haskell then surveyed the route over the summit with a maximum 4% grade. The 4½ miles between Cascade Tunnel Station and Wellington, which reached an elevation of 4,059' at the summit, required 12 miles of rails and included 8 switchbacks, 5 on the west side of the summit and 3 on the east side. The switchbacks, completed in 1892, had a vertical rise of 677' above the projected tunnel location on the east side and 898' on the steeper west side. Con-

struction on the line moved up the west slope from Skykomish; and on January 6, 1893, the final spike was driven near Scenic to complete the transcontinental line.

It was recognized that the 3.5% grades of the switchbacks on the east side, and the even steeper 4% grades on the west side would be a major impediment to heavy duty operation, but the situation was even worse than had been foreseen. The necessarily short tail tracks of each switchback — about 1,000' in length on the average — were a further handicap which would severely limit train length, even if the motive power was adequate to get the trains up and down the switchbacks. The little Moguls, that were standard power in the Cascades, could handle only two or three cars on the 4%, and were soon joined by the heavier Consolidations and Twelve Wheelers that had been delivered in 1892 for service in the Rocky Mountains. There was little room on the switchbacks, however, to utilize their services. With the heavy snow, trains dared not work in this area in the winter without a rotary plow ahead and behind. Operation was at best slow and unwieldy, taking between 1-½ and 2 hours to traverse the switchbacks. Under adverse conditions, it could take 36 hours. It became absolutely essential to build the tunnel as quickly as possible.

The tunnel to eliminate "Death Mountain" was surveyed and engineered by Stevens. Actual construction began in 1897, directed by his own staff, with no outside contractors employed. The tough granite yielded slowly, sometimes only a few feet per day, and additional problems were encountered with wind, water, explosives and a high labor turnover. The nearly 800 men, employed

SKYKOMISH VALLEY AND INDEX PEAKS

133

in the tunnel and support facilities, (at Wellington and Cascade Tunnel Station), spent their time off in Leavenworth. The citizens, mostly regular employees of the railroad, complained bitterly about the wild Saturday nights. The headings in the 2.63 mile long tunnel met in September, 1900, and regular service through the tunnel began in December.

The tunnel reduced the maximum elevation to 3,383', eliminated some 8.5 miles of track, and cut the running time by about two hours. The GN spoke of the new tunnel in glowing terms, stating that, "The immense white tube lighted with double rows of electric lights will be the wonder and admiration of all travelers across America, and as far as human foresight can predict will endure for countless ages, a monument to the daring ingenuity of the Great Northern's engineers."

Operation did improve with the opening of the new tunnel. With the addition of new power trains lengthened from 25 to 40 cars; and they could be hauled intact through the tunnel. The accumulation of smoke and gas within the tunnel, however, was a continuing problem. The coal burned was supposed to be free of sulphur and gas forming materials, but gas masks were standard equipment on all engines. Temperatures in the cabs sometimes reached 200 degrees, and the telephones installed every quarter of a mile for emergencies were often rendered inoperable by the smoke and gas.

On one occasion in 1903, more than 100 passengers narrowly escaped asphyxiation when the coupler, between the helper and the road engine failed in the tunnel. Valuable time was lost in a futile attempt to fix the coupler, and the engineer, fireman and conductor collapsed from the fumes. Another fireman, riding as a passenger, realized what had happened. He made his way to the engine and released the brakes. Fortunately he remained conscious long enough to apply the emergency brakes as the cars rolled into the Wellington yard with the crew and most of the passengers unconscious.

On July 10, 1909, a three-phase type electrification was completed, the only one of this type in the Western Hemisphere, and the only system developed at the time to permit regenerative braking on descending grades. Whenever speed exceeded the synchronous speed of the motors, the motors automatically became generators, returning power to the line, and holding back the train by the resulting drag. Train tonnage was limited, however, to maintain a 15 mph road speed to correspond to the 375 rpm synchronous speed of the motors, in order to prevent motor damage. Many of the crews did not like working on the motors. The street car type trolley poles were prone to come off the wire at every opportunity, and it still took time to couple on the electrics and release them again at Cascade Tunnel Station. Nevertheless, the little electric motors accomplished the purpose of moving trains through the tunnel without gassing the crews or the passengers; and they were particularly suitable for controlling the westbound trains downgrade through the tunnel.

Unfortunately, the electrification did not solve the problem of snow in the winter months. The railroad, exposed as it was, could be plugged by slides almost anywhere between Scenic and Leavenworth. The 21 miles between Skykomish and Wellington were to cause the railroad more trouble than most of the rest of the 1,800 mile line to St. Paul.

A prelude to the Wellington disaster had occurred in December, 1907. Preceded by a rotary plow, Baldwin Pacific 1438 pulled train No. 4 out of Skykomish headed for Wellington. Drifting snows, driven by high winds, filled the cuts. It took 5 hours to cover the 12 miles to Scenic, where the crew argued against continuing the remaining 9 miles to Wellington. Ordered on by the dispatcher, the train was within about 2 miles of Wellington when an avalanche roared down, sealing off the entrance to the snowshed that the rotary had just entered. Throwing the train into reverse, the engineer backed into the snowshed from which it had just emerged only seconds ahead of slides which sealed off both entrances to the shed. Here they remained for 10 days before walking out to Wellington. It was another 2 days before the train could be dug out.

A little more than two years later the situation did not end so happily. The winter of 1909-1910 had been a very difficult one over the 57 mile Cascade Division. Now near the end of February, Superintendent James H. O'Neill looked forward to the approaching spring. Instead of better weather, however, there followed two weeks of one of the heaviest snowfalls ever to hit the Cascades so late in the season.

On February 22, 1910, train No. 26, (an eastbound local), followed by No. 2, the Oriental Limited, arrived in Skykomish. At 10:15 PM they followed the rotary through Cascade Tunnel and reached Leavenworth without incident. The westbound freight they had encountered reached Scenic safely. At 1:30 AM February 23, train No. 25, a passenger local serving Spokane, Wenatchee, Everett, Seattle and Tacoma over a run of about 375 miles, and train No. 27, a four car fast mail from St. Paul, running late because of snow in the Bitter Roots, were ordered to proceed west from Leavenworth. The storm from the west increased in intensity, and the rotary that was to meet them was trapped by a slide at Windy Point. As there were no diners on the trains, and the only food available was at Cascade or Wellington, the decision was made to halt the trains at Cascade Tunnel

Station. It was the night of the 24th before the tracks were clear enough to move the trains through the tunnel to Wellington. During the night, an avalanche 50' wide hit Cascade, knocking the cookshack into the ravine and causing two deaths. It also prevented retreat back to Leavenworth.

The facilities were overtaxed at Wellington, the people worn to the point of exhaustion. There was too much snow, too many drifts, and the anxiety mounted on the part of the passengers over the possibility of an avalanche. The tunnel was too cold, damp and full of fumes (if they kept the engines steaming to provide heat and light) to consider placing the trains within its confines. Snowsheds would not cover a complete train, and they were also placed in the areas considered most dangerous. On the 26th, a slide 88' long, 35' deep, and filled with timber fell between the double rotary and its coal supply at Wellington. There was no way to break through; and now with no rotary to plow the spur tracks, it was impossible to move the trains even if this had been deemed the best choice.

O'Neill and two brakemen began the walk to Scenic. The 4 miles required 9 miles of track to reduce the elevation 1,000'. At Windy Point, there was an 800' drop to Scenic. Five passengers from the train set out on the 27th, and after an exhausting hike, slid down the ravine from Windy Point on their coat tails. Supplies were running low at Wellington, workers were quitting because their demands for more pay were refused, and the trains remained trapped by slides from the east as well as the west. Another group of 11 (5 of them trainmen) set out for Scenic on the 28th. That night there was an electrical storm and heavy rain. At about 1:45 AM, the hillside — denuded by a forest fire the previous summer — came down, sweeping the two trains and seven locomotives into the ravine. The slide, 2,000'

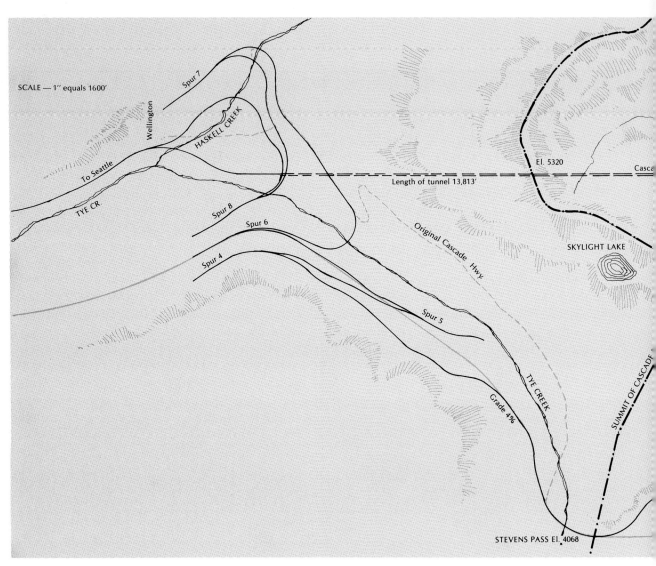

Spur 7

Wellington

HASKELL CREEK

To Seattle

TYE CR.

Spur 8

Spur 6

Spur 4

El. 5320

Casca

Length of tunnel 13,813'

Original Cascade Hwy.

SKYLIGHT LAKE

Spur 5

TYE CREEK

Grade 4%

SUMMIT OF CASCADE

STEVENS PASS El. 4068

wide, ½ mile long and 14' deep with snow and debris, took the lives of 96 people. There were confused, conflicting and erroneous reports on the casualties until the official GN report, issued on March 10, listed the number at 95. The spring run off revealed one more body, raising the count to 96 — 35 passengers, 55 trainmen and postal employees and 6 unidentified laborers. Suits were carried to the Supreme Court, which ultimately pronounced the disaster to be "an act of God". The GN changed the name of the town to Tye.

There were 25 to 30 miles of almost continuous slides through Stevens Pass at the same time, often mixed with rock and tree trunks. The rotaries were helpless, and blasting powder was used to clear the tracks. The first train broke through the tunnel from the east side to Wellington on March 9, and the way opened from Scenic

on March 12. The only way to protect the right-of-way located at the foot of the steep snow covered slopes was to build snowsheds. Through the rest of 1910, $1,500,000 was spent. This included the cost of building a 3,900' reinforced concrete shed at Wellington, 870' east of the existing wooden shed, with a new wooden shed to cover the distance in between, as well as new wooden sheds at 26 other locations. These covered 5,411' of track in addition to the 17 existing sheds, which covered 7,593' of track. A 6" pipe was laid alongside the track from Wellington to Scenic with standpipes in the sheds with hoses for fire protection. Coal bins were placed inside the sheds for emergency use by the locomotives and rotaries. Heavy relocation of 2.07 miles of the line at Berne and smaller changes at other points were made to eliminate the need to build more

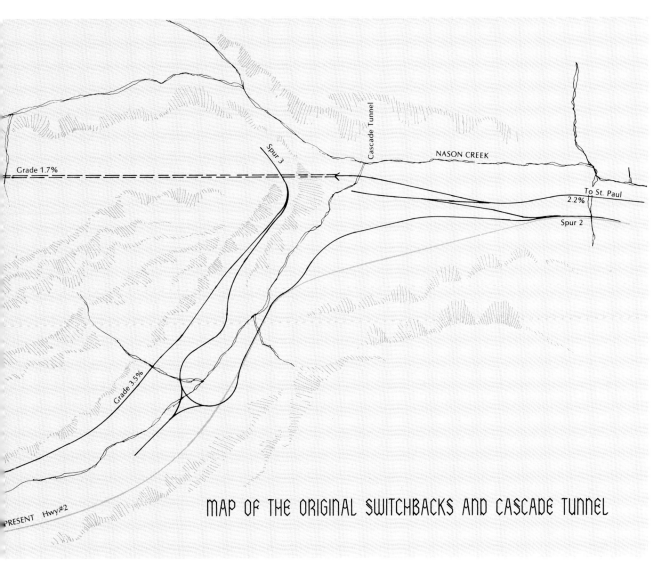

Grade 1.7%

Spur 3

Cascade Tunnel

NASON CREEK

To St. Paul

2.2%

Spur 2

Grade 3.5%

PRESENT Hwy #2

MAP OF THE ORIGINAL SWITCHBACKS AND CASCADE TUNNEL

snowsheds. In the following years, Windy Point was tunneled through and more snowsheds added, until 61% of the track between Wellington and Scenic were covered. Even so, the problem was not solved until the completion of the new Cascade Tunnel and the relocation of some 40 miles of track at a cost of $25,000,000.

In 1923, the Division Point was moved 22 miles east, from Leavenworth to Wenatchee. Economy demanded longer freight trains. The more powerful Mikes and Mallets put into service made it possible to haul greatly increased tonnage, but these longer heavier trains could not be pulled through the tunnel with the available 3 unit electric power. The addition of a fourth unit would overload the power plant, and therefore the trains were being broken in two, a time consuming oper-

ation. To solve this problem, the "Cascade" connection was developed by the electrical engineers. This was a system which allowed the traction motors to run at half speed without damaging the power plant, and also allowed the addition of the fourth unit. From then on, freight trains were hauled through the tunnel by the 4 units at 7.5 mph, and passenger trains at the regular 15 mph by 2 units. This in turn created an expensive surplus of electric motive power. To utilize these idle crews, locomotives, and power plants, and thereby decrease the operating costs, the GN decided to extend the electrification to Skykomish, even though plans being made for a new Cascade Tunnel would not only eliminate the electrification in the old tunnel, but 9 miles (between Scenic and Tye) of the new electrification as well.

The old 6,600 volt, three-phase system

by G.E. was not adapted for the extension to Skykomish because of its operating limitations. Instead, a new 11,500 volt, single phase trolley system was completed and put into operation between Scenic and Cascade Tunnel Station on February 6, 1927, and extended to Skykomish on March 5. New motive power was added in 1927 and 1928. The larger single units were built by G.E. and the smaller double units, which operated as one locomotive, by Baldwin Westinghouse. In addition, a single unit from the Spokane and Inland Railroad (Spokane Couer d'Alene & Palouse) was rebuilt for auxiliary use on the line. These were put into operation on the old line until completion of the new tunnel.

Studies for a new tunnel had been made in 1916-1917, another very bad winter in the Cascades. Ten possibilities were narrowed down to four, but World War I postponed any further plans. In 1921, locating surveys were resumed; and in 1925, John F. Stevens, recalled to the GN as consulting engineer, chose the ten mile Berne to Scenic route as the most practical. This survey included a 7.79 mile tunnel with a fall of 634' east to west, ¾ mile of new grade on the east slope to Berne and 1-½ miles of new grade on the west slope to Scenic.

The GN Board of Directors accepted Stevens' recommendation for the new tunnel on Thanksgiving Day, November 26, 1925, and gave the go ahead to President Ralph Budd. The contract was awarded to A. Guthrie & Company of St. Paul, Minnesota. The construction program, worked out by company Vice President J.C. Baxter, was under the direct supervision of Col. Frederick Mears, Asst. Chief Engineer of

the GN. To avoid maintenance on the deteriorating snowsheds for another winter, the project was to be completed in the winter of 1928-1929.

To expedite the work, drilling was begun simultaneously at both portals, with a third shaft sunk 622' to the tunnel level from Mill Creek, 2.41 miles west of East Portal. This heavily timbered 8'x24' shaft was later lowered to 659' to provide storage room and a sump for drainage. The Mill Creek shaft was completed in August, 1926, and work progressed west from East Portal and east upgrade from Mill Creek.

The western section, between Mill Creek and West Portal, was more than twice as long (5.38 miles) as the eastern section; and a pioneer tunnel was drilled 66' on the south side of and parallel to the main bore.

The drilling of both tunnels began on December 28, 1925, but the smaller size of the pioneer tunnel (8' wide and 9' high), compared to the larger tunnel (18' wide and 26' high), insured that the work in the smaller tunnel could progress well in advance of that in the main bore. Breakthrough in the pioneer tunnel occurred May 1, 1928, with President Coolidge setting off the final blast from Washington D.C. The pioneer tunnel was built 7' above the main tunnel subgrade, with crosscuts at 45 degree angles at approximately 1,500' intervals, thus maintaining work at many faces. Supplies and equipment could be moved in, and debris moved out, at several locations rather than at one. Later, when water became a serious problem, the pioneer tunnel floor was dropped so that it could serve to drain the main tunnel.

To complete the project in a little over

three years required that the tunnel be built twice as fast as any such tunnel had been built before. Many records were broken. At one time there were 1,793 men working underground, with work continuing night and day, Sundays and holidays. Four and three quarter million pounds of gelatin dynamite and ¾ million electric blasting caps were used. Concrete for the lining was mixed where it was poured. The first concrete was poured a year and a half after the start of drilling, and the last just 16 days after the last rock was removed. The work had been done so accurately on this nearly 8 mile tunnel that on "holing through" the two lines met only 9" apart and at levels only 3" different. The tunnel was completed on December 24, 1928, and the rails laid by January 4, 1929, in time for the opening on January 12.

The opening ceremonies were carried by N.B.C. over a hookup of 36 radio stations. Presided over by nationally known announcer Graham McNamee, the program included a speech by President Herbert Hoover, a song by Mme. Ernestine Schumann-Heink, and a dedication of the tunnel to James J. Hill by GN President Ralph Budd. Newspaper reporters and dignitaries waited to be hauled through the tunnel on a special train behind one of the new 2 unit electric locomotives. As the locomotives paused just inside the East Portal for the ceremonies, condensation created by the sudden change from the cold air outside to the warm air inside the tunnel, caused an arc-over on the transformer of the second unit. The first unit was unable to move the train alone, and as the 20 minute trip stretched into 35 minutes, the announcer at the West Portal ran out of words and filled in with band music. A third electric pushed the train through the tunnel, and it at last emerged triumphant through the paper covering the West Portal to the relief of all concerned.

The new tunnel reduced the summit elevation to 2,881' and eliminated 1,940 degrees of curvature. It also eliminated the track between Cascade Tunnel Station and Berne, the 2.2% grade between Scenic and Tye, and about 40,000' of snowsheds, two big steel trestles over Martin's Creek, and several smaller bridges.

Just as important as the new Cascade Tunnel, in improving the operation of the GN through the Cascades, was the relocation of the line up the eastern slope of the mountains, at a cost of approximately $5,000,000. Surveys on various routes for a new line had begun in 1921, and A. Guthrie & Company began construction on the chosen route in July, 1927. The relocation began at Peshastin, with a 2/3 mile connection built east of Leavenworth between the old and new lines. Proceeding up the Chumstick Valley, the new line reentered the Wenatchee Valley through the 2,601' Chumstick Tunnel, crossed over the Wenatchee River on a 360' steel bridge, and entered Dead Horse Canyon through an 800' tunnel. It then passed through the 3,960' Winton Tunnel to rejoin the original line.

The Chumstick Line replaced the old line winding along the Wenatchee River through the Tumwater Canyon, which had been blocked so often by heavy snow. It eliminated about 1-½ miles of snowsheds, as well as the need to build an additional 4,000' of cover. Although the new route was only about one mile shorter than the old, it reduced much of the sharp curvature and steep grades of the old line. There were 48 fewer curves, totalling 1,286 degrees, and the sharpest curves were now 3 degrees as opposed to 9 degrees. The maximum grade had been reduced about one fourth to 1.6%. The only 2.2% grades now left on the main line were the 12 miles between Skykomish and West Portal, and the 4 miles between East Portal and the start of the new Chumstick Line.

With the completion of the Chumstick cutoff in 1928, it was decided to electrify the remaining 50 miles of the line from Berne to Wenatchee and eliminate the need for steam entirely. Altogether 72.9 miles of main line and 17.04 miles of secondary track between Wenatchee and Skykomish were electrified at a cost of $6,000,000, not including the portion through the old tunnel. Power was provided by Puget Sound Power & Light, who established plants at Skykomish and Wenatchee, in addition to using the Tumwater plant leased to them by the GN.

While the new system speeded up the service and wiped out the losses of the steam operation, it was never used to its full potential. At the time of its installation, the GN and the NP were considering a merger. The system was therefore designed with the capacity to haul the main line traffic of both roads over the tunnel route, a demand never placed upon it. There was also the possibility of extending the electrification to Spokane. Massively over-designed, the system was also inherently complicated and inefficient. Electric power had to pass through a transformer, a motor and a generator to reach the traction motors, and the engines rarely exceeded a 40% efficiency.

As the GN turned to dieselization after World War II, a sharper look was given to the costs of the electrified operation through the Cascades. The result of those studies was that in 1956 the entire electrification project was scrapped in favor of diesel operation, and the Cascade Tunnel was equipped with a ventilation system, that through the use of two huge 6' fans placed at the east end, could blow air over the eastbound trains climbing upgrade.

The Baldwin-Westinghouse 2 unit motors and the G.E.-built W-1's were scrapped. Eight G.E. locomotives were sold to the Pennsylvania Railroad, and the power station at Tumwater was sold to the Chelan County P.U.D. The catenary and transmission lines were torn down, and today the long multipowered diesel freights move through the Cascades over what is still very much a mountain railroad.

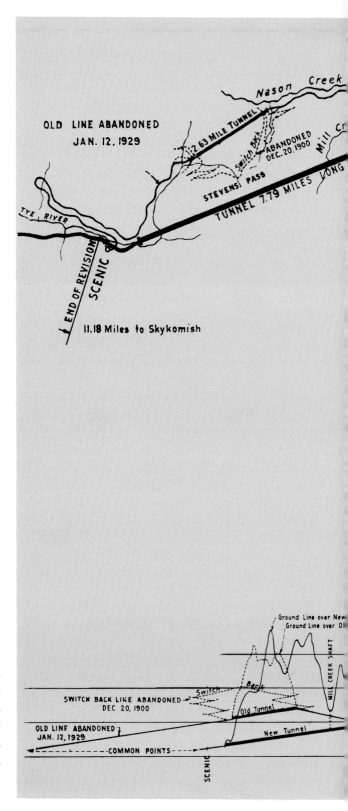

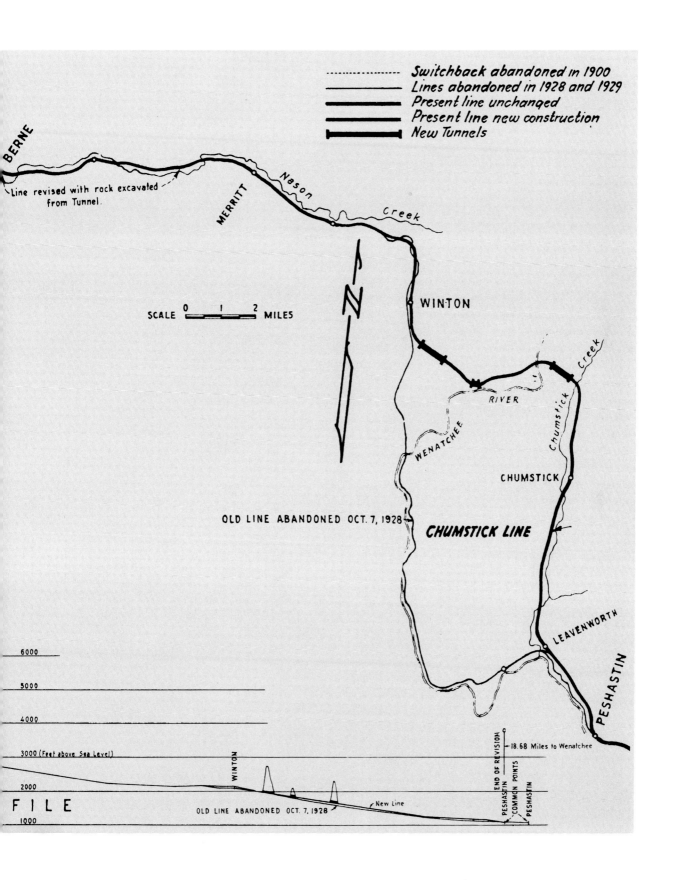

Switchback abandoned in 1900
Lines abandoned in 1928 and 1929
Present line unchanged
Present line new construction
New Tunnels

BERNE

Line revised with rock excavated
from Tunnel.

MERRITT

Nason

Creek

WINTON

RIVER

Chumstick

Creek

Wenatchee

CHUMSTICK

SCALE 0 1 2 MILES

OLD LINE ABANDONED OCT. 7, 1928

CHUMSTICK LINE

LEAVENWORTH

PESHASTIN

6000

5000

4000

3000 (Feet above Sea Level)

2000

WINTON

END OF REVISION

18.68 Miles to Wenatchee

PESHASTIN COMMON POINTS

PESHASTIN

F I L E

1000

OLD LINE ABANDONED OCT. 7, 1928

New Line

Walt Grecula

Eastern Washington State Historical Society

In June, 1890, John F. Stevens and C.F.B. Haskell were sent to Washington State to complete the location of the line from Spokane Falls (As Spokane was originally named) through the rugged Cascade Mountains to Puget Sound and tidewater.

Several views of early day Spokane. At upper left, in 1892, the Howard Street bridges cross Havermale Island, and the 1890 Exposition Building crowns the hill in the background. The GN's line and depot were located to the right of the second bridge, out of the picture. The second view is Spokane Falls prior to 1900, looking Northeast towards "Mt. Carlin" (now Mt. Spokane). The GN's beautiful depot on Havermale Island, built in 1902, was torn down to make way for Expo '74. Only the clock tower remains. The postcard shows a Westbound express, in 1912, pounding out of Spokane across the bridge over the lower falls.

LOWER FALLS, SPOKANE, WASH

Walt Grecula

143

The mineral waters of Soap Lake, 117 miles west of Spokane, were believed to
be medicinal in quality, and a large sanitorium was built on the lake
shore. For many years, the little GN station and the spa enjoyed a thriving
business, as the fame of the lake spread across the country.

Transportation along the Columbia to Central Washington was severely limited by Rock Island
Rapids. Access to Wenatchee and the rich country to the north was by horseback
or by an occasional wagon that braved the rough trails, until the arrival of the GN.
In this early photo, the railroad grade along the east bank, descending to the Columbia
from the horseshoe curve around Crater Coulee, is a light scar on the side of the cliffs. The
rapids below Wenatchee disappeared when Rock Island Dam was built in 1930.

The GN began construction of the Columbia River bridge, near Rock Island Rapids, in 1892.
A major undertaking for the railroad, and regarded as one of the finest cantilever structures in
the U.S., the bridge was built high enough to allow steamboats to pass beneath on
their way to a Rock Island terminal. For a period of seven months, prior to the completion
of the bridge in 1893, trains were ferried across the river on the car ferry, Thomas L. Nixon.

The Wenatchee World

The Wenatchee World

Wenatchee was to be the principal townsite of the GN between Spokane Falls and Puget Sound, and by the spring of 1892, James J. Hill had purchased for the GN a one quarter interest (500 shares of stock @ $50 a share) in the Wenatchee Development Corporation. Eight years later, the GN parallels the river on the Wenatchee (west) side, but most of the fruit warehouses that comprised "warehouse row" are yet to be built.

Walt Thayer

With the cliffs of Moses Coulee in the background, the Special pauses at Appledale, Washington on the Winchester/Mansfield branch. The sixty mile line, opened April 20, 1910, left the Columbia River below Wenatchee, near Cabinet Rapids, and for twenty miles followed the floor of Moses Coulee, an awesome mile wide rent in the basaltic rock that at one time was the old course of the Columbia River.

Steamboats plied the upper Columbia from Wenatchee to the head of navigation, near the tributary Okanogan River, until the building of the Wenatchee — Oroville branch in 1914. The boats, served by a spur from the GN yard, operated from a landing approved by Hill downstream from the GN station. They were under the control of Captain Alexander Griggs, an associate of Hill during the steamboat days on the Red River of the North. In the background is the Columbia River highway bridge, built during 1906/1908, partly financed by Hill who insisted that its span be designed to take the weight of a trolley line with a capacity of 58 tons.

SNOWSHOVELING ON STEVENS PASS FOR TRACKLAYING — DEC 14" 9[?]

ORDEAL IN THE CASCADES

The upper photos illustrate some of the difficulties encountered during construction through the formidable Cascades. Hundreds of workers had to be recruited to laboriously hand shovel the tons of deep snow out of the way before a tie could be laid or a bridge timber put into place. Heavy rock work, as is evidenced by this rock cut at station 780 on the main line west of the summit of Stevens Pass, was encountered by the construction crews working east from Everett. Blasting powder was used to loosen and break up the rock, most of which was then removed by hand tools and put into horse drawn carts for dumping. Trees comparable in size to this giant cedar — 60' in circumference — were also problems for workmen along the right of way. Most of the construction workers on the Great Northern in the 1890's were not Chinese as had been the case with the Northern Pacific a few years earlier, but Scandinavian, Irish and German immigrants — homesteaders who needed paying work to sustain their tenuous hold on the land.

To the right is the tree near the head of Nason Creek upon which locating engineer C. F. B. Haskell in 1890 carved the name STEVEN'S PASS.

U. S. Forest Service

Within the image: No 18 / Lower Portal of Tunnel at M... / Tye 150' High Trestle

Above: The lower portal of Martin Creek Tunnel is shown before construction of the trestle. Both the upper and lower portals of the tunnel faced east, as the railroad doubled back on itself, in this area, while climbing along the north wall of the Tye River Canyon.

Upper left: Looking downgrade east of Martin Creek on the old line near Windy Point, horse drawn carts are used to move the rock and earth from the tunnel at station 290. Left: The little town of Martin Creek was a welcome sight to the lumberjacks, the tracklayers and others laboring on the railroad in the Cascades. The log building in the foreground of the "business district" offers "Beds" and the Cascade Saloon advertises "Meals, cheapest and best in town".

TRACKLAYING ON BRIDGE N°4 OF SWITCH BACK WEST SIDE SUMMIT N°45

In 1893, prior to the completion of a tunnel, a series of switchbacks was constructed over the summit of Stevens Pass so that the main line of the GN could be put into operation. In just such a manner the NP had crossed Stampede Pass in 1887. The NP however had to live with their switchbacks for only a year, while the GN with a much more difficult tunnel to construct, had to live with theirs until 1900. There were five switchbacks on the west side, gaining an elevation of 898'. Although there was never a serious accident on the switchbacks, the 4% grades, 12 degree curves and short stub end tracks beyond the switches made the operation a real hair-raiser, and see-sawing back and forth up and down the mountain was slow and severely limited the capacity of the entire main line.

Burlington Northern and
Dr. George E. Fischer collection

SHEPHARD HENRY & CO.
STORE AT FOSS RIVER

154

At left: John Maloney, head packer for the GN during construction of the railroad, later founded the town of Skykomish. Below left: Contractors, Shepherd Henry & Company built their store at Foss River, just east of Skykomish, from materials cut near the site. The tent next door was a restaurant for construction workers. Above : The frontier town of Wallace began as a clearing in the woods along the Skykomish River, and later was renamed Startup at the insistence of the Post Office Department because of confusion with Wallace, Idaho.
Below : Index, 14 miles down river from Skykomish at the confluence of the north and south forks of the Skykomish River, is shown in 1892.

THE WORK IS FINISHED

TRACKLAYING - LAYING LAST RAIL (AT STA 758+74) ON MAIN LINE WEST

Snow was piled high at trackside in the Cascade Mountains on January 6, 1893, when two
Great Northern Railway officials drove the final spike in to the roughly-hewn crosstie to
complete a continuous track from the Twin Cities of Minnesota to Puget Sound. The site of
the impromptu ceremony was near the present western portal of the 7.79 mile Cascade
Tunnel, completed in 1929. The track-laying rig lowered the last rails onto the ties, and as the
heavy maul pounded the last spike, cheers rose from the workmen. They were drowned out by
sharp cracks from a six-shooter and the shrill whistles of work train locomotives that
reverberated throughout the Skykomish Valley. The first train over the tortuous switchbacks of
GN's original Cascade crossing arrived in Seattle on January 8, 1893,
but it was not until the following June that regularly scheduled passenger service was
inaugurated between St. Paul and the Pacific Coast.

In the photos on the left, the last rail was laid on the west side of the summit of Stevens Pass
on December 10, 1892, and with the work completed, old flatcars were used to carry out the
dismantled horse drawn carts and other construction material no longer needed.

157

Above: In this 1898 photo of the original GN switchbacks over the Cascades
the section of track in the immediate foreground leads downward curving into
Martin Creek Tunnel. Still curving and descending, the rails come out of the
other portal across the valley onto the 150' high Martin Creek Trestle. Both portals
of the tunnel faced east as the track made a half circle inside the mountain

Above right: A seven car passenger train is being worked up the 3.5% grades
of the east side switchback. The trestle in the foreground
crosses over Nason Creek.

Right: On the east side a three car train slowly eases around one of the 12
degree curves of the switchbacks. A forest fire has swept this side of the
mountain and the low brush is coming back to cover the burn.

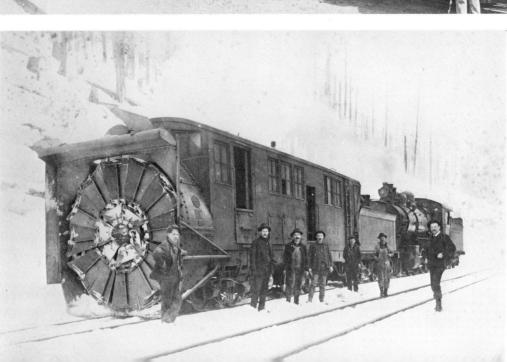

Two little Moguls pause for breath after working an eastbound passenger train up to Wellington. The lead engine is spotted just beyond the short girder bridge that crossed over Haskell Creek. In the immediate foreground, the track leads back to a very steep grade up the side of the mountain, ending in a dirt embankment. This was the safety or runaway track, used to prevent an out of control train from continuing on downgrade.

On the left, one of many Consolidations, delivered to the GN in the late 1890's to muscle freight trains across the Cascades, and one of the Ten Wheelers, that supplanted the little Moguls in passenger service, wait at Wellington. The steam powered rotary plow was a common sight between Leavenworth, Wellington and Skykomish. During periods of heavy snowfall, three or more rotary plows were in continuous service up and down Stevens Pass, stopping only to take on coal and water. Not everyone who was assigned there in the early days liked Wellington — the nearest doctor was in Skykomish, the nearest church was in Leavenworth, and at one time, the only non-railroad employee in Wellington was the hotel keeper.

Dr. George E. Fischer collection

The Original Tunnel 1900

The Great Tunnel

After the "Switch-Back"—the tunnel!
Scarcely less interesting than the "Switch-Back" will be the wonderful new tunnel now in process of construction by the Great Northern, through the Cascade Mountains, and which will take the place of the present "Switch-Back."

SKYKOMISH VALLEY AND INDEX PEAKS

The terminals of the tunnel at Cascade Tunnel and Wellington have already been referred to and will be seen by passengers while crossing on the "Switch-Back."

A reference to accompanying maps and diagrams will give an idea of the plan of the tunnel. This great piece of engineering will be two miles and a half long—13,200 feet. The roof will

16

be at one place of solid granite—5,350 feet thick. The tunnel will run in a straight line from the head of one canyon to that of another, with a slope of about ninety feet to the mile. The east portal is at an elevation of about 3,375 feet above sea level, while the west portal is about 3,125 feet above the same base. Work on the approaches to

AT THE HEAD OF THE WORKINGS, EAST SIDE OF TUNNEL WORKMEN DRILLING ROCK WITH DRILLS DRIVEN BY COMPRESSED AIR—TUNNEL LIGHTED BY ELECTRICITY

the tunnel began in January, 1897, but it was late in the summer of that year before the workmen got fairly under cover and had the compressor plants installed.

About 800 men, all told, are employed in and about the tunnel. Work is going on from both ends simultaneously.

17

Claude Witt collection

The original Cascade Tunnel, under construction for three years, was opened in December, 1900. The 2.63 mile bore, built on a 1.7% grade from east to west, eliminated 12 miles of switchbacks, uncounted degrees of curvature, and saved 8.5 miles in distance between Wellington on the west side, and Cascade Tunnel station at the east portal. Most of the tunnel was bored through solid granite, with only a little "lossen and seamy rock" at the west approach. [Above] A G.N. promotional booklet of the era explains the tunnels construction and length. [Above right] Not long after the opening, a freight "drifts" into the east portal. Because of the heavy smoke conditions, steam would be cut, and the trains would ".drift" on the downhill grade that ran from east to west. [At right] Also from a promotional brochure, a party of hikers pose at the west entrance to the tunnel.

Cascade Tunnel 1902
Great Northern Rly

Robert collection; Oregon Historical Society

271. Cascade Tunnel, Cascade, Wash.—G. N. R. R.

CASCADE

Charles R. Wood collection

Strandrud Family

Above: A trio of the three phase electric motors, delivered by GE in time to begin service on the newly completed electrification system, stand in Wellington yard. With all of their 115 ton weight on the drivers, the engines were rated at 47,600 lbs. of tractive effort (actually tested up to 80,000 lbs.) far exceeding original design specifications. Their synchronous electric motors turned at 375 rpm's to give them a road speed of 15 mph, and the three of them could take 1,600 tons and the steam road engine through the tunnel. A later modification, known as the "Cascade connection", made by changing the internal connections of the armature, allowed their motors to run at half speed, and enabled four of the units to work together at 7.5 mph. In this manner, they could take a 2,500 ton train through the tunnel, no small feat for a 1907 designed electric locomotive. Left: An eastbound passenger train enters Cascade Tunnel with a crew member riding the extended platform on the back of the helper so that he may assist with the trolley retaining ropes while holding on simultaneously to the hand rails. Trolley poles were used to collect current as pantographs were not practical on the widely spaced overhead wires, but the tendency of the trolley poles to jump the wire was a problem serious enough to require a member of the train crew to ride the back of the last unit to help stabilize the spring loaded retaining ropes and/or put the trolley wheels back on the wire if they jumped. Above left: Resembling an oversize street car with two trolley poles, one of the little electrics drifts out of Cascade Tunnel. Not all enginemen loved the electrics. Engineer Mike Finn left Wellington "to get to civilization" and because he "preferred a steamer in road service". Enginemen also thought inspection of the electrics was hazardous, with "full current in the car". As the years passed however the electrics improved, and by the time the new Westinghouse motors began to arrive in 1927, running the electrics was a preferred position.

Claude Witt collection

Above: Cascade Tunnel Station in 1910 was a turn-around and servicing point for helper engines coming up from Leavenworth. Also during the winter, extra section gangs were quartered here to assist in keeping the railroad open. The 66' enclosed turntable, located beyond the depot, is identified by the ventilator in the center of the roof, while not visible is a three stall engine house for the electrics used in the tunnel. Nearly buried in the snow above the trees is a trestle from the old switchback.

Left: The electric powerhouse and surge tank were built in the Tumwater Canyon, 30 miles from the electrified Cascade Tunnel, in 1907-09. The energy of the turbulent Wenatchee River was harnessed by the Tumwater Dam, transformed into 3 phase alternating current, and transmitted at 33,000 volts to the substation at Cascade Tunnel Station. At Cascade Substation the power was reduced to 6,600 volts and fed to the catenary, to power the 3 phase electric locomotives.

Right: At Cascade Tunnel Station a trio of B-B electrics have locked couplers with the steam helper on the point of No. 1, the Oriental Limited. In the era before the powerful class P-2 Mountains went into service in the Cascades, the heavy Oriental Limited needed the power of double-headed Ten Wheelers or Pacifics to get up the long grade from Leavenworth.

Walt Thayer collection

In the yard at Wellington, a work extra includes a car with an elevated platform for working on the overhead wiring. Carrying the markers, is one of the curious little 4 wheeled cabooses used by the GN prior to World War I.

Nippon Wash.

(Above) Nippon (later Alpine) was located on the 2.2⁰ grade between Skykomish and Scenic. Originally named for the many Japanese who settled in the area, at one time it was an important lumber center. (Upper right) The depot and tank at Scenic (originally called Madison). Just to left of the water tank, the small girder bridge crossed the Tye River. From here the line doubled back to Martin's Creek to gain elevation for the climb to Wellington (Tye) and the original Cascade tunnel. (Lower right) The agent poses for Lee Pickett's camera in front of the small station at Index. Located in the heart of the rugged Cascades, the residents never saw the sunrise or sunset because of the high peaks that surrounded the little town. It was for many years the home of the brilliant photographer and his wife Mrs. Dorothy F. Pickett, lives there to this day. Pickett was the railroad's official photographer for the entire Cascade region, and many of his outstanding photographs are reproduced in this volume for the first time.

PICKETT
INDEX-WN
4307
SKYKOMISH IN THE EARLY DAY

From the very beginning, Skykomish has been a railroad town, and the initial assault point on the Cascades from the west. The Beckler and Tye Rivers join just outside of town to become the beautiful Skykomish River — still renowned for trout fishing. Logging interests removed much of the timber in the surrounding mountains early in this century, but new growth has covered the mountains once again.

Claude Witt collection

Edward W. Nolan

Claude Witt collection

Above: At Skykomish yards looking east, a Mallet powered drag on the left, just down from the 2.2%, cools its brakeshoes.

Above left: Leavenworth in 1910, was the site of large machine shops, railroad yards, a roundhouse and the terminus of the Spokane Division. From an operational viewpoint, Leavenworth to Skykomish was the toughest sub-division on nearly 1,800 miles of main line between St. Paul and Seattle.

Left: Located right at the foot of the west slope of the Cascades along the Skykomish River, Gold Bar is a small community named for a bar in the river where gold had been panned. In 1916, when this photo of the GN station was taken, its estimated population was about 200. The 1% eastbound grade starts just west of here, and heavy trains picked up their helper, for the start of the battle up the mountain.

By 1908, the GN had tripled the tonnage per train hauled in the Cascades, and put into service the largest Mallet type engines in the world. In 1909, the GN put its biggest and most famous locomotives — Mallet No. 1909 and the William Crooks — on display at the Alaska-Yukon-Pacific Exhibition in Seattle. Below they are being moved onto the exhibition grounds.

Seattle Historical Society

Class L Mallet No. 1903 above, with another class L behind as a pusher, urges 2,500 tons of eastbound freight out of the Skykomish yard. On the left, the same train is now heading west along the low line after rounding the horseshoe curve at Scenic. It will be turned east again when it passes through Martin Creek's horseshoe tunnel and will appear on the line visible above the engine. When it passes Scenic again eastbound at Windy Point, the train will have gained 500' in elevation.

This remarkable early day action photograph was snapped at the instant an out of control freight piled up on the runaway track beyond Wellington. The switch leading to this track was always aligned for it, and it was not changed by the Wellington operator unless a train coming downgrade, out of the tunnel, signaled that it was under control. The L class Mallet, powering the freight, did not explode, as the photo would tend to indicate, but it did churn up a tremendous amount of dirt and dust. The result of the crash is evident above.

Strandrud Family 2 photos

Watercolor of No. 1964 by Mike Pearsall

Buildings Swept Away By the Slide

Where the Train Stood

where the

Picket
Phy
Co.
Snohomish

Wellington B

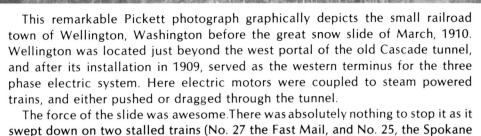

This remarkable Pickett photograph graphically depicts the small railroad town of Wellington, Washington before the great snow slide of March, 1910. Wellington was located just beyond the west portal of the old Cascade tunnel, and after its installation in 1909, served as the western terminus for the three phase electric system. Here electric motors were coupled to steam powered trains, and either pushed or dragged through the tunnel.

The force of the slide was awesome. There was absolutely nothing to stop it as it swept down on two stalled trains (No. 27 the Fast Mail, and No. 25, the Spokane to Seattle local). The hillside had been denuded the previous spring by forest fires and a severe rain storm had further weakened the snow.

The terrifying fact was that the two trains were trapped for six days by heavy snow drifts between Wellington and Windy Point. Retreat into the tunnel was impossible and the remaining side tracks were clogged by snow. Many of the passengers were in a complete state of panic and several on board had premonitions of impending disaster. Their premonitions were justified on that fateful night of March 1st.

Town Of Wellington
Unmolested

e The Snow Slide Disaster

PATH OF AVALANCHE AT WELLINGTON, WN. MARCH 1, 1910. J.D.WHEELER-1118
LEAVENWORTH.WN.

FIRST TRAIN THROUGH
WELLINGTON WN AFTER SLIDE
COPYRIGHT APPLIED FOR MCH/10.
J.D. WHEELER - 1131.
LEAVENWORTH, WN.

DISASTER AT WELLINGTON!

The awesome power of the avalanche is shown in the far upper left photograph of the wreckage of trains No. 25 and 27 in the snow and timber below Wellington. Much of this monstrous tangle of locomotives, cars, trees, brush and snow was not cleared until late spring. The photo below it shows the path of the 2,000' wide slide that roared down upon the trains, structures, and equipment, extending around the curve beyond the work crews. Great Northern people, and Superintendent O'Neil in particular, had worked beyond the point of human endurance attempting to get the stalled trains moving. It was not possible — the men and equipment were unable to cope with the unusual severity and duration of the storm that blocked the main line to the east and west, taking away what few alternatives the railroad had. The photo center left shows the blocked line between Windy Point and Wellington. The nearest assistance was at Scenic and help arrived on foot as rescuers climbed the near vertical mountain side to Windy Point then trudged over the slides and deep snow to Wellington. At upper left, the first Eastbound train through Wellington after the avalanche, passes a scene of snow choked tracks, powder blackened snow and shattered trees. [Lower left] Two of the locomotives involved in the wreck lie on their sides at the bottom of the ravine. The engine on the right was either an E-14 or E-15 class ten-wheeler, and powered train 27, the Fast Mail. The locomotive on the left, on train 25, the local, was an early H class Pacific.

Seattle Historical Society and Wayne Olsen collection

[Top] The trolley wire hangs limply as one of the first through trains reaches the site of the Wellington disaster. With much of the electrification wrecked and the four motors down in the gully, electric service was suspended until the summer of 1910, and steam engines once again worked their way through the smoke in Cascade Tunnel. Workers posed on the pilot of this locomotive, stand under a headlight so soot covered that the reflector cannot even be seen.

[Bottom] In the late spring of 1910, wreckers yard out of the gully the trains struck by the avalanche in March. Little remains to be picked up of the locomotives, rotaries and cars — mostly boilers, motors and heavy running gear.

Nearly a half mile of double track, reinforced concrete snowsheds were built across the path of the avalanche at Wellington in 1910 and 1911. After the disaster, the GN changed the name of Wellington to Tye. The Post Office Department, however, did not officially recognize the new name for several years, and mail addressed to either Wellington or Tye would be delivered.

Railfans pack out part of a coupler assembly, found near the site of the 1910 avalanche.

Howard A. Durfy

After the disaster of 1910 the railroad rebuilt the structures further east, closer to the west portal of the tunnel.

The two views of Tye Washington (formerly Wellington) are actually one remarkable photograph, taken by Lee Picket in 1914 with a wide lens. It covers the area from Bailets Hotel on the left to the new depot and engine servicing facilities on the right. While Tye could hardly be called beautiful, it has improved considerably from the grim little hamlet of pre-disaster years.

Coal chute at Tye, Washington

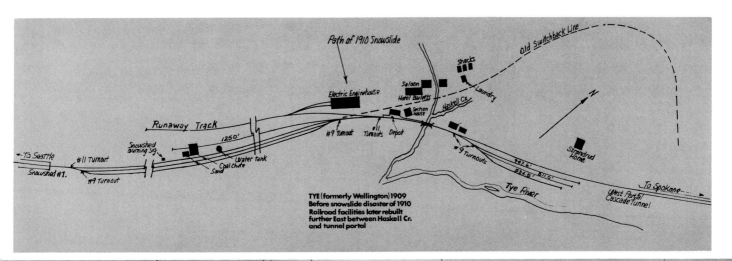

Path of 1910 Snowslide

Old Switchback Line

Electric Enginehouse

Shacks

Saloon

Hotel Barletts

Laundry

Haskell Cr.

Section House

Depot

#9 Turnout

#11 Turnouts

Standrud Home

Runaway Track

1250'

Snowshed warning sig.

#11 Turnout

Water tank

Sand

Coal chute

To Seattle

Snowshed #1.

#9 Turnout

#9 Turnouts

987.6'

834.8'

810.0'

Tye River

West Portal Cascade Tunnel

To Spokane

TYE (formerly Wellington) 1909
Before snowslide disaster of 1910
Railroad facilities later rebuilt
further East between Haskell Cr.
and tunnel portal

Standrud Family

In Tumwater Canyon, this series of five snowsheds was built
within a half mile to protect the main line
during the winter months from snow and from rolling rock in
the spring and summer.

Always promotion minded, the GN gave away or sold at a
nominal price tens of thousands of postcards featuring
scenes along the railroad. Particularly proud of its
accomplishments in the Cascades, the GN gave
special emphasis to this area, as evidenced by these pictures
taken near Scenic and Tumwater Canyon.

*Descending the Mountain Range on
Great Northern Ry. at Scenic, Wash.*

Entrance to Tumwater Canyon, on line of the Great Northern Ry

Freight train coming out of the Horseshoe Tunnel
near Scenic on the Great Northern R.R., Wash.

A few pages from the Strandrud Family Album

Alfred H. Strandrud stands by the tender of No. 32, a St.
Paul, Minneapolis & Manitoba engine, at the
beginning of his career on Great Northern locomotives.
Large for his age and mature acting, he had entered
service on the GN when age was more a matter of
appearance than being certified by a legal
document. A valued and trusted railroad man, he spent
most of his working life on the Cascade Division
as an engineer. His children have carefully
preserved his collection of pictures and documents.

A 20' deep rotary plow cut at Tye in the winter 1911-1912.

Winter at Tye can bring deep drifts, slides and avalanches, danger and exhausting duty hours. It can mean being confined for long periods to the cab of an engine or rotary while awaiting help from Skykomish or Leavenworth. However, there are many days when the sun shines beyond the shadow of the mountain, the air is still and the fresh snowfall is easily thrown clear by the plow as it moves up and down the yard tracks.

Alfred and me with daughter Mamie on the front porch of our home in Tye (Wellington) in late 1911.

Mamie and William in front of our house in January 1917.

Our Christmas tree at Tye December, 1916.

Winter comes early in Tye and stays late.
Here I am on the roof with Mamie,
William and the baby in January, 1917.

Our neighbors in Tye. Without the wooden
snowsheds inter-connecting the company homes,
it would be impossible to move from
one place to another in the heavy snow
without having to dig one's way out.

Alfred, winding up better than 50 years service with the G.N., and William at Seattle on the day of his last run, July 30, 1954.

This remarkable early day photograph is a composite of several wide angle pictures, very carefully put together to make one picture. It covers the area from Scenic Station on the left, to Scenic Hot Springs Hotel on the right. A freight works upgrade from Skykomish, and the smoke from the helper engine may be seen in the valley. The track crosses the Tye River over a bridge just past the water tank and enters the snowsheds going west towards Martin Creek. It switches back, at a higher level, to Windy Point and curves around the point towards Tye. The hotel was torn down during the building of the approach grade to the West Portal of the Cascade Tunnel, located in the mountain directly behind the hotel.

Strandrud Family

The loop at Martin Creek

This map further illustrates the tremendous operating difficulties the GN encountered between Scenic and the west portal of the old Cascade tunnel. The tinted areas covering portions of the old line depict the miles of snowsheds that protected the track in winter. Always costly and difficult to maintain, they were one of the many reasons why the railroad decided to eliminate the line. Over the years, until the opening of the new tunnel in 1929, many improvements and line relocations were made. On Windy Point for example, the curve was reduced and a new double track tunnel constructed in 1914. This tunnel is visible today while driving over Stevens Pass on highway No. 2. In fact, many of the old snowsheds can still be seen, tracing a ghostly path along the tree covered canyon walls.

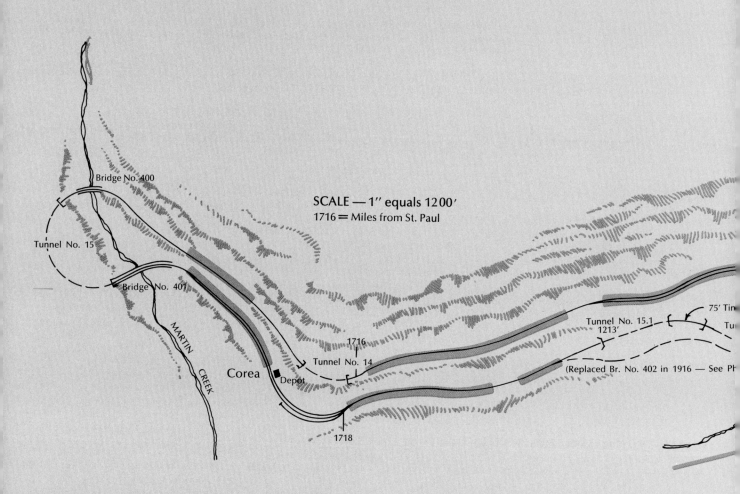

Bridge No. 400

Tunnel No. 15

Bridge No. 401

MARTIN CREEK

Corea
Depot

SCALE — 1″ equals 1200′
1716 = Miles from St. Paul

1716

Tunnel No. 14

1718

Tunnel No. 15.1
1213′

75′ Tin

Tu

(Replaced Br. No. 402 in 1916 — See Ph

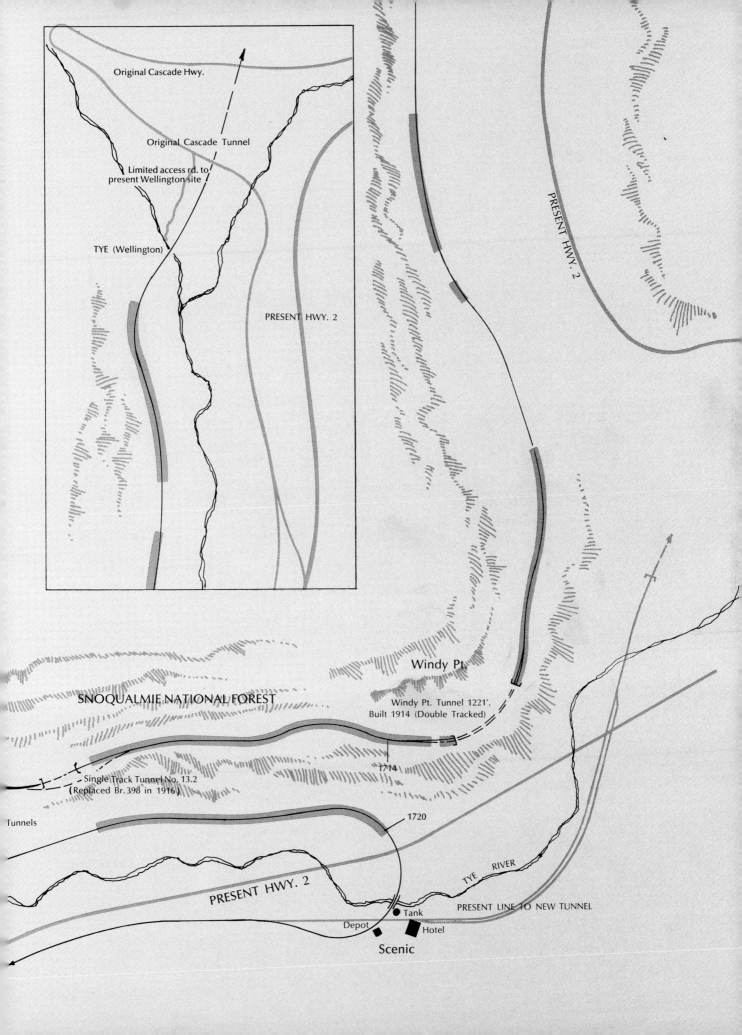

Original Cascade Hwy.

Original Cascade Tunnel

Limited access rd. to
present Wellington site

TYE (Wellington)

PRESENT HWY. 2

PRESENT HWY. 2

Windy Pt.

SNOQUALMIE NATIONAL FOREST

Windy Pt. Tunnel 1221'.
Built 1914 (Double Tracked)

1714

Single Track Tunnel No. 13.2
(Replaced Br. 398 in 1916)

Tunnels

1720

PRESENT HWY. 2

TYE RIVER

PRESENT LINE TO NEW TUNNEL

Tank

Depot   Hotel

Scenic

On the west side of the summit, 6.7 out of the 9 miles between Tye and
Scenic were under snowshed protection by 1917. Near Martin's Creek Tunnel,
the lower line passes through snowsheds to Corea at the far end, and on to
Scenic. The upper line, after emerging from the tunnel, continues on upgrade
towards Embro and Windy Point. The upper right photo is inside the snowshed
at milepost 1717.4 between lower Martin's Creek Trestle and Corea. On the
nearly vertical mountainside, any slide affecting the upper line invariably
affected the lower one, and virtually every slide area between Windy Point
and Scenic required snowsheds on both the upper and lower lines.

The remains of snowsheds in the Martin's Creek area.

E. Traficante

199

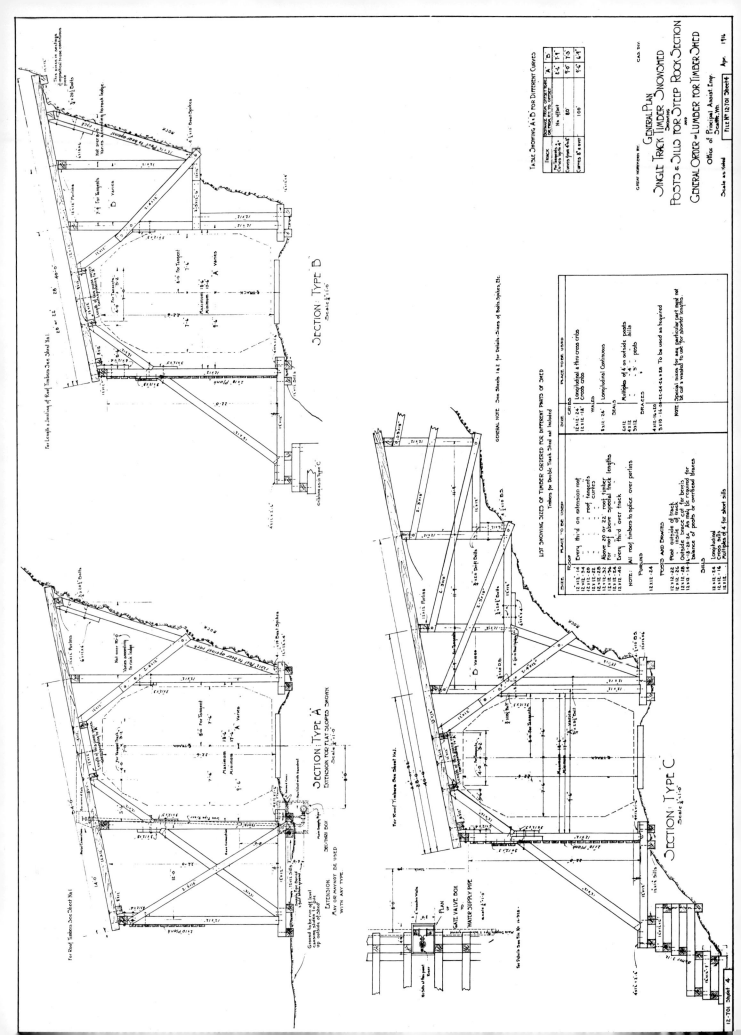

West Extension to Snow Shed 1676? looking east

8-27-'16

Dr. George E. Fischer collection

By 1917, there were only 2 miles of snowsheds on the east side of Stevens Pass — compared to 6.7 miles on the west side. These snowsheds, such as this one at milepost 1676.2, were constructed mainly in the Tumwater Canyon. Although shorter and more widely scattered, they were identical in general design to those built on the west side. The Great Northern experimented with several different types of construction, but ultimately returned to the all wooden snowshed, primarily because it was quicker and cheaper to build. The six middle rows of heavy planks on the track side of the sheds were removable. During clement weather, this afforded the entry of light and air, and a view of the scenery. By October 15, the planking was back in place. During the 1916 summer season, over 37,000,000 board feet of heavy timber was used in new construction and the repair of existing snowsheds. The increasingly heavy cost of maintenance and replacement was one of the compelling reasons for the Great Northern to consider locating a completely new line through Stevens Pass.

Dr. George E. Fischer collection

Slide of Jan. 22, 1916, which destroyed Snowshed
#1714.2, 1- mile east of Embro, at rest on
both high line and low line. Note path cleared
of timber by slide.

Dr. George E. Fischer collection

On January 22, 1916 a slide destroyed the snowshed at milepost
1714.2 just east of Embro. Even 12′ x 12′ posts and roof timbers,
stressed to take a load of 900 lbs. per square foot [100 lbs. sliding
load] could not withstand the enormous pressure.

Bridge 402, near Corea, was taken out of service by the same slide.
Huge trees, carried along by the sliding snow, served as battering
rams to demolish the heavy steel bridgework. The steel supports
were replaced temporarily with heavy timbers and the bridge was
returned to service a month later.

The remains of tunnel 13.2 and the snowsheds in 1971.   E. Traficante

To the left of the new snowshed construction, bridge 398 on the east side of Windy Point is being eliminated by a tunnel. The new tunnel bypassed a hazardous slide area and also improved track alignment by eliminating many degrees of curvature. In the lower photo, a combination concrete and timber snowshed is being built at milepost 1714.1 just to the west of Windy Point, to replace a timber snowshed that was badly damaged by a slide. The heavy concrete backwall, either a gravity type or tied to solid rock behind, was much stronger than log or timber cribbing, but the investment in time and money was so heavy that the more of them that were built, the less able the railroad was to consider the alternative of moving the entire line. Therefore combination type sheds were generally reserved for double track locations, and after 1917 the railroad reverted to the old timber snowsheds which had a useful life of around fifteen years.

Dr. George E. Fischer collection

Bridge 402, damaged in the January, 1916 slide and temporarily repaired, was located right above a steep gully that was a natural slide path. Because of its exposed position, it was decided to relocate the line and eliminate the bridge. In the fall of 1916, the Twin Tunnels [15.1 and 15.2] were built along the lower line, and a snowshed constructed between their portals to protect the track not covered.

Dr. George E. Fischer collection

E. Traficante

Upper left: A concrete arch extends out from the portal at the west end of the Twin Tunnels. Several hundred feet of these concrete arches were constructed at at least three separate tunnels to protect the exposed area not covered by the tunnel. Upper right: Tunnel 14.2 [west portal view] was the first tunnel east of Martin's Creek on the upper line. Above: Windy Point Tunnel, built in 1914, helped protect one of the most troublesome spots on the upper line. In this view at the west portal taken in June, 1971, there is still heavy accumulation of snow around the tunnel, and only rotting timbers still mark the location of the snowshed.

3½ miles west of Leavenworth — Feb. 19, 1916

1916 was a bad year for the GN in the Cascades. During the unusually severe winter, a series of slides occurred in the Tumwater Canyon, an area not usually as hard hit as the slopes on the west side. February 19, a slide 400' wide and nearly 50' deep covered the tracks. The mass of snow was packed so solid that it had to be blasted, and then hand shoveled so that the rotary wouldn't be buried in a snow tunnel of its own making. By February 22, the track was cleared and the difficult and hazardous job of getting derailed equipment back on the track began.

Dr. George E. Fischer collection

Lee Pickett [3 photos]

Clearing operations begin along the right of way of the approach to the new Cascade Tunnel at Scenic, in May, 1926. A pile driver shakes the Scenic Hot Springs Hotel to its foundation during the building of the trestle to the west entrance of Cascade Tunnel. The hotel, built around the turn of the century, was later demolished to make way for the approach grade, and rock from the tunnel work was dumped from the trestle as permanent fill. On the Tye River Bridge, immediately in front of the hotel, the temporary catenary for the electric operation from Skykomish to Tye was in place in the winter of 1926/27.

Walt Grecula collection

TYE RIVER – SCENIC WN.

The electrification, built by Stone and Webster in 1926/27 from Skykomish via Tye to Cascade Tunnel Station, was never extended east to Berne. With the opening of the Chumstick cut-off late in 1928, electric locomotives were operating from Wenatchee via Tye to Skykomish, with the exception of the short stretch between Berne and Cascade Tunnel Station where steam power was used to move the trains — electric locomotives and all. The opening of the new tunnel in January, 1929, eliminated the old line from Scenic to Berne via Tye, and with it the "temporary" electrification between Scenic and Cascade Tunnel Station. Some detailed views of this "temporary" catenary were presented in a book to the railroad by the contractor.

Dr. George E. Fischer collection

212

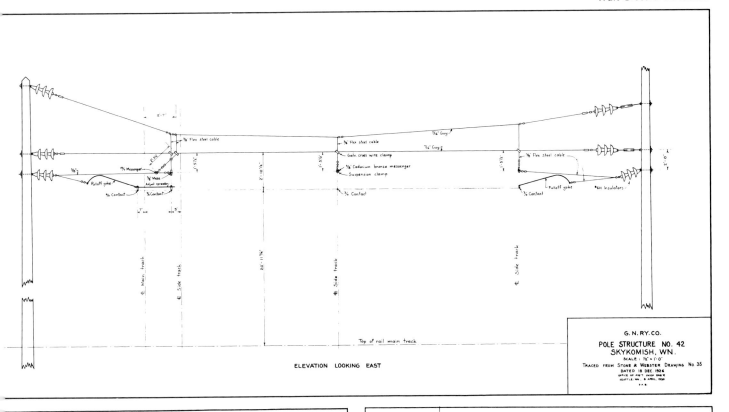

ELEVATION LOOKING EAST

G. N. RY. CO.
POLE STRUCTURE NO. 42
SKYKOMISH, WN.
SCALE : 1/2" = 1'-0"
TRACED FROM STONE & WEBSTER DRAWING No 35
DATED 18 DEC. 1926
OFFICE OF ASS'T CHIEF ENG'R
SEATTLE, WN., 8 APRIL, 1930

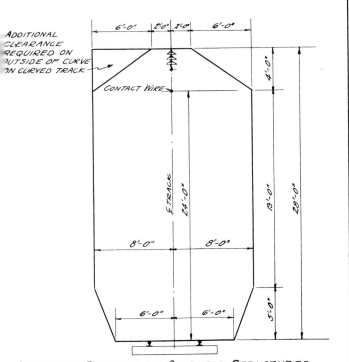

ADDITIONAL CLEARANCE REQUIRED ON OUTSIDE OF CURVE ON CURVED TRACK.

CONTACT WIRE

CLEARANCE REQUIRED OF OVERHEAD STRUCTURES ON ELECTRIFIED LINE BASED ON CONTACT WIRE HEIGHT OF 24'-0" & 150 FOOT SPANS. IN ALL OTHER RESPECTS G.N.RY.Co. STANDARD CLEARANCE DIAGRAM APPLIES

G.N.RY.Co. LINES WEST
TROLLEY LINE STANDARDS
CLEARANCE DIAGRAM
scale: 1" = 5'-0"
Approved. Y. Means
Asst Chief Engineer
Drawn by
Ch'k'd by DMB
Corr.
SEATTLE WASH. 10TH MAR. 1928   XA-23-1

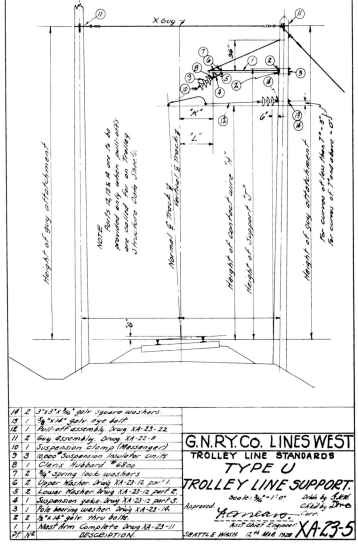

Pt. N.º		DESCRIPTION.
14	2	3"x3"x 3/16" galv. square washers.
13	1	5/8"x14" galv. eye bolt.
12	1	Pull-off assembly. Drwg. XA-23-22
11	2	Guy assembly. Drwg. XA-22-8
10	1	Suspension clamp (Messenger)
9	3	10,000" Suspension insulator units
8	1	Clevis Hubbard #6800
7	2	3/4" spring lock washers
6	2	Upper Washer. Drwg XA-23-12 par 1.
5	2	Lower Washer. Drwg XA-23-12 part 2.
4	1	Suspension yoke. Drwg XA-23-12 part 3.
3	1	Pole bearing washer. Drwg XA-23-14.
2	2	5/8"x14" galv. thru bolts.
1	1	Mast Arm Complete. Drwg XA-23-11

G.N.RY.Co. LINES WEST
TROLLEY LINE STANDARDS
TYPE U
TROLLEY LINE SUPPORT.
scale: 3/16" = 1'-0"
Approved. Y. Means
Asst Chief Engineer
Drwn by
Ch'k'd by
Corr.
SEATTLE WASH. 12TH MAR. 1928   XA-23-5

Lee Pickett

A Y-1 leads an eastbound passenger train, probably
the Fast Mail, across lower Martin Creek trestle
into Martin Creek Tunnel.

A brace of new class Y-1 electrics pose on upper
Martin Creek Bridge No. 400 in 1928. In their 28
years of operation very little was changed on the
locomotives. A "stinger" high voltage connection
was later put on the roof at each end of the units,
and the headlight lowered to a mounting above the
multiple unit connections in front of the cab door.
Rarely were a pair of class Y's operated with all 4
pantographs raised. The Electrified Zone rules
stated that 2 pantographs were to be raised on
multiple cab locomotives — one on the leading unit
and one on the trailing unit. The high car passes
Scenic Station in 1928. The Scenic Hot Springs Hotel
had been torn down to make way for the ¾ mile
approach grade to Cascade Tunnel upon which the
station was built.

A class Y-1 electric leads a Mountain and a Pacific type, on the point of the Oriental Limited across lower Martin Creek trestle in 1928.

Lee Pickett

C. M. Rasmussen collection

A horse drawn sled crosses a bridge over the Tye River at Scenic, Washington, the west portal entrance to Cascade Tunnel, to bring supplies into the engineering camp headquarters.

MUCKING IN THE WEST PORTAL WITH MYERS WHALEY SHOVEL — SHOWING THE ELECTRIC ENG. & ONE CAR

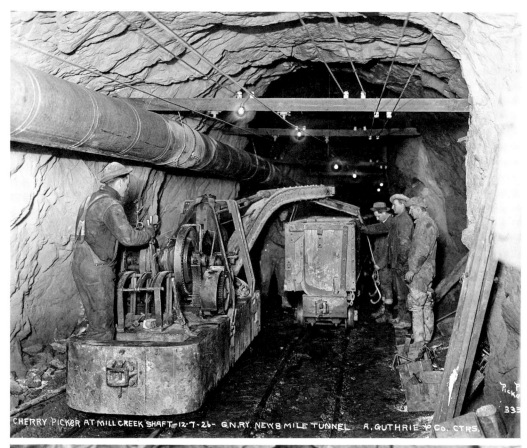

CHERRY PICKER AT MILL CREEK SHAFT 12-7-26 G.N.RY. NEW 8 MILE TUNNEL A. GUTHRIE & CO. CTRS.

In contrast to the "Currier and Ives" type scene, the work on the tunnel progressed underground in less pleasant surroundings. On the far left, a Myers Whaley shovel removes rock and debris [muck] in the pioneer tunnel [parallel to the main tunnel] between West Portal and Mill Creek shaft. At Mill Creek shaft, a movable car-transfer machine called a "Cherry Picker" picks up empty 50 cu. ft. Koppel cars and sets them in place ahead of the last loaded car, obviating any need for switching in the tight confines of the tunnel. Standing on the muck-pile, Supt. Frank J. Kane and Herbert J. King offer congratulations on the breakthrough May 1, 1928 between the east and west headings in the pioneer tunnel.

Dr. George E. Fischer collection

THE KIDKELLY - JACK HUMPHREY FIGHT AT SCENIC WASH OCT. 27 27

(Above) The tough and capable construction crews are getting ready to muck out the last shot in the Pioneer Tunnel. Even though construction of the new tunnel proceeded 7 days a week, 3 shifts a day around-the-clock, it was not a case of all work and no play. Social functions were arranged for the men at regular intervals.
(Above left) A prize fight between Kid Kelly and Jack Humphrey on October 27, 1927 at Scenic.
(Below left) A dance at Mill Creek Camp. One wonders, even though it was at the height of prohibition, if there weren't a few hip flasks hidden under those well-pressed suit jackets.

Above is a rare view of East Portal, original Cascade Tunnel. Overhead is the catenary and trolley wire of the new electrification that terminated here at Cascade Tunnel Station. At the upper right, a pair of Z-1 class electrics power a special assignment. Motion picture crews on a flatcar are taking pictures of the old line up through Tye.

After a day of stringing wire, a work train, headed for Cascade Tunnel, winds along the Skykomish River just below Index. Work continues on the transmission line and new tunnel.

Lee Pickett

C. M. Rasmussen collection

Dr. George E. Fischer collection

Louis W. Hill, Jr., grandson of James J. Hill, rides the motor of train No. 4, the last regular train over the abandoned snowshed route of the Great Northern, January 12, 1929.

Upper left: A deck girder bridge crosses the Wenatchee River, on the Chumstick Cutoff just west of Chumstick Tunnel, August 27, 1928. The new line between Winton and Peshastin, while only a mile shorter than the old line following the turbulent course of the Wenatchee River through Tumwater Canyon, eliminated three complete circles of curvature and 1½ miles of snowsheds, and reduced the ruling grade 25%.

Lower left: An R class pusher pauses on the old route across Stevens Pass, January 11, 1929, as the electric locomotives on the head end of the Oriental Limited raise their pantographs to catch the catenary. The next day, the new 8 mile long Cascade Tunnel was opened and the old route was abandoned.

The grade to the west portal of the new tunnel-then and now. (Above left) the
new track passes the old water tank and bridge at Scenic.
(Left) The new line curves around past Windy Point, located by an "X" on
the photograph. Lee Pickett took these two photos just before the opening of
the new line. The color photograph shows the area today. Highway #2 crosses
over the tracks at a point near the location of the water tank. In the distance
Amtrak's North Coast Hiawatha dips into the tunnel. Surprisingly Amtrak's
Empire Builder goes the other way, over the old NP route.

The Oriental Limited slowly eased by No. 5012, just outside the entrance to
the concrete snowsheds immediately below Tye, as cameras were poised to
record the last westbound train over the old snowshed route. Instead of a
happy group of tourists on the back platform of the observation car however,
there was a solitary passenger bundled up against the chill. This unhappy
circumstance was remedied by replacing the lone passenger
[by photo retouching] with the Apple Festival Queen and her
Ladies in Waiting before release to the press.

FIRST ORIENTAL LIMITED ENTERING THE CASCADE TUNNEL

Dr. George E. Fischer collection

On January 12, 1929, No. 5003 on the head end of the westbound Oriental Limited was the first locomotive [officially] to pass through the new tunnel. At the switch where the old route diverged from the new main line, the Wenatchee Apple Festival Queen and her court christened and decorated No. 5003 before boarding the train for the ride through the tunnel.

Shortly after the opening of the new Cascade Tunnel, Tye was abandoned by the railroad. By the summer of 1929, all salvageable material had been removed, and the wooden buildings were left to rot. Later, the remaining structures were razed and burned to prevent an accidental burning that could touch off a forest fire. Above: The remains of Tye and the concrete snowsheds in the 1970's.

C. M. Rasmussen collection

E. Traficante

Above: The final leg of the switchback on the east side of Stevens Pass has been used, for many years, as a rough access road from the main highway.

Stevens Pass Highway [U. S. #2] opens in the Tumwater Canyon after the grade was abandoned in 1929.

Some deterioration of the west entrance to the old Cascade Tunnel is evident, but the portals were well built, and the old portal with its winged abutments will continue to stand for many decades. The Tye station board is from the collection of Dr. George E. Fischer.

Baldwin-Westinghouse class Z-1 No. 5002, outside the shops at Appleyard, is one of ten built in 1926 and 1928. No. 5004 A&B, 5006 A&B and 5008 A&B worked together as double cab locomotives, while Nos. 5000-5003 were operated as both double cab and single cab locomotives. Designed for double cab operation [two units] the Z-1 with a 1-D-1 + 1-D-1 wheel arrangement, exerted 88,500 lbs. tractive effort on a continuous rating basis, and weighed 715,400 lbs. While used mainly as freight motors, they also could double in passenger service with a speed limit of 45 miles per hour.

In the two photos to the right, Train No. 6, the Cascadian, with moto 5006-B in the lead and a Cafe-Observation bringing up the rear marker pulls up the 2% just west of Scenic. The little Spokane Seattle local wa the only passenger train to traverse the Cascades durin daylight hours. With 35 conditional stops listed in the timetable betwee Spokane and Seattle [330 miles], it still made the run in 10 hours — i fast as the Builder. On the mountainside in th background, the old line to Wellington still shows as a concrete sca Today much of it is hidden by the evergreens that have grown up sinc the line was abandoned in early 192

234

W. R. McGee

Westbound No. 37			Eastbound No. 38
7:30 AM	Lv.	Spokane...Ar.	8:30 PM
9:00 AM	"	Harrington Lv.	6:44 PM
9:43 AM	"	Odessa..... "	6:03 PM
10:56 AM	"	Soap Lake.. "	4:55 PM
12:50 PM	"	Wenatchee.. "	3:15 PM
1:45 PM	"	Leavenworth "	2:15 PM
f 2:50 PM	"	Berne...... "	f 1:05 PM
f 3:10 PM	"	Scenic...... "	f12:45 PM
3:50 PM	"	Skykomish.. "	12:10 PM
5:10 PM	"	Monroe..... "	10:40 AM
5:25 PM	"	Snohomish. "	10:23 AM
5:53 PM	"	Everett..... "	10:05 AM
7:00 PM	Ar.	Seattle..... "	9:00 AM

The first published timetable of the Cascadian, known originally as train Nos. 37 and 38, September 15, 1929.

The Great Northern Goat

W. R. McGee

Helper units class Z, 5008A — 5008B and 5003 enter the west portal of Cascade Tunnel on train No. 402 [99 cars — 5,263 tons]. To their right, the remains of the narrow gauge construction track that ran into the pioneer tunnel, lies rusting away some 12 years after the completion of Cascade Tunnel. In the lower photo, all but the caboose and last four cars of train No. 402 have disappeared into the tunnel. The bright vermillion caboose, distinctive in itself, is further enhanced by the Rocky Mountain goat herald painted on the side and lettered "See America First — Glacier National Park".

W. R. McGee

"Little Mitch", at the throttle of 5012 on the head end of the Cascadian, pulls out of Sky bound for Wenatchee. Both pantographs are raised, a normal operating procedure. The rule book called for two pantographs to be raised regardless of how many units were coupled together to make one locomotive. A folded down pantograph was an innocent looking piece of equipment, but connected by a heavy "bus cable" to the raised pantograph, it was just as deadly. About one man a year lost his life by coming in contact with the high voltage, and Mr. Joe Gaynor, Superintendent of Electric Operations in Wenatchee, worked long and hard to train his crews to stay clear. Even a motor derailing was hazardous. A derailed motor, still in contact with the overhead "trolley", was a dangerous piece of equipment, and hand rails were not used in stepping to the ground. It was necessary to jump clear to be safe.

As long legged Northerns and monstrous Mallets that could pull a mountain down characterized Great Northern operations in the Rockies, so the electrics were the symbol of the Great Northern in the Cascades. In a routine operation, three Y's on the point and three or four Z's cut in about two thirds of the way back, pulled and pushed 5,000 to 6,000 ton trains over the hill. The speed was slow — about 17 mph upgrade, and nearly the same coming down, with the regenerative braking of the big electrics invaluable in controlling the speed of the train on 2.2% descending grades. Starts were smoother than was possible with steam, and there was no smoke or gas. Here 5014-15-16 move train 401 [122 cars — 5,000 tons] on the 1.6% grade at Winton, Washington in May, 1941.

W. R. McGee

Train 401 tops the summit of the Cascades at Berne, just
outside the east portal of the Cascade Tunnel. The lead motor,
5014, begins to nose down toward the tunnel
entrance, while the rest of the long 122 car drag hangs
back over the 2.2% grade.

V. R. McGee

239

Arriving at Skykomish from Wenatchee, Engineer Clemens looks back from the cab of Y-1 class No. 5014 to see if he has pulled the head end up far enough to cut out the helper. Before the days of radio communication, between head end, helper and rear end, this was always a guessing game. When the helper has been released, 5014-5015 and 5016 will be cut off, and an R-2 class 2-8-8-2 will take the train on into Seattle.

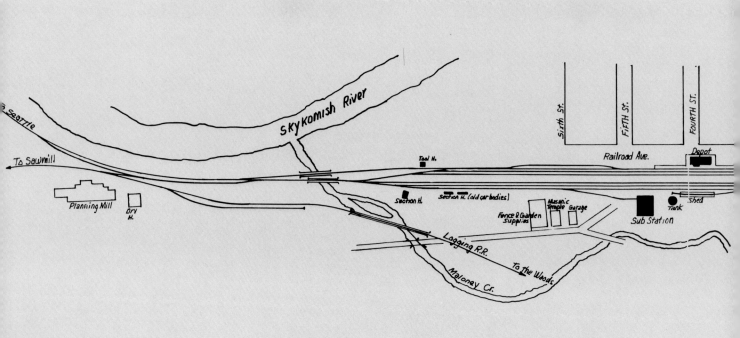

Walt Thayer

Engineer Leo Clark oils around 5010 while waiting for the Cascadian, train No. 5 to come in from Spokane. Engine crews changed at Wenatchee — as did the motive power — and the steam engine on No. 5 will be cut off as soon as the train comes to a halt. The diesel switcher has brought 5010 up to the station from Appleyard. Circumstances varied, and at other times a hostler would bring the electrics up to the station and take back the power that had been cut off, but freight crews usually took their train right into Appleyard where the power was changed.

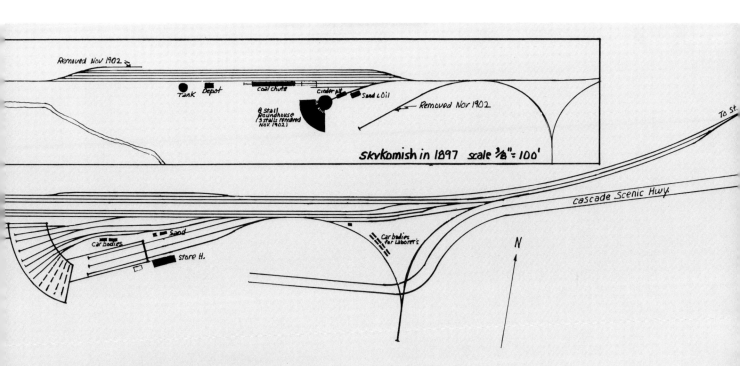

A pair of Y-1's, in the streamlined Empire Builder color scheme, and a huge class W lead a
freight over the bridge crossing Nason Creek, in the 1950's.

The diesel powered "High Car" was a rebuilt and extensively modified gas-electric, used for working on the catenary, or "trolley", as many GN people prefer to call it. Under its own power the car was noisy, so noisy in fact — from the short exhaust stacks of the diesel — that conversation in the operating end was impossible. Nevertheless, it was a fine piece of equipment. For many years Mr. Shirley Alger was the pilot/conductor, and it was for his convenience that the steps on the car ends were more closely spaced than usual.

Above: Class Y-1a 5011 prepares to leave Wenatchee with the westbound Cascadian train No. 5. The unusual appearance of 5011, the only streamlined Y-1, is due to an extensive rebuild by the GN shops using many superstructure parts purchased from EMD. In the early 1940's, 5011 took a tremendous spill at the west approach to Foss River Bridge, while on the head end of No. 27. All that was salvageable were the frame, motors and running gear. At left: 5011 waits at Sky for an eastbound train. Service on the electrics was a prized assignment, requiring highly skilled men with a thorough knowledge of the internal and external equipment. Firemen had to pass one test to be assigned to electric service, and a second after three years of experience — requiring the ability to answer 245 detailed questions on the operation of motors — to be considered for promotion to engineer.

Walt Mendenhall

Burlington Northern

244

5018 waits at Sky for full tonnage and the long pull to the summit. Since all of the GN motors fed current back into the "trolley" when in regeneration, it was possible by watching the meters at the superintendent's office, at Wenatchee, to tell approximately how fast the train was coming down the "hill". An even closer check could be made on the train speed, by timing the intervals at which the pantographs crossed the regularly spaced air gaps [insulated sections of wire that do not carry current]. Mr. Gaynor, Superintendent of electric operations at Wenatchee, was an expert at "reading" the train speed. Trains coming down the 2.2% were strictly limited to 20 mph, and more than one engineer was both surprised and chagrined to find Mr. Gaynor waiting at Wenatchee, or to receive a telephone call from him at Skykomish.

Casey Adams

In 1946 General Electric Company delivered to the Great Northern two of the most powerful single unit electric locomotives ever built — Nos. 5018 and 5019, the sole members of class W. Capable of delivering 5,000 horsepower each, they were as powerful as any diesel combination on the road, but they were to see only a decade of service. The over all efficiency of operating diesels straight through between Wenatchee and Seattle, brought an end to the electrification in 1956, and Nos. 5018 and 5019, too big and too complex to be interesting to other roads, were scrapped in 1959.

This photo of Appleyard, just south of Wenatchee, was taken in the early 1950's before the motors were pulled out of service, as evidenced by the units outside the electric repair shops. In the near foreground the main line cuts around the yard area, choked with freight cars. On the far right of the picture, are the icing facilities. Most reefers then still were filled with ice and salt to lower the temperature via the ice bunkers in the ends of each car. Today, little is left of the yard except a few classification tracks.
Walt Thayer

Vern Nelson, then electrical superintendent at Appleyard in Wenatchee, steps down from No. 5011, the only streamlined class Y-1.

Walt Grecula

Walt Grecula

The motor-generator from a Y-1 is on the work stands at Appleyard Shops during an overhaul of the commutator in 1947.

How do you put an 11,000 volt catenary inside the shops so that the motors can be moved in and out under their own power? You don't. With men in the shop area, working in close to the catenary is too dangerous. The motors were moved towards the shops under power at about 10 mph. Then the pantograph "down" button was punched, lowering the pantograph, and the motor continued coasting into the shop area, stopping at a designated location. When work was concluded, they were towed out of the shop.

With the completion of a ventilating system for Cascade Tunnel in July 1956, diesels began operating across the entire Cascade Division without a change of power at Skykomish or Wenatchee. At right, the first eastbound diesel powered freight roars out of the tunnel under the watchful eye of personnel from the engineering department

The GN had studied extending the electrification to Spokane in 1930, and to Seattle in the early 1950's, but could find no economic justification for the extensions. Further studies in 1955 concluded that while the electrics were half as costly to operate as steam power, they were nearly twice as costly as the diesels. After a brief trial period, the catenary came down and diesels became "King of the hill" on the Cascade Division.

From left to right: In late July, 1967 all seems quiet at the east portal of Cascade Tunnel, except for the chirping of crickets along nearby Nason Creek. Behind the closed tunnel door, however, a gale of fresh air is being blown through the tunnel by 600 horsepower fan motors, activated by the operator at Scenic. Then the tunnel door begins to open, triggered by the approaching train in the tunnel. Next the glaring white beam of a headlight appears — its eight mile trip in darkness nearly over. At last the Empire Builder emerges from the tunnel with five units on the point attesting to the brisk summer business.

Walt Grecula

Robert E. Oestreich

Sailing ships on Elliott Bay, and the Seattle
waterfront, with the Denny Hotel in the
background, in 1887.

4. MORE THAN MOUNTAINS...

251

In the 1880's the Northern Pacific, terminating in Tacoma, brought men and capital to the Pacific Northwest in search of fortunes to be gained in land, lumber, mining, wheat and industry.

With Washington statehood in 1889, the influx grew. From the depot in Tacoma, thousands moved north along Puget Sound, eager to seize their portion of the last frontier.

A struggle began among the Puget Sound communities of Olympia, Tacoma, Seattle, Mukilteo, Everett, Anacortes and Bellingham to become the terminus for the westward building GN; and in the fall of 1893, Mr. E.H. Beckler, Chief Engineer for the GN, discussed the reasoning involved in the GN's selection. Only one possibility other than Puget Sound existed for the GN's western terminus — Portland, which was in control of the Inland Empire trade. The line leading to Portland would have been by way of an extension from Butte to Lewiston, a line plagued with problems. It would also have required the construction of four long bridges (two each) over the Snake and Columbia Rivers at an estimated cost of over $2,000,000. In addition, three other rail lines were in the area between Lewiston and Wallula; and the OR&N was already on the south bank of the Columbia. Because of the nature of the line, Portland was rejected.

Along Puget Sound, there was almost 100 miles of continuous harbor from Tacoma north. The location of the terminus depended largely on where the Cascades were crossed, as the line would have to follow one of the river valleys out of the Cascades. The Snoqualmie led to Seattle or Everett; the Skykomish led to Everett; and the Skagit led to Anacortes on Fidalgo Island, an early selection for the NP terminus. The Skagit also had an outlet at Bellingham Bay, where Fairhaven was said to have the best harbor on the sound.

The Fairhaven & Southern Railroad had completed 26 miles of road from Fairhaven to the Skagit in 1889, and Mr. Beckler, in referring to this construction remarked, "These parties may have thought that some transcontinental railroad would come down the Skagit and fail to find Bellingham Bay, or they may have thought that with 26 miles of constructed road on the western end, it would be an easy matter to fit in several hundred miles to the eastward".

With the purchase of the Fairhaven & Southern, the GN could tap into the coast line at the most favorable point for its official terminus or designate any nearby harbor or city it chose. It would not be the first time that a terminus was selected on the coast and a line run to it afterward. Whichever city was chosen, Seattle as the largest city on Puget Sound would have the largest share of the business for some time to come.

Passes at the head of the Skagit were never really carefully examined when the road was constructed. If a suitable pass had been found and used, the line would have run from Newport, building more than 100 miles along the Columbia River and by-passing Spokane with a population of 25,000. This would have been a longer line through more difficult terrain than the route chosen, with not enough population and business to support it. The route through Spokane, across the Big Bend plateau south of the Columbia, via Stevens Pass and down the Skykomish into Everett had the advantage of the shortest distance, the least rise and fall of the line, the least curvature, the lowest summit and the cheapest construction costs.

The promises of Everett on the peninsula above Port Gardner Bay excited the imaginations of a group who gathered there in 1892. They envisioned it as a Pittsburgh of the west with sawmills, a shipyard, paper mills, a smelter, factories and a rail line to connect with Tacoma and Seattle. A leader in this group was Henry Hewitt, often referred to as the father of Everett. Born in England in 1840, the son of a minor timber baron, he had survived the panic of 1873 with millions in holdings intact. He had left Wisconsin for the Pacific Northwest in 1888, and later joined with Charles L. Colby and Colgate Hoyt to purchase land and to incorporate the Everett Land Company.

Colby, wealthy New York banker and financier, was president of American Steel Barge Company and an executive board member of the NP. Colby and Colgate Hoyt, also an executive of the NP, were both members of the Baptist Church on Fifth Avenue where John D. Rockefeller worshipped. Rockefeller, believing that his would be a minor commitment, was amenable to Colby and Hoyt's proposals for investment in Everett. Instead, his money became the major resource that attracted others and created a speculation explosion.

In February, 1892 James J. Hill arrived in Everett where an elaborate banquet was held in his honor. Lumber was their greatest resource, he told the group assembled, and he emphasized their need for a cheap railroad connection. He spoke also of putting in a line of ships to Japan, and hinted that he might find it necessary to haul tonnage no further than Puget Sound. When he added that they need fear no city to the south, he fired the hope that Everett would be the terminus of the GN. He would require land however, including some of that square mile known as the "school section". In January, 1893 Hill got 200 acres of the school land at $76 an acre in an unopposed bid. The Everett Land Co., which had previously withheld land, now put up for sale 25' lots at $200 each (10% down) for workers' homes. Other business lots in town went for thousands of dollars.

The jubilation and frenzy of activity were cut short by the panic of 1893. Three of the five banks in Everett closed, construction halted, lumber prices fell and in-

vestors (including Rockefeller) withdrew leaving the region in a general collapse. In 1897 the Everett Land Co. dropped into receivership and its assets were auctioned off in 1899, ending Hewitt's dream. Hill picked up the pieces and organized the Everett Improvement Company under John T. McChesney — banker, former mayor of Aberdeen, S.D. and friend of Hill.

Timber from the NP land grants would feed freight to the GN, and Hill encouraged the timber barons to come with free mill sites and low railroad rates. Weyerhaeuser, already the most powerful timber baron in the U.S., negotiated in 1900 for 900,000 acres of the NP land at $6 an acre or about 10¢ per 1,000 board feet. He organized the Weyerhaeuser Timber Company and opened the largest lumber mill in the world in Everett. Hill also brought out in his private car, David M. Clough, a former governor of Minnesota. Clough organized the Clark-Nickerson Lumber Company and later the Clough-Hartley Company, the greatest producer of red cedar shingles in the world. In fact, so many were brought out by Hill and so many forests opened, that the market became glutted by the over production.

By 1904 the timbermen, feeling that the railroads were robbing them, joined with the Populists to push for a commission to regulate the rates. Hill retaliated by raising the rates, creating a shortage of cars and virtually imposing an embargo on Washington timber. They sued the GN and NP via the ICC and won, but this action also brought taxes that they hadn't expected. Most of these timbermen had come up the hard way. They were rough and tough with little formal education. They were also heavily in debt to eastern capital and therefore had to produce heavily to pay off. The incentive then was to cut and get out rather than to conserve, further contributing to the glut. There was no control to the industry. Only Weyerhaeuser, with his own capital and more sophisticated management, could plan for sustained yield.

It was still easy to acquire cheap land

for homes and farms however, and the GN depot on the hill above the harbor continued to welcome the new citizens. The population rose from 8,000 in 1900 to over 35,000 in 1910. It was said that "Everett rested on Jim Hill's land and Butler's gold". Butler was William C. Butler, brother of Nicholas Murray Butler, President of Columbia University. A Rockefeller protege, he had emerged after 1893 with the Everett First National Bank and the Everett Trust and Savings Bank; and controlled virtually all new building in Everett. Hill, through the Everett Improvement Company, had a monopoly on gas, electricity, water, wharfage and land.

Although Everett had been led to believe that it would be the terminus when the GN was completed in 1893, the actual goal had always been Seattle. Unlike Everett, Seattle was not a company town. Eastern capital, which extracted the wealth that the land provided in timber, minerals and farm products, produced the company town, a common occurrence in the west. It was the belief of men such as Arthur A. Denny that if a city could remain economically independent, it could develop its own capital to provide the depots, ports, banking, medical and legal services, manufacturing and retail trade for the surrounding community.

Denny was in the group of 10 adults and 12 children dropped off at Alki Point by the steamer Exact on November 13, 1851. On February 15, 1852, Arthur Denny with Boren, Bell and their families moved to the east side of Elliott Bay, establishing the new city of Duwamps. The name was changed later that summer to Seattle at the suggestion of Dr. David Maynard.

Seattle's early growth was tied to San Francisco. The logs shipped from Seattle were paid for by goods brought back on the return trip for sale on commission. Denny, in partnership with Dexter Horton, opened a 20'x30' store at 1st S. and Washington Sts. He went to San Francisco to purchase the stock and by so doing he assumed the risk, made the profit and lessened Seattle's dependence on San Francisco for shipping and capital.

From the first, Denny had contemplated a railroad from the Atlantic Coast to Puget Sound. Isaac Stevens, the first Governor of the Washington Territory, had confidently predicted in 1853 that a railroad would cross the Cascades to Puget Sound within five years. Denny did not seek eastern capital, but rather settlers with the needed skills to build a city of sufficient size and wealth to attract a railroad. Settlement on Puget Sound was slowed in the 1850's, however, with the opening of Kansas and Nebraska to homesteading. Indian skirmishes and the Civil War further delayed the migration.

Hope for a railroad was renewed in 1870 when the Northern Pacific, now financed by the house of Jay Cooke, began building west from near Duluth, Minnesota, with a branch line from the Columbia River to Puget Sound. In 1873, scraping together all that they could, Seattle, now a community of about 1,100, offered the NP $250,000 in cash and bonds, 7,500 town lots, 3,000 acres of undeveloped land and half of the waterfront to locate the terminus in Seattle. Although this comprised better than two thirds the value of the entire county, it was not enough for the NP. In what Vernon Parrington describes as the Great Barbecue, the NP had acquired title to millions of acres of land for right-of-way whether it built the railroad or not. In what amounted to a shameful swindle, they were provided with a virtual blank check by Congress. With amendments to its charter, the NP had increased its land grants to the point where the land reserved for the railroad and held back from settlement amounted to almost half the territory of Washington. Therefore the railroad, financed by the land, became subordinate to its land subsidiary company. Since the officers of the company owned the land on Commencement Bay, they chose to build their own city, destroy Seattle, and keep all the profits. They announced the decision to make Tacoma the terminus of the NP July 14, 1873.

In answer to this insult, outraged citizens of Seattle met on July 23, 1873 to incorporate the Seattle & Walla Walla Railroad & Transportation Co. Judge McGilvra provided the legal services in drawing up the company and in issuing the stock, while Arthur Denny became its first president. The entire populus turned out at Steele's Landing on the Duwamish River May 1, 1874 to begin grading the 3' gauge line that was planned to cross Snoqualmie Pass into the grain fields of Eastern Washington to terminate at Walla Walla. It was a gala occasion for which the women had prepared a sumptuous picnic lunch. By 1875, however, the line had progressed only 3½ miles to Argo on its way to Renton. It was simply too large an undertaking to be accomplished on a part time basis. In 1876, James M. Coleman offered to put up one third of the capital to extend the line, and in November the new Seattle & Walla Walla Railroad began construction of the remaining 9 miles to Renton. In 1878 a 6.3 mile extension was pushed northeast to New Castle to serve the coal mines.

November, 1880 Henry Villard bought the New Castle mines and formed the Columbia & Puget Sound Railroad to purchase (for $250,000) and complete the Seattle & Walla Walla. Villard gained control of the NP in 1881, and under his direction the NP built the standard gauge Puget Sound Shore Railroad to link Seattle with its Columbia River line. From Black River Junction (near Renton) the line reached Seattle over a third rail on the Columbia & Puget Sound. In 1884 Villard lost control of the NP, and it fell back into the hands of the pro-Tacoma group, which immediately suspended the Puget Sound Shore operation. Even with service restored on the "Orphan Road" in 1885, and the 21 mile Cedar River extension to Maple Valley and Franklin completed on the C&PS, it had become apparent to Seattle that the line would never be more than a local road.

Still the Seattle & Walla Walla had carried the name of Seattle across the continent. Some had heard of Seattle for the first time, and were impressed with people of such spirit, that when denied a railroad, they would set out to build their own against overwhelming odds. One who had read of the May Day picnic in 1874 was Thomas Burke, a law student at Ann Arbor, Michigan. Upon completion of his studies the following year, he came to Seattle and later married the daughter of Judge McGilvra. Now ten years after arriving in Seattle, Judge Burke joined with Daniel Hunt Gilman in asking for community support to form the Seattle, Lake Shore & Eastern Railway Co. On April 14, 1885 the line was chartered to build along the shore of Lake Washington north to Sumas to connect with the CPR. A second portion of the line, planned to cross Snoqualmie Pass into Eastern Washington, was abandoned when the NP crossed Stampede Pass. The line north still did not really serve Seattle's purposes, for at best it would make Seattle only a city at the end of a branch line. In the early 1900's control of the Lake Shore & Eastern was sold to the NP by the eastern stockholders.

Meanwhile in the late 1880's news of Jim Hill's westward moving Manitoba aroused a cautious optimism in Seattle. When Hill visited the cities along Puget Sound, he spoke with the leading citizens and returned to St. Paul without any actual commitment having been made. Some months later Burke received a quiet visit from Col. W.P. Clough, Hill's attorney. He announced that if the right-of-way and land for terminals could be obtained without obstruction or legislative difficulties, Seattle was Hill's choice for the western terminus of the GN. An astonished and delighted Burke accepted the position as Hill's representative in the matter.

Burke set out immediately to secure a franchise for the GN right-of-way entering the city from the north, running along the waterfront via Railroad Avenue, and ending at the tide flats south of the city. Railroad Avenue had been laid out previously by Judge Burke and Judge Cornelius Hanford in providing a right-of-way for the Seattle, Lake Shore & Eastern Railway. In order to avoid conflict with the Seattle & Walla Walla, which meandered along the shore line, the 120' wide Railroad Avenue was constructed outside the high tide line. When it became known that Burke proposed to grant the GN a 60' path along Railroad Avenue, the NP played on the fears of Seattle citizens by insisting first that the GN was only using Seattle to squeeze better terms from Fairhaven for the terminus; and secondly that if such a franchise were granted it would bottle up the city.

The city newspapers fought for the franchise and the City Council swiftly granted it. There was only one holdout among the private citizens in relinquishing rights to the land along the tide flats for the terminals. Burke and nine others raised the $10,000 to buy him out, providing Hill with a section of land one mile long and two blocks wide south of Dearborn St.

The GN was completed to Seattle in June, 1893. On July 4th Hill arrived for a two day celebration which has been described as "the grandest demonstration in the history of the Northwest". Special excursion rates on trains and boats attracted thousands from neighboring communities to participate in bicycle and torch light parades, elaborate floats, song fests, speeches and dancing. The showpiece was the Coal, Lumber and Mineral Palace at Pioneer Square. Over its north entrance was a design in electric lights of the "J.J. Hill" locomotive. Powered by a 50 horsepower generator, the electric lamps forming the wheels flashed off and on to create the illusion of constant motion.

With through service established to St. Paul and Chicago, a rate war began. First class fare to St. Paul was reduced to $25. A "3,000 mile ticket", good for one year's use anywhere on the entire system, could be purchased for $75. Rates on lumber were cut from 90¢ to 40¢ a hundred to fill the empty freight cars returning east. This amounted to 2/5¢ per ton mile to St. Paul, an unheard of rate. Both the interests of the lumber industry and the GN prospered.

Hill wanted land for the freight terminals closer to the wholesale district, and instructed Burke to purchase 4 blocks for this purpose. Burke approached the owners directly and asked for the lowest possible price. All complied but one, a friend and former business associate of Hill's from St. Paul. When Hill said that he would give the man what he asked, Burke shot back a telegram informing Hill that if he paid his friend more than he would pay Burke's friends for comparable land, he could consider that he held Burke's resignation in his hand. Impressed, Hill referred his friend back to Burke, and the man settled for the lower price. All of this land was purchased by Hill personally and when it was transferred later to the GN, it was done so at the purchase price without consideration for its increased value or interest.

The GN depot at the foot of Columbia St. was a sore point with Seattle, but Hill, busy developing his system, had insisted "He is a wise farmer who develops his farm before he builds a palace on it. It is more important to Seattle to have goods delivered to it cheaply than to have a fancy depot, and I am devoting my attention to the more important thing."

In 1889 an appealing offer was presented Seattle by the NP, now convinced that Seattle's trade was worth going after. NP President Charles S. Mellen announced that the NP was prepared to build Seattle a $500,000 depot between Madison and Marion Sts. on the waterfront. A huge section of the Seattle waterfront from Washington

St. to University St. had been purchased, and the NP proposed to convert much of this area into a giant freight yard.

James J. Hill rushed to Seattle by special train, and the Seattle Times commented on his arrival in an editorial. "It is probably true that Mr. Hill has done more for the upbuilding of Seattle than almost all other interests combined, and it is most natural that the public should regard Mr. Hill as the protector of the city's rights and the main cause and impetus of her future growth and prosperity . . . ." Hill spoke in favor of a union depot on the south side at or near King Street, but rejected the idea of any such facilities along the waterfront. He admonished Seattle that, "If you put such an obstruction across the front of your city, you will commit commercial suicide. You cannot obstruct traffic without driving traffic away. It would be a grave mistake for the city to make. Thus far in your career you have made no mistake; keep the record clear."

Early in 1900, Burke presented his argument before the City Council. He compared the NP's antagonism toward Seattle with the generosity accorded the city by Jim Hill, and asked them which one they believed would treat Seattle better. The answer was contained in a telegram sent to Hill by Burke. "City Council stood by you 12-1, and that one came in to make it unanimous."

In 1902, the GN began work on a tunnel under the business district of Seattle, that would leave the traffic on Railroad Avenue undisturbed. The tunnel was completed in 1905, and trains ran through it to the magnificent new depot serving both the GN and the NP at King Street.

With his work completed, Burke wished to retire and recommended L.C. Gilman to Hill as his replacement. Brother of Burke's former partner Daniel Hunt Gilman, L.C. Gilman proved to be so able a railroad man that in 1916 he became president of the Spokane, Portland & Seattle.

Seattle was no longer a city that needed a railroad, but a city that could not be ig-

nored by the railroads. The Chicago, Milwaukee & St. Paul reached Seattle over Snoqualmie Pass March 29, 1909. On January 1, 1910, Harriman's Union Pacific arrived via the OWR&N. The Columbia & Puget Sound (formerly the Seattle & Walla Walla) had been purchased by the Pacific Coast Co. (a holding company) in December, 1897, along with the rest of Villard's Oregon Improvement Co. properties, and converted to standard gauge. In March, 1916 the name was changed to the Pacific Coast Railroad; and on October, 1951, the railroad was sold to the GN, which had long wanted it for its Seattle terminal facilities. The alliance between Seattle and the GN had proved to be a fortunate one. A mutual bond of admiration formed between the determined citizens of Seattle and Jim Hill, a scrapper himself, had brought their common interests together for the benefit of both.

While June, 1893 was the date formally linking the GN with Seattle, the railroad had actually entered the Seattle scene nearly two years earlier with the opening of the Coast Line. Three separate divisions comprised the Coast Line — the Seattle and Montana Railway, the Fairhaven and Southern Railroad and the New Westminster and Southern Railway. The latter was an outgrowth of the Bellingham Bay Railroad and Navigation, chartered in August, 1883 by Illinois Senator Eugene Canfield to build from Fairhaven (Bellingham) to Sumas. With the completion of the CPR to Port Moody (just east of New Westminster) in 1885, and through service to Vancouver established in 1886, Canfield changed his mind concerning a connection at Sumas. In 1888 he organized the New Westminster and Southern Railway.

Because of financial difficulties, the New Westminster and Southern was sold to Canadian interests, and Nelson Bennett was awarded the primary contract for the completion of the line. Bennet also purchased the BBR&N charter from Canfield in July, 1889, and then abandoned the paper railroad to form the Fairhaven &

Southern Railway. He pushed this line north through Ferndale and reached the boundary December 1, 1890. Both the NW&S and the F&SR passed into the control of Hill, and the line moved south to Burlington, with a branch to Sedro-Wooley, in 1891. On October 12, 1891 the final spike was driven about 18 miles north of Everett (between Silvana and Stanwood) to connect the F&SR with the Seattle and Montana Railway, a line incorporated in the Hill interests March 9, 1890 and financed by the GN.

In late November, the first 10 car passenger train left Seattle with 275 prominent civic, business and railway officials and their ladies. By the time the elaborately decorated train crossed the border, there were nearly 600 passengers aboard. Each lady was provided with a bouquet, and the men wore badges inscribed, "The Great Northern, November 27 and 28, 1891. We rejoice in the completion of the Washington and British Columbia sections". On the south bank of the Fraser River, the train was met by steamers to transport the passengers to New Westminster, where a Chamber of Commerce luncheon and a greeting by the Mayor awaited them.

Hill had long contemplated the US/Canadian border in more of a geographical than a political context. His view held that each country could and should be the others best customer. Raw materials and trade should flow freely between the two countries, preferably on the GN of course. This philosophy led him into conflict with a spirit of Canadian nationalism; and a bitter battle with the Canadian Pacific Railway and his former associate and protege, Cornelius Van Horne, for the transportation supremacy of half a continent. This was a battle to rival his war with Harriman and the UP/SP during the building of the Spokane, Portland and Seattle. Nowhere was the struggle more in evidence than in Southern British Columbia, for of the sixteen border crossings by the GN, twelve of them entered British Columbia.

Vancouver, with its fine deep water harbor and Oriental trade, was cut off from the rich resources of the interior of the province. The CPR entered BC at the most northerly point on its line, some 200 miles north of the US border. Eastern interests, therefore, dominated the CPR and the wealth of BC. Hill began acquiring existing charters for railroads in Canada and obtaining new ones. Within a few years, the Vancouver, Victoria and Eastern Railway & Navigation Company became the amalgamation of all GN subsidiaries operating in BC.

The VV&E was chartered in 1896-7 by William Templeton (Mayor of Vancouver); Lachlan, Hugh and Norman Mclean (brothers heading a large engineering firm in Vancouver); and Dr. George Milne (prominent Victoria citizen who added a spur line and ferry connection). The line, designed to serve the coastal cities, was caught between the American lines and the CPR. In the summer of 1897, with financing denied by Ottawa, the group approached William MacKenzie and Donald Mann (later to build the Canadian Northern), and an agreement was reached by them with the CPR. The CPR would build west to Midway and the VV&E would build west from Midway to the coast. This plan was abandoned when a change in the BC Government resulted in a withdrawal of the provincial subsidy. When MacKenzie returned at a later date to revive the VV&E, it was suspected that Hill was behind the new move; for control of the VV&E would give Hill the legal authority he sought to enter Canada.

On March 21, 1901, Hill acknowledged by letter that he indeed was a partner in the venture. In mid-June Hill acquired a majority interest, and without a subsidy, began building toward the border from Marcus. This was the first move of his massive offensive against the CPR in Southern BC. John F. Stevens had arrived in Marcus at this time with the new charter for the Washington & Great Northern Railway, under which the US portion of the line would be constructed. Marcus was on the line of the Spokane Falls & Northern Railway, chartered by Daniel Chase Corbin in April, 1888. Hill had gained controlling interest of this line July 1, 1898 through secret purchases of large blocks of stock in New York.

The New Westminster & Southern had stopped at the south shore of the Fraser River. In 1903-1904, the Fraser River Toll Bridge was constructed, paid for entirely by the Provincial Government. The GN was the only railroad to take immediate advantage of the bridge to link its lines from the US border with New Westminster and Vancouver. Hill gained entry into Vancouver in 1904 with an illegal diamond crossing over the CPR made after dark at Sapperton. The line between New Westminster and Vancouver was the Vancouver, Westminster & Yukon Railway, chartered in 1897 and financed by the GN. It was sold to the VV&E in July, 1908.

It was through the VW&Y that the GN, on October 5, 1902, purchased the Victoria Terminal Railway & Ferry Company, formed November 29, 1900 to enlarge the scope of the Victoria and Sidney. The V&S, chartered in 1893, and later known as the "Jim Hill Special", needed a connection to the mainland to remain viable. Thus the formation of the Victoria Terminal Railway which ran a ferry from Sidney up the Fraser River to Liverpool on the south bank to link with the New Westminster & Southern. Upon completion of the 17½ mile line on the mainland between Port Guichon and Cloverdale in 1903, the ferry terminated at Port Guichon. In the fall of 1907, the Victoria Terminal Railway began the construction of a sea level branch south from Colebrook through Crescent and White Rock to Blaine, to eliminate the hilly section between Cloverdale and the US border on the New Westminster & Southern. In 1909, the branch was completed north to Brownville on the Fraser River.

In 1905, Hill had pushed the VV&E into Phoenix (near Grand Forks) and bought heavily into the mining company and smelter. He also announced that he would build west from Curlew, under the charter of the VV&E to the coast. By fall, the line moved from Curlew to Ferry and across the border to Midway on its meandering route to Oroville. Simultaneously, grading crews worked northwest of Oroville up the Similkameen Valley towards Princeton; and surveys were ordered east from Cloverdale to link this new line with the Seattle Vancouver line.

Hill's thrust into Phoenix, and the resulting loss to the CPR, began to hurt the Province. It was now lukewarm to Hill's coast road, especially after Louis Hill's April 14, 1905 announcement that part of the line would go through the US. There was strong suspicion that Hill would build his Coast to Kootenay line only to ensure Spokane dominance over BC. The Victoria Columnist described the incursion of the GN into British Columbia as "like so many fingers on a hand, with the State of Washington as the palm".

The CPR was not standing idly by while Hill made his moves. In 1905, Corbin, whom Hill had squeezed out of the Spo-

kane Falls & Northern, chartered the Spokane International Railway to connect with the CPR and reduce the GN/NP monopoly over the region. This Spokane to St. Paul line, when completed, was shorter and faster than the GN; and competition for the American Northwest was now wide open. When the US Government dropped the mail contract with Hill and gave it to the CPR, Hill was furious. In April, 1907, he announced that he would build the VV&E through the Hope Mountains. The GN Crow's Nest Pass line would connect with the VV&E on the west and push east to join the Grand Trunk Pacific in Winnipeg, giving Canada two transcontinentals. A depression running from late 1907 into 1909, however, cancelled many projects including the extension to Winnipeg.

A new threat arose during this time from the Kettle River Valley Railway Company, originally incorporated by Corbin in the State of Washington on March 19, 1898. Corbin had been unable to obtain the charter in Canada. This remained for Tracy Holland to accomplish two years later. The line was raced down the Kettle River Valley from Curlew to Republic in competition with the GN, but was a disappointment as far as revenue was concerned. James John Warren of the Trusts and Guarantee Co., which had supplied the largest share of the capital to build the KVR, approached Thomas Shaughnessy of the CPR in April, 1908. He proposed to use the KVR to build the line to the coast; and also to push it south and east from Republic to join the Spokane International. This would provide an easier line to the Boundary smelters and help regain the area from Hill.

The VV&E, moving up the Similkameen Valley, reached Karemeos on July 10, 1907, and Princeton in December, 1909. Work west of Princeton slowed, however, as the GN concentrated on building its line from Oroville to Wenatchee. This only increased the suspicions of Canadians, many of whom were convnced that the purpose of the line was to transport Canadian coal

to the US for use in GN locomotives. The people of Princeton, who in their joy at the earlier arrival of the GN had unofficially renamed the Similkameen River the "Jim-Hillameen", now referred to the GN as the "Great Now & Then".

Slowly the VV&E pushed east from Abbotsford and west from Princeton. By the spring of 1912, there was still the section in Coquihalla Pass over the Hope Mountains to complete. The KVR, guided by the CPR's brilliant locating engineer, Andrew McCulloch, was also bearing down on Coquihalla Pass. For almost 20 years, Hill and the CPR had waged war for the control of Southern BC, the rich minerals of its interior, and the Vancouver tidewater trade. This would be the most important battle of them all. The narrow defile of the pass precluded building more than one line; and the expense and difficulties would be enormous.

The stage was set for a duel to the death. Instead, Gillam of the VV&E and Warren of the KVR met in October, 1912 to reach an agreement on joint trackage. By April, 1913 it was agreed that the CPR would build the line through Coquihalla Pass for the joint use of the GN and CPR. This compromise was in truth a surrender to the CPR, and signaled the beginning of the gradual withdrawal of the GN influence from Southern British Columbia. The Canadian fear of US domination had always been a formidable obstacle. The GN built without subsidy, while the Canadian lines received the backing of their government. A further drain on the finances of the GN had been the costly battle through the Columbia Gorge and down the DesChutes. Perhaps an era of overbuilding and duplication of lines was simply coming to an end. It was also true that an aging Hill had less influence on the decisions of the GN management which now questioned further expansion of the GN into BC. The VV&E Coast to Kootenay line was completed just a few weeks after Jim Hill's death, and abandoned almost immediately. On September 27 and 28, 1916, Louis

Hill and a few GN officials rode a special GN train from Vancouver to Princeton and on to Spokane. This was the only GN train to ever run over Coquihalla Pass.

In May, 1912 the GN had joined forces with the Canadian Northern. (The Canadian Northern was taken over by the Canadian Government during World War I and became part of the Canadian National — arch rival of the Canadian Pacific.) In 1912, the Canadian Northern purchased the old GN line on the south bank of the Fraser and gave the GN running rights into Winnipeg over the rails of the CN. This was in exchange for running rights over the Great Northern's new line into Vancouver, and to obtain some of the Hill owned land on False Creek in Vancouver for a CN station. The new GN line into Vancouver was completed in 1913, five years after the start of construction. The steep bluffs along the Fraser that separated New Westminster and Vancouver allowed no room for the track to loop back and forth to reduce the steep gradient encountered in both directions. The only possible solution was a long, deep cut to reduce the grade. Excess material from this Grandview Cut was used to fill the low lying property at False Creek where the GN terminal facilities and station would be located.

In the spring of 1916, after nearly two years of construction, the GN station on Main Street was opened to serve the lines south to Seattle and east to the Kootenays. The imposing red brick structure covered nearly a city block and its elegance was described as "out of this world". The Canadian National dropped its plan to share the GN station and instead constructed its own magnificent station next door. The CPR, across town, also replaced its small station with a costly new edifice. Vancouver was now served by three major railroads and three separate terminals, far beyond what was needed for the traffic generated.

In early 1962, faced with a steadily declining passenger business, costly maintenance and heavy taxes, the GN found it no longer practical to continue operating its own station. An application to the Board of Transport Commissioners to abandon the station and move next door into the CN station was approved, and in 1965, the GN station was torn down. Passenger service on the famed "Internationals" was replaced in May, 1971, and it is the Amtrak operation that now moves over the Coast Line.

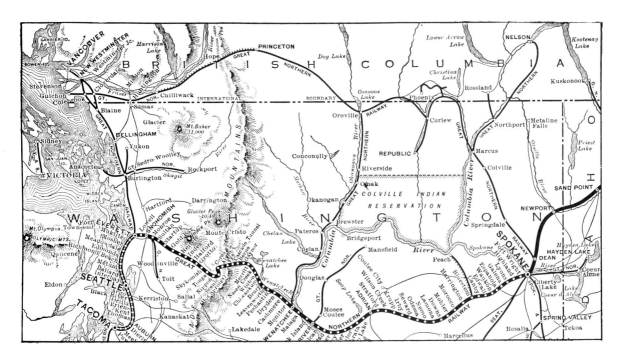

Everett Community College

The rails reach Tidewater...

Claude Witt

Everett Community College

Above are mills along Port Gardner Bay about 1910, when Everett envisioned
becoming "the Pittsburgh of the West".

The GN crossed 1,800 miles of prairies and mountains to reach Tidewater at
Everett in 1892. Direct access to Seattle was provided over the rails
of the Seattle & Montana, organized and built in the interests of the GN.
Left is the GN Everett Depot in the early 1900's, built near
the site of the depot of the Seattle & Montana, shown in the top photo.
The former, greatly changed, still serves in the 1970's.

U. S. Forest Service

Locomotives of the Columbia & Puget Sound Railroad are displayed near Renton in 1889,
shortly after the great Seattle fire which destroyed the station, shops, roundhouse,
wharves and some of the rolling stock. The Columbia & Puget Sound had been
reincorporated by Henry Villard November 26, 1880, by combining the Seattle & Walla
Walla RR & Transp. Co. and the Seattle Coal & Transp. Co. The 33 mile line
which ran from Seattle through Renton, Maple Valley and Black Diamond to Franklin,
became the Pacific Coast RR in 1916.

Seattle's King Street Station, shown during construction, was completed in May, 1906 in a joint undertaking by the NP and the GN, as part of a terminal improvement project to relieve congestion along the waterfront. In 1907, a train caller stands inside the beautiful new station, the style of which was inspired by the architecture of Venice, Italy.

Seattle Historical Society (2)

Along the Seattle waterfront in 1896, a 2 car Seattle & International (NP) local, bound for Sumas, Wa. and Huntington, B.C., stands in the foreground. Behind this, the 8 car GN passenger train prepares to leave for St. Paul, and the string of cars beside it all but blocks the view of the small station.

Joe D. Williamson collection

Wally Swanson

Charles R. Wood

Train No. 27, the Fast Mail, passes the small station at Edmonds just north of Seattle.

An aerial view shows the GN, NP, PC, UP and Milwaukee yards in December, 1925. The Seattle/Tacoma Interurban heads south along First Avenue past the OWR&N freight house, and in the lower left corner is the wooden street car trestle which ran between Washington and Spokane Streets. The King Street Station, in the upper left corner, and the tunnel are still in use, although many of the rail facilities south of the station are now gone, and the land is being used for the King County Domed Stadium.

The GN leaves Seattle headed north through a mile long tunnel underneath the downtown business section of the city. The tunnel was completed in 1905. Due to the relatively soft ground and the proximity to the foundations of existing buildings, some settling and damage occurred. Several law suits were brought and payment made, but Seattle's waterfront was freed of main line railroad traffic. Many years later, a freight destined for Interbay yard disappears into the south portal of the tunnel. As the long freight moves at restricted speed, the conductor leans from the caboose steps to spear his orders.

Joe Williamson

Near Shilshole, a Consolidation works south towards the Salmon Bay drawbridge and Interbay, with a long freight that nearly exceeds the old hog's capacity. Prone to slip when rain soaked, the clay and sand bluffs, rising steeply beside the tracks, have caused delays and derailments which have resulted in the relocation of several miles of track.

After passing the yard at Interbay, the Spokane Local clumps northbound across the rail joints of the Salmon Bay drawbridge over the Lake Washington Ship Canal, in the late 1920's. With bell ringing, the Pacific locomotive sets the pace at a fast walk until the last car has cleared the bridge.

Warren Wing collection

In 1940, a Mountain and two Pacifics are inspected in the roundhouse at Interbay, principal yard and shops of the GN west of the Cascades.

Stanley H. Gray

Stan Styles

In 1952, No. 511 stops at Bellingham with the International. The first coach behind
the locomotive is the odd Pullman "Pendulum coach", tested extensively
on the GN for several years.

White Rock appears on the hillside by the bay, as a northbound freight passes the
International Boundary signs after a stop for customs.

Blaine is the last stop in the United States before crossing the
border into British Columbia.

Charles R. Wood

Stan Styles

A Seattle bound train stops at White Rock in 1911 for Canadian customs. Because there were few good roads to the small B.C. towns along the Sound, the GN provided extensive and important commuter service, as the major artery of transportation south and west from Vancouver and New Westminster.

A southbound freight stops at White Rock in 1969.

Stan Styles

Stopped on the ten degree approach curve to the mile long Fraser River bridge at New Westminster, the International loads passengers at the old GN/CN station in 1952. Prior to the completion of the bridge in 1904, GN trains were ferried across the Fraser River.

A pile driver works on bridge 69 at Crescent Beach. Heavy maintenance is often necessary in the area between here and White Rock because of frequent mud and rock slides and damage to the trestles, caused by the winter storms and high tides.

Claude Witt

372 THE GREAT NORTHERN AND CANADIAN NATIONAL DEPOTS, VANCOUVER, B.C. CANADA

The GN arch in Vancouver, on Hastings Street near Hamilton, was erected for the September, 1912 visit of the Duke of Connaught, Governor General of Canada from 1911 to 1916. The 5 mile long, double track CPR tunnel through the Selkirk Mountains bears his name.

The GN station in Vancouver, B.C., completed in 1915, was planned to house both the GN and the CN. Instead, the CN built its own station next door. The steel and brick station, trimmed with marble, was vacated in 1962 when the GN moved into the CN station, and was torn down in 1965.

The massive gray stone Canadian National station, officially opened in November, 1919, is occupied today by the CN, and by the successor to the GN and BN passenger services, Amtrak. It will soon be occupied by VIA, the successor to CN and CPR passenger services.

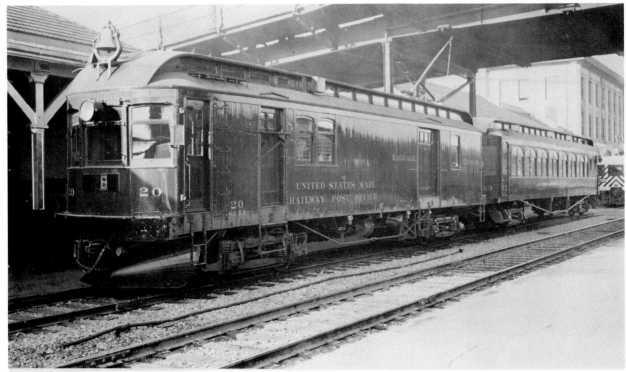

SC&P No. 20, an Express-Mail motor heads up the two car Coeur d'Alene train at the GN station in Spokane in 1939.

Spokane Coeur d'Alene & Palouse

In September, 1909, the Idaho Central Railway Company was organized in the interests of the GN in order to acquire from the Panhandle Electric Railway & Power Company its water rights, power sites and projected line from Priest River, Idaho north toward the Canadian border. No construction of the line ever took place, and all right of way through U.S. public lands was relinquished. On December 7, 1926, the name of the Idaho Central was changed to the Spokane Coeur d'Alene & Palouse Railway Company, and on June 1, 1927, the SC&P joined the GN in purchasing the electrified lines of the Spokane and Eastern Railway and Power Company and the Inland Empire Railroad Company. With this acquisition the GN moved to expand its operation into the rich farming country south and east of Spokane in competition with the Northern Pacific, Union Pacific and Milwaukee. In the late 1920's, equipment from the traction road, the first single phase road in the country, was modified in the Spokane shops of the SC&P, and materially assisted in the construction of the new Cascade tunnel. Passenger service was ended on the SC&P in 1939, and in 1941, the electrification was scrapped in favor of diesel operation. In 1943, the GN purchased all property of the SC&P in settlement for its debts to the GN.

The sharply curved trestle and covered bridge of the Spokane, Coeur d'Alene and Palouse Railway, span the Palouse River in Southeastern Washington, not far from the Idaho border and the terminal at Moscow.

Dr. Philip R. Hastings

SC&P Baldwin-Westinghouse Motor No. 606 shuffles cars at Spring Valley, Washington in September, 1940. Spring Valley, about 30 miles south of Spokane, was the junction point for a branch extending 42 miles to Colfax on the Palouse River, in the midst of the rolling wheat country of Eastern Washington. Motor 606, capable of a top speed of 27.5 miles per hour, was one of four electric locomotives built between 1906 and 1908 for the SC&P. Two of the Motors, 603 and 604, were modified to take the 11,000 volt trolley on the GN main in the Cascades, while 605 and 606 remained as 6,600 volt locomotives on the SC&P.

Vern Nelson collection

Express/passenger No. 43 is at the Spokane shops in 1939.

SC&P motor No. 502, a 51 ton steeple cab design freight motor, was built by Baldwin-Westinghouse in 1912. Rated at 300 tons trailing with a 36 mph safe speed, it was identical in speed and capacity to the somewhat newer motors such as No. 503. The SC&P operated a total of 13 freight motors which could also double in passenger service. In two round trips between Spokane and Parkwater, two motors pulling ten standard GN coaches carried 3,500 people to the National Air Races in 1927.

Vern Nelson collection

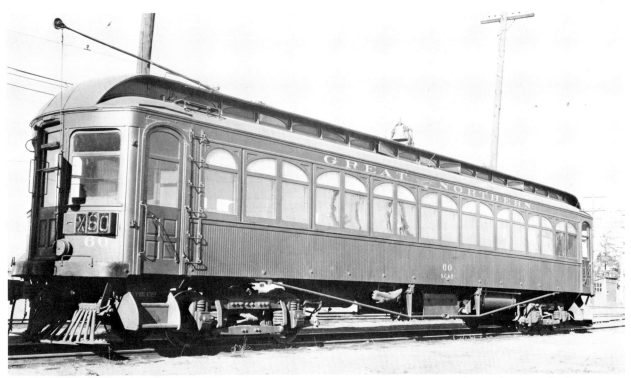

Great Northern (SC&P) passenger coach No. 60, at Spokane in the mid 1930's, had a seating capacity of 64. The 60′ coach was originally equipped with both a pantograph for operation on 6,600 volts AC and a trolley pole for operation on 600 volts DC. In later years, the entire single phase system was modified to operate exclusively on the 600 volts DC, eliminating the need for pantographs.

Vern Nelson collection

No. 20 with a trailer, at Coeur d'Alene in 1939, has been fitted with a permanent snow plow pilot in deference to the heavy snow often encountered on this run in the wintertime.

The Wenatchee-Oroville branch

In 1910, the GN turned its attention to the building of a branch line from Wenatchee to Oroville. Although Oroville was served by the GN branch that left Dean and passed north through Marcus to cross and recross the Canadian border, the country along the Columbia and Okanogan Rivers between Wenatchee and Oroville, some of the finest fruit growing country in the United States, was virtually inaccessible. Service along the Columbia north to Brewster was provided by river packets, and along the Okanogan by stage. Moreover, the Kettle Falls Branch, as it wound westward along the border, passed through some of the roughest country in the northwest, with steep grades and a series of hairpin curves that unduly lengthened the mileage between the small towns. Recognizing the vast potential of the area, it became imperative for the GN to build the 134 mile heavy duty branch line.

Contracts were awarded to Guthrie, McDougall & Company of Portland, Oregon, with the line to be built under the direction of A.H. Hogeland — chief engineer of the GN, and Ralph Budd — formerly chief engineer and then assistant to the president. A.F. Whitcomb was the district engineer in immediate charge.

Work began south from Oroville in the spring of 1910, while the construction north from Wenatchee was delayed until 1912 for the relocation of a 27 mile portion of State Road No. 10. In many areas along the steep bluffs of the Columbia, there was not room for both the wagon road and the railroad, and the wagon road was relocated higher on the bluffs, with grades specified by the Washington State road engineer not to exceed 7%.

Heavy rock work was encountered by the railroad between Wenatchee and Pateros at mile post 58. At Destruction Point one steam shovel worked for nine months moving rock that had been blasted loose to provide the right-of-way. The 200,000 cubic yards of hard rock was then used further up the line to cross a bay in the Columbia River north of Knapps Hill. In all, ten steam shovels were kept at work moving over 3,000,000 cubic yards of material — half of it rock — to grade this stretch of railroad. Three short tunnels were necessary along the Columbia where promontories were too steep for roadbed construction, and five creosoted timber bridges were built along the line. A first class railroad was completed in 1913, with light 0.4 percent grades northbound and 0.3 percent grades southbound. Curves were kept to a gentle 4 degrees except for three 5 degree curves at mile post 40.

Shortly thereafter, the line between Oroville and Curlew was abandoned as too costly and too limited in capacity to operate. Traffic from north of Oroville was routed over the new branch to Wenatchee and thence to Spokane. Settlement of the entire area north of Wenatchee proceeded rapidly, and from these lush valleys thousands of carloads of fruit are now shipped to markets all over the world.

The paddle-wheel steamboat Selkirk, owned by Hill and Griggs, works its way through the rapids at Entiat, twenty miles above Wenatchee on the Columbia, enroute to the landing at Chelan Falls, circa 1900.

Lake Chelan, lying in a tremendous glacial cirque basin carved out thousands of years ago, begins high in the North Cascades and ends in the semi-arid country above the Columbia River. The narrow fifty mile long lake, fed by melting snows and glaciers, is fifteen hundred feet deep and surrounded by mile high mountain peaks. In the late 1920's, the level of the lake was raised by 25 feet upon completion of a ten million dollar hydro-electric project by Washington Water Power Company. It was planned at that time that part of the electric power generated by this plant would be used to electrify the railroad east of the Columbia River, but this project never went beyond the initial planning stage.

For many years Lake Chelan was promoted by the railroad as a scenic and recreational area to rival Glacier National Park. The Lake Transfer & Stage, owned by Wm. Spring and W.R. Higgins, carried mail and passengers from the Chelan Depot about 5 miles to the hotel at the foot of Lake Chelan.

The water tank at Chelan, now torn down, was kept full by gravity flow from Beebe Springs, about ¼ mile north of the tank. The orchards, once owned by Junius Beebe, father of author Lucius Beebe, are nearby.

Walt Thayer

A construction train on the Wenatchee-Oroville branch pauses at Entiat in 1914.

On June 2, 1913, No. 463 heads the first passenger train through Omak,
40 miles south of Oroville.

Construction of the Wenatchee-Oroville branch along the Okanogan River, between Oroville and Brewster, was easier and progressed more rapidly than the construction below the high bluffs of the Columbia. Track laying crews are at work in the Okanogan Valley, April, 1913.

Okanogan County Historical Society

Walt Thayer

Azwell is typical of apple growing communities where the dominant structure is the apple grower's warehouse. During the late summer and early fall, the long siding next to the warehouse is filled with cuts of refrigerator cars. The loaded reefers are then moved to Appleyard, destined for storage warehouses or movement east and west.

Walt Thayer

Engineer Jack Dennis looks
down from the cab of
Alco 213, the regularly
assigned power for passenger
train No. 253 and 254, on
No. 254's last run to Oroville.

Walt Thayer

Alco 213 idles at the Oroville station as the crew and passengers await train No. 253's departure on its last run to Wenatchee. Oroville, the end of the 4th subdivision, was also the beginning of the 8th subdivision that connected at one time with the Kettle Valley Railroad at Princeton, B.C., 80 miles further north.

Robert Cannon, the mail clerk, leans out of the door of the R.P.O. car at Omak, July 14, 1953, the "Last day of Mail" on the Wenatchee-Oroville Branch. It was also the last day for the passengers on train No. 253 and 254, and one of the biggest crowds ever to ride this train got on and off at various stops as their way of bidding farewell to a friend.

In 1911, a Victoria Vancouver & Eastern construction train is at work between Princeton and Coalmont, B.C. The GN subsidiary was the beginning of a planned east/west main line that would have given the GN a direct route into Vancouver from Wenatchee or Spokane via Oroville. The strong influence of the GN along the Canadian border was a real concern to the Canadian Government, and the Kettle Valley Railroad along the border was built primarily to counter this growing political and economic influence.

Gas-electric car 2317 was put in operation in 1926, on the GN branch that ran north and east between Marcus, Washington and Nelson, B.C. on Kootenay Lake.

Seattle Times

The Oroville-Hedley tri-weekly mixed train No. 397, crosses the Similkameen River just inside the
U.S. border, enroute to Hedley, B.C. in 1949. As the crow flies, it is only about 5 miles to the
Canadian border, but as the railroad goes — sometimes following, sometimes crossing the Similkameen
River — the distance is nearly 21 miles. The further north and west the train goes, the rougher and
more primitive the country becomes. The line was constructed in the early 1900's, when the
mines at Hedley and the sawmills at Princeton, B.C. were booming. In 1955, after the gold mines
in Hedley petered out, the line was removed between Keremeos and Hedley.

The GN in California

A. Guthrie Construction Co. enters Northern California in July, 1931, laying track along part of the
GN "backdoor route" to San Francisco. This route is via the GN extension of the SP&S/Oregon
Trunk from Bend, Oregon to Bieber, California and a connection with the Western Pacific main
line. Below, the GN special arrives at Bieber for the Golden Spike celebration, November 10, 1931.

Above: In 1938, class 0-1 Mikado No. 3077 waits at Lookout, California, just north of Bieber. Water is scarce in this high lava bed country, not far from Mt. Lassen, and the 2-8-2 trails an auxiliary water car, as did most other GN power along the California extension.

Below: Little remains of the once extensive yard, trackage and terminal facilities at Bieber. BN/WP freights growl right past the station, where once crews changed, and thundering GN Mallets pulled into town during World War II with all the tonnage they could haul.

Charles R. Wood

Two hundred forty two miles and 6½ hours out of
St. Paul, the westbound Builder eases to a stop at
Fargo, North Dakota. From this point west, for
hundreds of miles across North Dakota and
Montana, the land is one vast prairie.

Great Northern Railway

5. ORIENTAL LIMITED/EMPIRE BUILDER

In the few short years between the creation of the Great Northern in 1889 and its completion to the Pacific Coast in 1893, it would appear that little thought had been given to naming the first class train between St. Paul and Seattle. Indeed, evidence suggests that James J. Hill, during this time, was not overly interested in a prestigious passenger train, but rather that he was primarily interested in transporting immigrants, agricultural products, lumber, minerals and manufactured goods. In 1892, the Montana Express ran to Butte, Montana, and local service was offered further north along the main line as it progressed over the Rockies. After the completion of the road, there was the Great Northern Flyer, the Great Northern Express, and others simply identified by train number. In the late 1890's, with the Yukon gold rush booming and every train and ship into and out of Seattle jammed with gold seekers, there was the Alaska Limited.

In January, 1905, twelve years after the completion of the main line, the Oriental Limited was inaugurated as the name train of the Great Northern. Perhaps James J. Hill had this name in mind for many years, for it had been his boyhood dream, when leaving his home in Canada, to work his way to the Pacific Coast and then to the Orient. The name may have seemed a bit incongruous for a train that traversed 1,800 miles of prairie and mountains to terminate at tidewater, but James J. Hill's vision reached far beyond where the rails terminated. It extended, in fact, another 7,000 miles to the ports along the eastern rim of the Pacific. The lucrative Oriental trade, moving mainly out of California ports, was increasing every year, and Hill had moved several years

earlier to involve the GN in this trade.

In 1896, he had sent Captain James Griffith to Japan to negotiate with officials of the NYK line, and these discussions led to the signing of a contract in St. Paul later that same year. On August 31, 1896 the steamer Miike Maru sailed into Elliott Bay, and later in the day a

huge parade celebrated its arrival. Seattle's first steamer in trans-Pacific service, the Miike Maru marked the ascendancy of Seattle as a world port. The GN now had regular trade connections reaching half way around the world from St. Paul. Flour, cotton, lumber, steel, and manufactured goods moved on GN rails to Seattle, and then via Japanese ships to the Orient.

Anyone who knew Hill, expected that this "flaw" in the operation would not long endure. In 1900, the Great Northern Steamship Company was organized with a capitalization of $6 million. Contracts were signed for the construction of two 28,500 ton steamships (with two more to follow); the Dakota and the Minnesota, and in 1901, the Great Northern's Asiatic Dock was completed at Smiths Cove, next to the principal yard of the GN at Interbay. The NYK Line occupied the Asiatic Dock, Pier 88. The new Minnesota and Dakota arrived at Pier 88 in December, 1904. The twin steamers, wide of beam and with a deep draft, were the largest combination passenger and freight ocean carriers afloat. Hill applied the same principle to the water as to the railroad — larger ships, like longer trains with huge engines, could carry more goods and move them more efficiently. It was now possible for Great Northern passengers and goods to travel all the way from St. Paul to the Orient on Great Northern equipment.

But the volume of trade envisioned by Hill at the turn of the century never fully materialized. The close of the Russo-Japanese War in 1905 brought a decline in trans-Pacific shipping, resulting in more bottoms available to carry goods than there were goods to move. In 1907, the Dakota ran aground on a reef outside Yokohama Harbor and sank before it could be salvaged. As a final blow, the passage of the Hepburn Act of 1906 enabled the Federal Government, through enforcement of the "commodity clause", to force the railroads to divest themselves of steamship lines and coal mines that they had acquired to stifle competition. By 1915, the Minnesota and the brief career of the Dakota had cost the GN an operating loss of $3 million. With the sale of the Minnesota in 1917, the Great Northern's own trans-Pacific service ended, but the agreement with the NYK Line and a profitable trade with the Orient continued.

On a 58 hour schedule between Seattle and St. Paul, the 1905 Oriental Limited (trains Nos. 1 and 2) beat the running time of the rival North Coast Limited by 4-1/2 hours. The Northern Pacific, of course, had a much longer main line between the two cities, as well as heavier grades and higher summits in the Rockies. The trains themselves were remarkably similar, which was not surprising in view of the fact that the steel-framed wooden equipment for both lines was built by the same companies -Pullman, Barney & Smith and American Car & Foundry. Also, until just a few months previously, the NP had been part of the "Hill Lines", and there was even a hint of the Oriental on the North Coast Limited. The tailgate sign displayed the "Monad", a red and black design of Chinese origin and the trademark of the NP

since about 1900. Both trains, composed of head end equipment, coaches, diner, sleepers, and an observation car, were usually about eight cars long. The diners featured an "English Pub" atmosphere, while the plush, carpeted sleepers and the observation cars were ornate and heavily decorated with imported wood. Many of the sleeping cars on the Oriental Limited were named for locations in the Orient—Tokio, Yokohama, Manila, Foochou, and Fujiyama. Others were named for earlier associates of Hill in forming the St. Paul & Pacific, while still others were named for areas along the line, such as Tumwater and Cashmere. The observation cars were not named, but simply carried the title "Compartment Observation Car".

In 1909, the Oriental Limited began operating on a 72 hour schedule through to Chicago, via the rails of the Burlington between St. Paul and Chicago. On a slower schedule than the Oriental, its running mate the Oregonian (train Nos. 3 and 4) also offered daily service between St. Paul and Seattle, making many more station stops than the premier train. The Oregonian offered a late evening departure from St. Paul, arriving in Seattle and Tacoma in the morning hours, while the Oriental reached its western destination in the evening. Eastbound, the departures were reversed, with the Oregonian leaving Seattle in the morning and the Oriental in the early evening. Both the Oriental and the Oregonian served Portland with cars cut out at Spokane and transferred to the rails of the SP&S. Eastbound passengers from Portland arrived in Spokane on SP&S trains Nos. 2 and 4. Through sleepers to St. Paul and Chicago were cut into the Oriental and Oregonian, while coach passengers merely transferred from one train to the other.

1909 was also the year of the Alaska-Yukon-Pacific Exposition, a summer long event that promoted Alaska, Orient and Pacific Northwest trade. The Exposition was held in Seattle on what is now the site of the University of Washington, and many of the Exposition buildings remained as a nucleus for the University campus. In the same year the famous Silk Trains began to run on the GN. Japanese and English ships moved the raw silk to the U.S. ports of San Francisco and Seattle. Arriving in Seattle, some cargo passed through Pier 41 (now Pier 91); and much of the silk passed directly through Pier 88 for trans-shipment east via the GN. Originally, the silk was handled in regular train service, but as the volume grew with the increased demand for silk, special fast trains were assigned. About a week's advance notice of the cargo's arrival was received, during which time the best equipment was assembled and conditioned. The Silk Trains were going strong by 1912, and continued to run through 1933.

In 1922, the wooden cars of the Oriental Limited were steel sheathed in keeping with the move toward the safer and more

durable all-steel equipment. This rebuilding was a temporary measure employed until new equipment could be delivered, at which time the rebuilt equipment was assigned to the Glacier Park Limited, which had supplanted the Oregonian on the schedule.

1922 was also the year the Pullman Company took over the operation of the sleeping cars, which up to that time had been both owned and operated by the railroad. It was a good promotional move by the railroad, widely accepted by the traveling public, and less costly in the long run. So pleased was the Great Northern by the Pullman Company operation, that it had the Pullman Company build the entire sleeper, dining car and observation car consist (seven sets of equipment) for the new Oriental Limited of 1924.

The new Oriental Limited went on display in Chicago and other cities as far west as Portland, Oregon in the late spring of 1924, and went into service on June 1st. The consist of each train included a dynamo baggage car, a smoking car, a first class coach, a tourist sleeping car, three first class sleepers, a diner, and an observation car. All equipment was of heavyweight steel construction, painted GN olive green with olive green letter boards on which the name Oriental Limited appeared in large dulux gold letters. The ends carried Pullman or Great Northern in smaller type.

The Oriental names for the sleepers and dining cars were dropped. The dining cars now carried the names of states served by the Great Northern, and the sleepers were named for the cities and areas so served. The observation cars were all named in the Great Circle series, referring to the shorter route out of Northwest ports across the North Pacific to the Orient. Windows in the ends of these huge observation cars were built unusually high and wide to allow for better viewing of the magnificent western scenery; and the large deeply recessed observation platforms allowed room for as many as eight people at once.

Interior decor of the cars was a striking change from the lavish design and exotic woods of the older equipment. The interiors were painted in soft, restful tones of gray, green and sand. The English Pub atmosphere in the dining cars was dropped for a more contemporary theme. Pullman cars now had permanent headboards placed between what had formerly been open sections. Every afternoon, tea and cakes

were served in the observation lounge, which served as the social center for activity on board the train. In addition, a maid and bath in the women's lounge complemented the same services offered the men in their lounge by a barber and valet shop.

While the schedule to Chicago was speeded up by four hours, the train, over the long run, wasn't really a great deal faster than its predecessor of 1909. This was due in part to the new heavier equipment and in part to the fact that ABS signalling had not yet been completed along the main line. Then, too, there wasn't a real need to dramatically speed up the service. Highways in the Northwest, except for small segments, were still primitive, and autos or buses offered little competition. The airlines were in their infancy, with slow, noisy planes restricted largely to daytime hours and clear weather. Service, not speed, was the keynote of the entire operation. It remained for Nos. 27 and 28, The Fast Mail, to be the real speed burners of the GN, delivering the mail between St. Paul and Seattle as quickly as the numerous stops would permit.

Locomotive power assigned to the Oriental Limited was varied. The Oriental Limited of 1905 was powered by the new class H-1 Pacifics across the more difficult divisions, while Ten Wheelers and Atlantics powered this comparatively light and short train across the level districts. As the Oriental became longer and heavier, the Ten Wheelers and Atlantics could no longer cope with the situation. By the early 1920's, even booster-equipped Atlantic types could not keep the Oriental Limited to time on the flattest stretch of GN track, between Wolf Point and Havre, Montana. Heavier Pacific types, class H-4 and H-5,

were assigned, and in 1923 the famous P-2 class Mountain was specifically ordered for the Oriental Limited, Glacier Park Limited and Nos. 27 and 28. These locomotives were so successful that the GN was never able to replace them in heavy passenger service.

In May, 1929 Mr. C. O. Jenks, Vice-President, Great Northern Railway, announced the forthcoming arrival of a new train that would run on a 63 hour schedule between Chicago and the Pacific Northwest. The announcement stated, "It is a train that embodies all the latest improvements that the skill of the Pullman Company has created. From the new observation cars — the longest yet built — to the powerful locomotives that will haul it over the Rocky Mountains it is a new train, a train dedicated entirely to the comfort of its patrons and designed to meet the requirements of the faster schedules demanded in transcontinental service."

Left unsaid by Mr. Jenks was the fact that it was also time to brighten the image of the Great Northern Railway — "A Dependable Railway" in 1925. The new train would make a significant contribution to this brighter image and align the railroad even more firmly with the territory it served. The new dining cars would be named for the states and Canadian provinces serviced by the Great Northern; and each new sleeper and observation car would be named for . . . "some man illustrious in the building of the Northwest, including James J. Hill and his associates, some explorer who led the way into the unknown, some pioneer who opened up new areas of settlement, some soldier whose protection was so necessary to the growing communities, or some man of vision who built

The Grea

orthern Flyer

up the great industries of the region. These men found the Northwest a wilderness and they have left an empire, so to honor them and to honor particularly the greatest of these practical dreamers — Mr. James J. Hill — the new train will be known as The Empire Builder".

The timing of the announcement was good. In January, 1929 the Great Northern had officially opened the new 8 mile long Cascade Tunnel. The extensive line relocation up through the Chumstick Canyon that eliminated the old route through Tumwater had been completed. In addition, the new electrified division between Skykomish and Wenatchee was in full operation, using the most modern electric locomotives that money could buy. The Great Northern was in fact brightening its image with $25 million worth of new railroad and locomotives (both steam and electric), as well as the new premier train.

With appropriate fanfare, the new Empire Builder (six sets of equipment) entered regular service on June 10, 1929 as train Nos. 1 and 2. Its running mate, the Oriental Limited, now re-numbered as train Nos. 3 and 4, continued on its 68 hour schedule. The Glacier Park Limited, comprised largely of the refurbished equipment of the old (prior to 1924) Oriental Limited, was withdrawn from service.

The first of the Northerns — the S-1's — delivered for the Builder in the summer of 1929 were found wanting in high speed operation. Later in the year, the locomotives most often identified with the Builder — the S-2's — were delivered. These 80" drivered Northerns, although somewhat temperamental in starting a heavy train, provided superb passenger power for the 1930's and 1940's. They were the last steam locomotives ordered by the GN from any commercial builder.

Painted the same olive green, the new Empire Builder did not look a great deal different from the Oriental Limited. Painted proudly in dulux gold on the wide letterboards, however, was the name EMPIRE BUILDER in railroad-extended Roman lettering. The name was repeated on the coaches, baggage cars, and Railway Post Office car. The new sleepers carried names that were indeed familiar in the Northwest - Charles A. Broadwater (builder of the Montana Central), Marcus Daly (the copper king), Arthur A. Denny (Seattle pioneer), Isaac Stevens (railroad surveyor of the 1850's), General Frederick W. Benteen, General George A. Custer and General Philip Sheridan. In all, 17 cars were named for generals and 19 others were named for famous civilians. The older tourist sleepers continued to carry numbers rather than names, as did of course the coaches and head end equipment. The "Observation Solarium-Lounge" cars, nearly 89 feet long over the coupler faces, were the longest observation cars ever built for the Great Northern and featured an enclosed sun room rather than the traditional open observation platform. These new cars could also be used in mid-train if desired — a definite operating asset. Since they were fully enclosed, they relieved the train crew of the responsibility of watching over passengers on an open platform.

The interior of the cars featured the light pastel grays and greens that had proven so popular on the 1924 version of the Oriental Limited. Carved walnut panels, and touches of old gold enhanced the Observation Lounge. The parchment shaded lamps, easy chairs, writing desks, and candelabrum side lamps all contributed to the Tudor decor; and an expert mixologist served at the buffet. It was, as the publicity brochure described, "like a lovely living room."

On the first anniversary of the inauguration of the Empire Builder, Mr. A.J. Dickinson, Passenger Traffic Manager, reported that the transcontinental running time of the Builder, twice cut during the previous 12 months, was now down to 60 hours and 45 minutes. Compared to the 68 hour schedule of the Oriental Limited, the Empire Builder saved a full business day for travelers between Chicago and the Pacific Northwest. The report also noted that the faster schedules and the new train had met with an instant response from the traveling public and a gratifying increase in transcontinental passenger business. Just nine months after this glowing report, the full impact of a nationwide depression hit the country and business dropped dramatically. By March, 1931, with just enough business to support one train, the Oriental Limited was dropped from the schedule. It would be nearly two decades before it reappeared.

In June, 1935, the Union Pacific's articulated streamliner — City of Portland — made its first trip out of Portland for Chicago. An immediate sensation in the Northwest, the little streamliner made the trip every six days, cutting 12 hours off the usual Portland/Chicago schedule. Even though the primitive diesel power unit broke down frequently, so that the train had to be rescued by a steam engine, the train was so popular that reservations were made far in advance. Many passengers traveled the additional 180 miles from Seattle to Portland just to be able to ride the City of Portland.

In November, 1934, the Burlington — jointly owned by the GN and the NP — had introduced streamliner service with the Pioneer Zephyr between Lincoln and Kansas City. The Twin Zephyrs between Chicago and Minneapolis quickly followed, and then the Denver Zephyrs in November, 1936. Widely exhibited before being put into service, these Budd built streamliners attracted huge throngs of spectators. Everyone

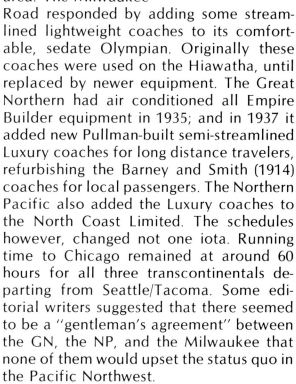

wanted to ride the streamliners, including the people of the Pacific Northwest.

Editorial comment in the region's newspapers pressed for streamliner service to the Puget Sound area. The Milwaukee Road responded by adding some streamlined lightweight coaches to its comfortable, sedate Olympian. Originally these coaches were used on the Hiawatha, until replaced by newer equipment. The Great Northern had air conditioned all Empire Builder equipment in 1935; and in 1937 it added new Pullman-built semi-streamlined Luxury coaches for long distance travelers, refurbishing the Barney and Smith (1914) coaches for local passengers. The Northern Pacific also added the Luxury coaches to the North Coast Limited. The schedules however, changed not one iota. Running time to Chicago remained at around 60 hours for all three transcontinentals departing from Seattle/Tacoma. Some editorial writers suggested that there seemed to be a "gentleman's agreement" between the GN, the NP, and the Milwaukee that none of them would upset the status quo in the Pacific Northwest.

The fact of the matter was that the extension of streamliner service to the Pacific Northwest in the 1930's was not considered a good investment. The country was involved in a deep depression that threatened the very existence of many of the railroads. The Great Northern and the Northern Pacific had huge investments in the Empire Builder and the North Coast Limited. The Milwaukee, in and out of receivership since shortly after World War I, needed all of its limited resources to invest in the extremely popular Hiawatha. Then too, the traffic density of the West was light when compared to that of the Mid-west and the East. In 1930, the combined population of North Dakota, South Dakota, Montana and Idaho was 2,500,000. Washington had a population of 1,600,000 and Oregon 1,000,000. By contrast, Illinois had a population of 7,000,000 while Minnesota and Wisconsin had nearly 3,000,000 each.

By early 1940 the picture had changed, however. The war in Europe created an urgent need for better and faster transportation between the Mid-west and the Pacific Northwest. Orders for huge numbers of ships, airplanes, and manufactured goods of all kinds resulted in a West Coast boom that was unprecedented. As ship repair and building yards, aircraft factories and other plants began to expand to meet the demand, the need for workers on the Pacific Coast outstripped the available labor force, and companies began recruiting and hiring in the Mid-west. The United States Government federalized the National Guard, opening huge training camps in the Northwest, and by 1941, the Builder began running in two sections to try to fill both the civilian and military need for transportation. With the entry of the United States into the global conflict on December 7, 1941, the three Northwest line carriers had more traffic — both freight and passenger — than they could handle. The Builder, the North Coast Limited, and the Olympian often left Seattle for the two day and three night journey to Chicago with passengers standing in the aisles. Passenger equipment that hadn't seen transcontinental service in years began to make the round trips between Chicago and Seattle as fast as it could be serviced and turned. The Empire Builder became so heavy that even the new diesel freight units were pressed into service to help it over Marias Pass. Obviously the day was now rapidly approaching when the heavyweight Builder would

not only be outdated, but worn out as well, and it was equally obvious that the entire Northwest was experiencing an era of growth that would not end with the war. The time had come to replace the 1929 Builder.

Accordingly, on November 4, 1943 the GN placed an order with the Pullman-Standard Car Manufacturing Company for five new 12 car sets of streamlined equipment at a cost of $7,000,000. The consist of each train would include a baggage-mail car, one 60 seat coach, three 48 seat coaches, a coffee shop dormitory car, a diner, four sleeping cars, and an observation lounge. Four of these trains would be owned by the GN, and one by the Burlington, which operated the trains between St. Paul and Chicago. These new trains would operate on a 39 hour schedule to St. Paul and 45 hours to Chicago, cutting 13-1/2 hours off the previous Builder schedule.

The 45 hour schedule was not completely new. During the 1920's the Silk Specials had operated on such a schedule, but under different conditions than the regularly scheduled trains. The comparatively light Silk Specials were given rights over every other train on the railroad. The only stops made were for changing crews and power. The best power available was carefully inspected and waiting at each division point; and the crews were selected for their ability and judgment in getting the Specials over the road as quickly as possible. It simply was not possible to operate the Builder in the same manner. The stops were too numerous, the equipment too heavy, and there were not enough fast passenger engines to keep such a schedule, even if the station stops had been reduced (as was done with the streamliner). Furthermore, heavyweight Pullmans and coaches rocketing down the main line for long distances at speeds in excess of 80 mph would have been uncomfortable and hazardous for the passengers. Nor was the dining car service geared for such speed. The heavy 80 foot diners and the Pullmans rode very well at speeds of around 60 mph, but push this type of equipment faster and the sway, bounce, and undulations of the cars would have made the service intolerable for many passengers.

The new trains, delivered early in 1947 — streamlined, lightweight, and with lower centers of gravity — were designed to be smooth riding at high speed. The EMD E-7-A locomotives, two 2,000 horsepower units per train, were delivered some time ahead of the passenger equipment (1945). They went into trial service on both the Fast Mail and the 1929 Empire Builder to acquaint the crews with their operation and to familiarize the shops with their service requirements. The diesels, with their tremendous power and smooth acceleration, could start the train without a single jar from either engine thrust or slack between the cars. The train started and stopped as one unit. This was due to the "tight lock" couplers which eliminated the slack and to the electrically activated brakes.

Mr. John Budd, Assistant General Manager, Lines East, in charge of the transcontinental exhibition run, pointed out to the reporters riding the Builder that while the new diesels were capable of a top speed of 117 mph, the GN did not envision running the new train at much more than 85 mph; and at that speed there would not be any passenger discomfort. The train would attain its top speeds on the plains of Minnesota, North Dakota and Eastern Montana. Its speed also would be improved in the Rocky Mountain area by the new tunnels built to eliminate the 10

degree curves. There was little sway or lean on the curves at speed; and the reporters were as much impressed by this feature as they were by the higher speeds, which were not noticeable except for the more rapidly passing telegraph poles.

Following its press debut in Chicago on February 6, 1947, the Builder was moved to St. Paul on February 7th for its christening ceremony. In 6 degree weather, the Queen of Snow and King Boreas Rex of the Winter Carnival broke bottles of Puget Sound and Mississippi River waters over the engine pilot. In the eight hours that it was on exhibition in St. Paul, over 4,000 people visited the Builder. Even larger crowds greeted the Streamliner the next day in Minneapolis, and hundreds of requests for reservations were received.

Over the next few days, the Builder was previewed at Duluth, Superior, Minot, Fargo, Great Falls, Spokane and Portland. Leaving Portland on the 15th for Puget Sound, the Builder lay over for an afternoon viewing in Tacoma before moving on to Seattle.

The people of Tacoma had been greatly disappointed when GN President F.J. Gavin had announced on April 23, 1946 that the new Streamliner would not serve Tacoma directly. Protests and heroic efforts on the part of Chamber of Commerce President Kenneth M. Kennel and other business leaders were to no avail. The fast scheduling of the new Builder was largely responsible for the decision. Some stops at other cities across the country were also eliminated. The old Builder, soon to become the Oriental Limited, would still serve many of them.

Viewed at Seattle's King Street Station on the 16th, the Builder moved to Wenatchee and then to Everett, where it was on display for Snohomish County residents on the 17th between 6:30 and 7:30 PM. It was at Vancouver, B.C. on the 18th; and as it rolled towards Bellingham on the 19th, hundreds of school children from Custer and Ferndale and their teachers turned out to watch. Scores more gathered at the crossroads and stations along the way. For these people it was also a preview of the Puget Sounder Streamliners (Internationals) which were put into service later in the year between Seattle and Vancouver, British Columbia.

With the first scheduled run to begin February 23rd, the 307 passenger capacity was sold out. The day of the streamliner had arrived for the Northwest. The westbound Empire Builder rolled out of Chicago at 1:00 PM over the rails of the Burlington and followed the Mississippi River for some 300 miles of its journey to the Twin Cities. Leaving Minneapolis at 8:30 PM, the train passed through the farming and dairy country of Minnesota and out onto the prairies of North Dakota through the night, arriving at Williston at 7:20 AM. Here the time zone changed to Mountain Standard, and the train departed at 6:20 AM. The Builder crossed Montana and climbed the backbone of the Rockies, reaching Glacier Park Station by mid-afternoon. For 60 miles the Empire Builder rolled along the southern boundary of the park, then down the west slope of the Rockies through the Flathead Valley and along the Kootenai into Idaho. Clocks had been set back another hour at Troy for Pacific Standard Time; and the train glided into Spokane at 11:30 PM. Here a coach and a sleeper were cut out of the train for the trip to Portland via the SP&S. The ten car Builder continued to Wenatchee, where it picked up the electrics (for 73 miles) to cross the Cascades, descending

into Seattle at 8:00 AM. Following a check, clean up, and change of crew, the Streamliner left for its return trip to Chicago at 3:00 PM.

There were many innovations in the new equipment. The sleeping cars, the first built and delivered to any railroad since the war, featured the duplex-roomette. The ingenious staggering system offered a private room for little more than the cost of a lower berth. Another innovation was the installation of the reclining Heywood-Wakefield seats for passenger comfort in the 48 seat coaches. The brightly decorated coffee shop car had seating for ten at the counter and another ten in the lounge. Standing in line for the diner was eliminated by a system of reservations. Fog-proof double-paned windows helped to insulate the cars. Running ice water was provided in each room and car, and a public address system was placed in all of the cars with the exception of the Pullmans for both announcements and entertainment.

Color was also an important element in the design of the postwar Empire Builder. Everett DeGolyer (famed railfan, historian, and owner of one of the most comprehensive rail photo collections) once described the Builder as the most beautiful train in the world. Reflecting the mood of his company and the GN in this regard, Ralph Haman, Engineer of Color and Design for Pullman-Standard, stated, "With the end of the war, the world is coming out of uniform. Everyone is tired of olive drab and sameness. We are ready for gaiety and beauty, and the new Empire Builder will have these qualities."

And come out of uniform it did — the train was a gaily striped ribbon of color moving along the shores of Puget Sound and over the prairies of Montana and Dakota. The high visibility of the olive green and Omaha orange served to identify the train at a great distance and was a safety factor at crossings. The solid bands of olive and orange were highlighted and separated with stripes of synthetic gold. A pale silvery gray band along the bottom sill of the cars and engines separated the car side from the running gear. The train, road, and car names appeared as stripes of synthetic gold against a background of olive green.

The individual car names were carefully chosen to link the Empire Builder closely with the country through which it passed. Most of the names were taken from the lakes, mountain passes, and glaciers in Glacier National Park. The lunch counter-lounges bore the names of Waterton, St. Mary, Two Medicine, Cour d'Alene and Red Eagle Lakes. The diners were named for Lakes Superior, McDonald, Chelan, Josephine and Michigan. The observation cars carried the names of the Mississippi, Missouri, Flathead, Kootenai and Marias Rivers. Of the four sleepers assigned to each of the five trains, two were named for the passes — Gunsight, Ptarmigan, Dawson, Piegan, Logan, Triple Divide, Lincoln, Cut Bank, Red Gap and Swift Current. The other two carried the names of glaciers within the park — Blackfoot, Ahern, Grinnell, Hanging, Many, Oberlin, Sexton, Harrison, Sperry and Siyeh.

Interior color and decor were also drawn from the territory served by the Builder. Working closely with Pullman-Standard, the Great Northern and the Burlington selected the colors and designs after researching literally hundreds of colored pictures of the vast Northwest Empire. Again Glacier Park dominated, influencing most of the color schemes. The blues used in the coaches and dining cars were inspired by the hue of the glacial lakes; and the greens derived from the park's flowers and foliage. The bark of trees suggested the reddish brown seat covers of the coaches. Spruce trees provided the blue greens. Prairie wheat supplied the yellow tones.

The theme of the observation cars honored the Blackfeet Indian tribes with Winold Reiss paintings, and the pioneers with water colors by Charlie Russell reproduced on the bulkheads. The drapes were replicas of Hudson Bay blankets. Indian picture writing and Hudson Bay colors were also used in the coffee shop cars.

Coaches were in monochromatic blue, green or yellow, with the dominant tones used below the windows. Shades of tan, apricot, green, gray and yellow were used for the sleeping cars.

In the diners, Walter Loos' oil paintings of the wild flowers of Glacier Park were duplicated by a photographic process, handpainted, and built into the panels between the tables. Draperies, rugs, and upholstery in glacial blue provided a setting for the exquisite paintings.

In May, 1948, in order to meet the heavy demands for private rooms, the Great Northern ordered two more sleepers for each Builder, (one for Seattle passengers and one for Portland), which would make the Builder a fourteen car train east of Spokane. Delivery of the sleepers — each containing a drawing room, three compartments and five bedrooms — was expected within 18 to 24 months. In addition, an extra observation car, diner, and club car were ordered for the Empire Builder; and a number of new day coaches were ordered for the Oriental Limited.

In October, 1948 the GN delivered a real surprise with the announcement that it had ordered six new sets of equipment which would include thirty sleepers, and six each of coaches, diners, coffee shops, observation cars, baggage cars and baggage-mail cars, at an estimated cost of $8,500,000. With the arrival of this equipment for the Empire Builder in 1951, and with the Build-

er's old equipment reassigned to the Oriental Limited (which now became the Western Star), the GN had two Seattle-Chicago Streamliners. The cost of the new equipment reached $12,000,000, and in 1955 another $6,000,000 was spent on sixteen dome coaches and six Great Dome lounge cars to complete the equipping of the Mid-Century Empire Builders.

With the 1951 Empire Builder (actually five sets of equipment), the GN departed for the first time since 1924 from the all Pullman consist. The diners, coffee shop-lounges, and observation-lounge cars were built by American Car and Foundry. Named for Appekunny, St. Nicholas, Going-To-The-Sun, Cathedral and Trempealeau Mountains — the observation cars featured taller windows for better viewing and in some respects resembled the cars used on the 20th Century Limited. The diners — bearing the names of Lake of the Isles, Lake Wenatchee, Lake Ellen Wilson, Lake Union, and Lake Minnetonka — featured a softer more subtle color scheme, hidden valance lighting and etched glass partitions. "The Ranch" cars (coffee shops) were perhaps the most unique cars on the entire train, with authentic Western decor complete to the G-Bar-N brand registered in Helena, Montana. They carried the names of Crossley, Running Crane, Hidden, Iceberg, and White Pine Lakes.

The Pullman built sleepers displayed the paintings and art designs of the Northwest Indian tribes. Three of the sleepers on each train were named for rivers — Chumstick, Tobacco, Skykomish, Sheyenne, Fraser, Sun, Skagit, Spokane, Snohomish, Mouse, Pend O'Reille, Milk, Poplar, Bois De Sioux, and Snake. The other three bore the names of mountain passes — Jefferson, Suiattle, Rogers, Hart, Haines, Pitamakan, State, Blewett, Akamina, Firebrand, Inuya, Santiam, Horn, Lewis and Clark, and Wapinitia.

The dome coaches and Great Dome lounge cars were built by Budd. They provided a magnificent panoramic view, and passengers rushed for the cars and the choice front seats in particular. The full length dome cars seated 75 passengers, and the popular cocktail lounge below could accommodate 34. Weighing nearly 100 tons, and riding on six wheel trucks, they offered the best ride of any car on the train. Yet, because of the high window sills on the Great Domes, the smaller dome coaches actually provided the better view.

From its inception in 1929, the Empire Builder was always assigned the best motive power available from the passenger power pool. During the steam era, Northerns and Mountains were regularly assigned to the Builder. On occasion, modernized Pacifics powered the Builder across the level districts, although this was not common practice with a 1,000 ton train running on a faster schedule than its predecessor, the Oriental Limited. At the major terminals — St. Paul, Fargo, Minot, Havre, Whitefish, Spokane, Wenatchee and Seattle — standby protection power was always within a few minutes call if the need arose due to an engine failure or malfunction.

When E-7 diesels were purchased for the 1947 Builder, no one could have anticipated that these massive, fast, handsome units would quickly be withdrawn from the service for which they were specifically intended. The big E-7's could indeed whip the lightweight consist down the long tangents and around the easy curves across the plains of Minnesota, North Dakota and Eastern Montana. When the Builder grew from a 12 to a 14 car train, however, the power needed in the mountainous terrain was simply more than the two 2,000 horsepower units on the head end could provide. An abortive attempt was made in 1950 to keep E-7's on the head end of the Builder by adding F-7-B units between the two E-7-A units. Even though these new 1,500 horsepower B units (500B-505B) were built for this service, their gear ratio did not match the ratio of the A units, and the old bugaboo of overheated traction motors on the A units persisted.

Following this trial period, the E-7-A's were withdrawn from the Empire Builder and replaced by sets of the ubiquitous F units which had been modified for passenger service, complete with train heat boilers. The F units that replaced the E units were an interesting breed of diesel locomotives. Geared for an 89 mph speed — but restricted to a maximum of 79 mph by the ICC, since the GN did not have either automatic train control or cab signals — they were a mixed lot of F-3's, F-5's and F-7's virtually indistinguishable from each other due to modifications in the GN shops that made them all look like early F-7's.

The Empire Builder was the showcase of the GN; and it was therefore important to the railroad that the Builder present the best possible appearance inside and out. Not the least of these considerations was the continuity of line of the engine units themselves. Rare was the occasion when A units would be coupled nose to tail or a B unit would be coupled directly to the leading head end car. Instead the GN ran the engine units in a logical sequence, such as A-B-A or A-B-B-A.

Between Wenatchee and Skykomish in the Cascades — from 1947 to 1956 — the Builder was of course powered by electric locomotives coupled to the diesel units. The E-7-A's were rated at only 225 trailing tons on the 2.2% between Skykomish and Merritt, and the combined power of the two A units was insufficient to move the Builder over this grade without helpers. Further complicating the operation, in the

tunnel the diesels had to run in idle position to avoid causing excessive smoke and gas. The early diesels also lacked dynamic braking, and the regenerative braking of the electrics was invaluable coming down from the summit on either the east or west slope. No specific class of the electrics was assigned exclusively to the Builder at Wenatchee or Skykomish. Rather, assignment was dictated by need and was solely at the discretion of the dispatcher. Therefore, at various times, numbers 31 and 32 could be seen powered by a pair of Y's, a mixed set of Y's and Z's or even one of the huge W's.

The class W motors, delivered to the railroad in 1947, were painted in Omaha orange and olive green. At the same time, the GN shops began to repaint the class Y electrics in this color scheme. As succeeding units were shopped, they too were repainted until the entire class was resplendent in the streamliner colors. The class Z motors were never repainted, but remained in their olive and black color scheme until the day they were scrapped.

During 1967/68 the Empire Builder changed its color scheme of Omaha orange and olive green to Big Sky Blue, which did little to enhance its appearance. In 1970, with the creation of the Burlington Northern, the equipment was repainted in Cascade green with white accents. Scarely had this color scheme been applied, when AMTRAK took over the operation and the identity of the Builder was almost completely lost. Now, with much of its original equipment in service elsewhere on the AMTRAK system — or scrapped — only the EMPIRE BUILDER name remains on the schedule.

Great Northern Railway

Above, a Great Northern passenger train, possibly the Great Northern Flyer, pauses at Jennings, Montana in 1898 on its way east. In the days before the Oriental Limited, GN passenger trains simply carried the railroad name on the letterboard. To the right, the new Oriental Limited is posed along the shore of Puget Sound in the late spring of 1909. Pacific class H-4 No. 1443 was only a year old when these pictures were taken, and its jacket gleams like a steel mirror.

The Oriental Limited 1909

Great Northern Railway

Elegance & Luxury

The new observation parlor car 7577 and dining car 7118 [second car forward] were built by Barney and Smith in the summer of 1909, when the Oriental Limited began operating on a 72 hour schedule through to Chicago. The sleepers were built by Pullman, and the coaches by American Car & Foundry. In the lounge of the Oriental Limited, tea and cakes were served every afternoon at 4:00.

Great Northern Railway

Overleaf: From the observation car, travelers enjoy
the magnificent scenery along the Wenatchee River,
deep in Tumwater Canyon, as the Oriental Limited
rolls slowly eastward.

National Park Service

The Oriental Limited of 1905 crosses the Stone Arch Bridge between Minneapolis and St. Paul. Still in daily use, the famous bridge, now modified and strengthened on the Minneapolis side of the Mississippi River, has been designated in 1975, a "National Historic Civil Engineering Landmark" by the American Society of Civil Engineers.

Edward W. Nolan

Along the waterfront in Seattle in 1968 [left to right] are Father Murphy, Louis Hill Jr.'s daughter, and Mr. and Mrs. Hill. The occasion was the dedication of the "Historical Point of Interest" plaque, at the site of the landing of NYK steamship MIIKE MARU with a cargo of tea in August, 1896—establishing Seattle as an international port.

Kim Forman, Burlington Northern

In this 1905 photo, the Oriental Limited passes Smith Cove in
Seattle. Moored nearby are the Minnesota and Dakota, built by the
Great Northern Steamship Company to ply between Seattle,
Yokahama and Hong Kong. These huge ships, both of them nearly
28,500 ton capacity, were the biggest ships of their time in
trans-Pacific trade, and were the culmination of Hill's dream of a
transcontinental railroad moving goods to and from ports that
served the Orient.

As a safety measure, wooden cars of the Oriental Limited, such as observation car 9029 and dining car 7118, were rebuilt and steel sheathed in 1922. They were included in the consists with the new Pullman built all steel cars until the seven sets of all new equipment arrived in 1924—including compartment-observation car Great Lakes above.

Great Northern photos Dr. George Fischer collection

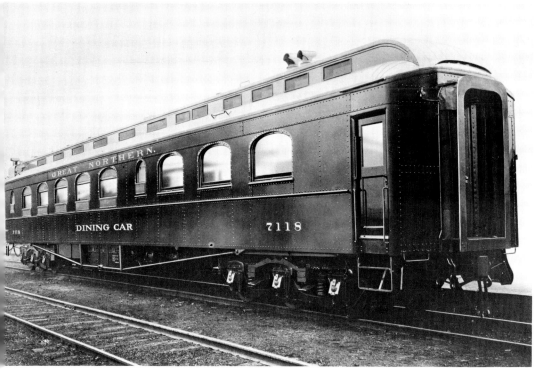

6A-H1362

Collection of Walt Grecula

Hill had perceived early the need for adequate terminal facilities to be owned and used jointly by all railroads entering St. Paul. After much consideration, he sold the property at the foot of Sibley Street to the St. Paul Union Depot Company (of which the Manitoba was one-eighth owner), and the depot, built in 1886, became a "blue-chip" investment. Both the depot and the enormous train shed built in 1889 (interior and exterior view shown) were replaced in the 1920's by the Union Station shown above.

Above: A Ten Wheeler helps a Pacific fight its way up the tough 2.2% in
Stevens Pass. They pause as the train has caught a red block near
Cascade Tunnel station.

Above left: A heavy, double headed Oriental Limited of the 1920's works its
way west through the Tumwater Canyon.

Left: A new open observation car is just out of the builder's shops.

THE NEW ORIENTAL LIMITED OF GREAT NORTHERN RY.
AT FULL SPEED

J. Foster Adams photo

Class P-2 Mountain No. 2505 brings the Oriental Limited into Portland. The 85′ long compartment-observation cars were built with deeply recessed platforms that could seat eight people on folding chairs. These cars—seven of them, were built by Pullman with taller than usual lounge windows for better viewing of the scenery, and were painted in the standard GN olive green. Shown also are the mens lounge and the dining car.

Burlington Northern

ORIENTAL LIMITED 1924

Great Northern Railway

Handsome New Dining Cars in Service on the New Oriental Limited, A De Luxe Train, No Extra Fare.

Bill Johnson

A Pacific type, on the Fourth Subdivision of the Kalispe
Division, has its train, The Oriental Limited, well in hand as
accelerates on the slight downgrade going into Libb
Montana. In the late 1920's, Pacifics were the usual assigne
power over the relatively flat subdivisions. The Northerns we
still in very short supply, and the P-2 Mountain class w
utilized on the heavier mountain grade

Behind a modernized and booster equipped Atlantic, the
Oriental Limited pauses for its photograph on the old Montana
Division. On this nearly flat subdivision out of Wolf Point, the
Atlantics were given another try at keeping the Oriental to
schedule. The Atlantics, however, could perform as expected
only under ideal conditions, and the
experiment was not successful.

Class Y-1 electric leads the steam powered Oriental Limite
out of Skykomish in late 1928, before the opening c
the new Cascade Tunne

Lee Pickett

C. M. Rasmussen collection

THE 1929 EMPIRE BUILDER

Mountain No. 2517 is at St. Paul Union Depot, June 11, 1929 for the inaugural run of the Empire Builder. The 28 engines of the P-2 class, although initially restricted to a maximum of 50 miles per hour, were capable of sustained high speed, and established many speed records between St. Paul and Seattle. They worked every name train on the GN, and in later years when bumped off the Limiteds, they performed well in freight service. Always searching for bigger and better power, the GN had bought 15 Mountain types—class P-1—from Lima in 1914. Never really successful, they were rebuilt in 1928 to 2-10-2's, class Q-2 by the GN shops, but the P-2's built by Baldwin—the GN's favorite builder—never underwent extensive modification, and remained essentially the same until they were scrapped in the 1950's.

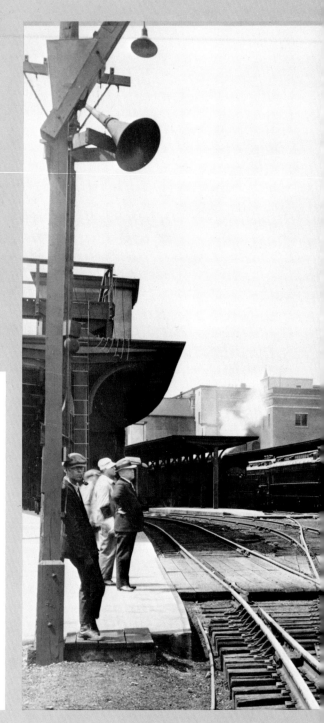

Empire Builder	Oriental Limited		Oriental Limited	Empire Builder
No. 1 Daily	No. 3 Daily		No. 4 Daily	No. 2 Daily
		Chicago, Burlington & Quincy Railroad		
9:00 P. M.	11:00 A. M.	Lv. Chicago Union Station. Ar.	7:30 P. M.	9:15 A. M.
8:00 A. M.	10:00 P. M.	Ar. St. Paul............Lv.	8:30 A. M.	10:45 P. M.
		Great Northern Railway		
8:30 A. M.	10:30 P. M.	Lv. St. Paul............Ar.	8:00 A. M.	10:30 P. M.
9:05 A. M.	11:15 P. M.	Lv. Minneapolis.........Ar.	7:25 A. M.	10:00 P. M.
10:40 A. M.	....	Lv. St. Cloud...........Lv.		8:20 P. M.
①1:15 P. M.	....	Lv. Fergus Falls........Lv.		5:32 P. M.
....	2:00 A. M.	Lv. Willmar............Lv.	4:50 A. M.	....
....	5:15 A. M.	Lv. Breckenridge........Lv.	1:25 A. M.	....
2:50 P. M.	6:35 A. M.	Lv. Fargo..............Lv.	11:45 P. M.	4:10 P. M.
5:50 P. M.	....	Lv. New Rockford.......Lv.		1:00 P. M.
....	8:45 A. M.	Lv. Grand Forks........Lv.	9:30 P. M.	....
8:40 P. M.	3:20 A. M.	Lv. Minot..............Lv.	3:35 P. M.	10:20 A. M.
11:05 P. M.	6:00 P. M.	Lv. Williston...........Lv.	12:01 P. M.	6:55 A. M.
7:15 A. M.	3:55 A. M.	Lv. Havre..............Lv.	2:30 A. M.	10:10 P. M.
10:00 A. M.	6:55 A. M.	Lv. Shelby.............Lv.	10:55 P. M.	7:00 P. M.
11:35 A. M.	8:40 A. M.	Lv. Blackfoot...........Lv.	9:25 P. M.	5:35 P. M.
12:27 P. M.	9:30 A. M.	Lv. Glacier Park........Lv.	8:35 P. M.	4:15 P. M.
3:40 P. M.	12:25 P. M.	Lv. Whitefish...........Lv.	5:20 P. M.	1:35 P. M.
6:33 P. M.	4:10 P. M.	Lv. Troy...............Lv.	1:20 P. M.	9:33 A. M.
10:45 P. M.	9:00 P. M.	Ar. Spokane............Lv.	8:00 A. M.	4:15 A. M.
11:00 P. M.	9:30 P. M.	Lv. Spokane............Ar.	7:30 A. M.	4:00 A. M.
3:50 A. M.	1:55 A. M.	Lv. Wenatchee..........Lv.	2:55 A. M.	11:15 P. M.
8:58 A. M.	6:28 A. M.	Ar. Everett.............Lv.	10:32 P. M.	7:02 P. M.
10:00 A. M.	7:30 A. M.	Ar. Seattle.............Lv.	9:30 P. M.	6:00 P. M.
11:40 A. M.	9:10 A. M.	Ar. Tacoma............Lv.	7:50 P. M.	4:20 P. M.
		Spokane, Portland & Seattle Railway		
11:15 P. M.	9:15 P. M.	Lv. Spokane............Ar.	7:30 A. M.	3:50 A. M.
10:00 A. M.	7:30 A. M.	Ar. Portland...........Lv.	9:00 P. M.	6:00 P. M.

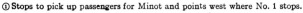
① Stops to pick up passengers for Minot and points west where No. 1 stops.

Great Northern Railway

Great Northern Railway Dr. George Fischer collection

Great Northern Railway

In June, 1929 the first westbound Empire Builder pauses at Everett before resuming its journey southward along Puget Sound on the last lap into Seattle. The nearly 89' long Observation-Solarium-Lounge sported a radio antenna on the roof, and featured an enclosed sun room rather than the traditional open observation platform. A wreath decorates the Great Northern tailgate sign, and a huge crowd has gathered for the momentous occasion.

In a scene not to be repeated until the days of the second World War, the Empire Builder of 1929—15 cars long—is stretched out across the Stone Arch Bridge between Minneapolis and St. Paul. The usual consist of the Builder was about 10 cars, or 1,000 trailing tons.

Dining cars Indiana [above] and Wisconsin [below], assigned to the 1929 Empire Builder, could seat 36. The air conditioned cars, in beautiful Tudor decor, were roller bearing equipped, and due to their size [83' 10'' over the buffers] and weight [83½ tons—18½ tons heavier than streamlined diners], rode solidly on their 6 wheel trucks.

The Great Northern Goat

Thousands of bouquets like this are assembled each year for the Empire Builder and Oriental Limited dining cars.

The Great Northern Greenhouses
By Malcolm Breese

THE Great Northern Railway maintains at Monroe, Washington, its own greenhouses from which dining cars, observation cars and ticket offices all over the system are supplied with flowers at all seasons of the year. These greenhouses were established in 1926 and since that time have supplied literally millions of flowers to brighten the trains and offices of the railway.

The greenhouses run full blast the year round supplying as high as 1,500 to 2,000 blooms daily. The flowers include carnations, narcissus, tulips, iris, gladiolus, sweet peas, asters and numerous others.

Eighteen

During Easter week 3,300 Easter lily blooms were shipped out, so that passengers on the Empire Builder, Oriental Limited and other trains and partons of the Great Northern ticket offices might have the pleasure of enjoying luxuriant Easter flowers.

In addition to supplying the trains and offices, during the summer season the Monroe greenhouses provide flowers for the four big **hotels** and many chalets in Glacier National Park. It also sends out thousands of plants for gardens and window boxes at stations along the line and supplies other thousands of lilacs, evergreens and shrubs for planting along the right-of-way.

Great Northern Goat

In 1926, the Great Northern established its own greenhouses in Monroe, Washington. They supplied flowers for the dining cars, ticket offices and for the hotels and chalets in Glacier National Park. In addition, boxes of plants, shrubs and evergreens were supplied for stations and for along the right-of-way.

The coaches were originally built by Barney & Smith in 1914, and modernized for assignment to the 1929 Empire Builder.

Great Northern Railway

THE EMPIRE BUILDER—Train 1

WESTBOUND.
All new Pullman Equipment.
Observation Club car, Chicago to Seattle-Tacoma. Sun room, observation room, lounge, buffet with soda fountain, women's dressing room and shower bath, barber shop and men's shower bath, ladies' maid and valet service, radio reception.
Special Pullman sleeping cars, Chicago to Seattle-Tacoma, 8 sections, 2 compartments, 1 drawing room, large men's and women's toilet rooms.
Special Pullman sleeping car, Chicago to Portland, 8 sections, 2 compartments, 1 drawing room, large men's and women's toilet rooms.
Special Pullman sleeping car, Spokane to Seattle.
Dining car service Chicago to Seattle.
Day coach and smoking car, Chicago to Seattle-Tacoma.

THE EMPIRE BUILDER—Train 2

EASTBOUND.
All new Pullman equipment.
Observation Club car, Seattle-Tacoma to Chicago. Sun room, observation room, lounge, buffet with soda fountain, women's dressing room and shower bath, barber shop and men's shower bath, ladies' maid and valet service, radio reception.
Special Pullman sleeping cars, Seattle-Tacoma to Chicago, 8 sections, 2 compartments, 1 drawing room, large men's and women's toilet rooms.
Special Pullman sleeping car, Portland to Chicago, 8 sections, 2 compartments, 1 drawing room, large men's and women's toilet rooms.
Special Pullman sleeping car from Spokane to Chicago, from Seattle to Spokane on No. 38, leaves Seattle 9:00 a. m., arrives Spokane 8:00 p. m., 8 sections, 2 compartments, 1 drawing room, large men's and women's toilet rooms. Open for occupancy at Spokane at 9:30 p. m.
Dining car service Seattle to Chicago.
Day coach and smoking car, Seattle-Tacoma to Chicago.

THE ORIENTAL LIMITED—Train 3

WESTBOUND.
Observation car, Chicago to Seattle-Tacoma. Drawing room, 2 compartments, observation room, women's lounge, bath, men's smoking room, buffet, ladies' maid, valet service, library.
Special Pullman sleeping car, Chicago to Seattle-Tacoma, 12 sections, 1 drawing room.
Special Pullman sleeping car, Chicago to Portland, 12 sections, 1 drawing room.
Pullman tourist sleeping car, Chicago to Seattle.
Pullman tourist sleeping car, Spokane to Portland via S. P. & S.
Pullman sleeping car, St. Paul-Minneapolis to Helena, 12 sections, 1 drawing room.
Pullman sleeping car, Minneapolis to Fargo on No. 3, returns on No. 30.
Pullman sleeping car, Minneapolis to Yankton, open for occupancy 9.30 p. m.
Pullman sleeping cars, Spokane to Seattle, 12 sections, 1 drawing room.
Pullman sleeping car, Wenatchee to Seattle on No. 3, returns on No. 28, the fast mail, leaves Seattle 9.50 p. m., arrives Wenatchee 3.40 a. m. Car may be occupied until 7.30 a. m.
Dining car service Chicago to Seattle.
Day coach and smoking car Chicago to Seattle-Tacoma.

THE ORIENTAL LIMITED—Train 4

EASTBOUND.
Observation car, Seattle-Tacoma to Chicago. Drawing room, 2 compartments, observation room, women's lounge, bath, men's smoking room, buffet, ladies' maid, valet service, library.
Special Pullman sleeping car, Seattle-Tacoma to Chicago, 12 sections, 1 drawing room.
Special Pullman sleeping car, Portland to Chicago, 12 sections, 1 drawing room.
Pullman tourist sleeping car, Seattle to Chicago.
Pullman tourist sleeping car, Portland to Spokane via S. P. & S.
Pullman sleeping car, Helena to St. Paul, 12 sections, 1 drawing room.
Pullman sleeping cars, Seattle to Spokane, 12 sections, 1 drawing room.
Pullman sleeping car, Seattle to Wenatchee on No. 28.
Dining car service Spokane to Chicago.
Day coach and smoking car Seattle-Tacoma to Chicago.

Time from 12.01 midnight to 12.00 noon shown in light face type; time from 12.01 noon to 12.00 midnight shown in heavy face type.

During April and May of 1930, the Great Northern sponsored a series of radio programs, timed as publicity for the summer vacation and tourist season. The programs, broadcast to twenty four cities, were arranged, written and produced by the Great Northern, and released from the New York studios of NBC. Some of the subjects featured were: Mt. Rainier and the City of Tacoma, Glacier National Park as seen from the Empire Builder, Minneapolis the Mill City, Mt. Baker and Bellingham, and a program about forest fires and their prevention.

The Great Northern Goat

"Empire Builders" National Radio Programs

THE Great Northern Railway is sponsoring a series of weekly half hour programs over the Coast-to-Coast Chain of the National Broadcasting Company. These programs are on the air every Monday evening from 10:30 to 11:00 P. M., Daylight Saving Time, 8:30 to 9:00 P. M., Central Standard Time, 7:30 to 8:00 P. M., Mountain Standard Time, and 6:30 to 7:00 P. M., Pacific Standard Time.

The four programs listed here will conclude the 1929-1930 Empire Builder series, which the Great Northern Railway has been sponsoring over a coast-to-coast radio network for the past nine months. This series has been planned to appeal to a wide diversity of tastes and personal preferences. Essentially a dramatic series, each production nevertheless has been set against a rich musical background and embellished with vocal and instrumental ensembles, solos and novelties, so that their appeal may also extend even to those listeners whose preferences run to music.

JUNE 2. One of the almost legendary romances of the Canadian Royal Mounted Police will be the basis for the first June program. British Columbia will be the locale.

JUNE 9. A romance built around the initial journey of the Empire Builder a year ago will be the theme of this Monday's program. The Old Timer, who was a passenger on this inaugural journey, tells the story of this trip.

JUNE 16. The Honorable R. L. Wilbur, Secretary of the Interior, will be heard in the third June program, which will announce the opening of Glacier National Park for its 21st season.

JUNE 23. The final program of the 1929-30 series will be a fast moving railway drama in which trains, the dispatcher's office and the other units necessary to train operation will be featured.

With the closing number of this series, the second that the Great Northern has sponsored over a coast-to-coast radio chain, the Great Northern Railway would appreciate a brief statement from those who have heard these programs, telling their reactions to the present series and any suggestions for their improvement.

The following stations will broadcast the Empire Builders Series:

WJZ, New York; WBZA, Boston; WBZ, Springfield; WHAM, Rochester; KDKA, Pittsburgh; WJR, Detroit; WLW, Cincinnati; KYW, Chicago; KWK, St. Louis; WREN, Kansas City; KSTP, St. Paul-Minneapolis; WTMJ, Milwaukee; WEBC, Duluth-Superior; WKY, Oklahoma City; WBAP, Dallas-Fort Worth; KPRC, Houston; WOAI, San Antonio; KOA, Denver; KSL, Salt Lake City; KGO, San Francisco; KFI, Los Angeles; KGW, Portland, Ore.; KOMO, Seattle; and KHQ, Spokane.

Broadcasting Company; the continuity editor is
Edward Hale Bierstadt.

Stations

The Empire Builder series will be on the air
every Monday night as follows:

10:30 to 11:00 p. m. - Eastern Standard Time
9:30 to 10:00 p. m. - Central Standard Time
8:30 to 9:00 p. m. - Mountain Standard Time
7:30 to 8:00 p. m. - Pacific Standard Time

They will be broadcast over a network of the
National Broadcasting Company, which includes
the following stations:

City	Station	Meters
Boston, Mass.	WBZA	302.8
Chicago, Ill.	KYW	293.9
Cincinnati, Ohio	WLW	428.3
Dallas-Fort Worth, Texas	WBAP	288.3
Denver, Colo.	KOA	361.2
Detroit, Mich.	WJR	399.8
Duluth-Superior	WEBC	234.2
Houston, Texas	KPRC	325.9
Kansas City (Lawrence)	WREN	245.8
Los Angeles, Calif.	KFI	468.5
Milwaukee, Wis.	WTMJ	483.6
New York, N. Y.	WJZ	394.5
Oklahoma City, Okla.	WKY	333.1
Pittsburgh, Pa.	KDKA	305.9
Portland, Ore.	KGW	483.6
Rochester, N. Y.	WHAM	260.7
St. Louis, Mo.	KWK	222.1
St. Paul, Minneapolis, Minn.	KSTP	205.4
Salt Lake City, Utah	KSL	265.3
San Antonio, Texas	WOAI	252.0
San Francisco (Oakland)	KGO	379.5
Seattle, Wash.	KOMO	325.9
Spokane, Wash.	KHQ	508.2
Springfield, Mass.	WBZ	302.8

The New
EMPIRE BUILDER
The Luxurious
ORIENTAL LIMITED

The Empire Builders

A Nationally Broadcast
Series of Radio
Programs

Sponsored by the
Great Northern Ry.

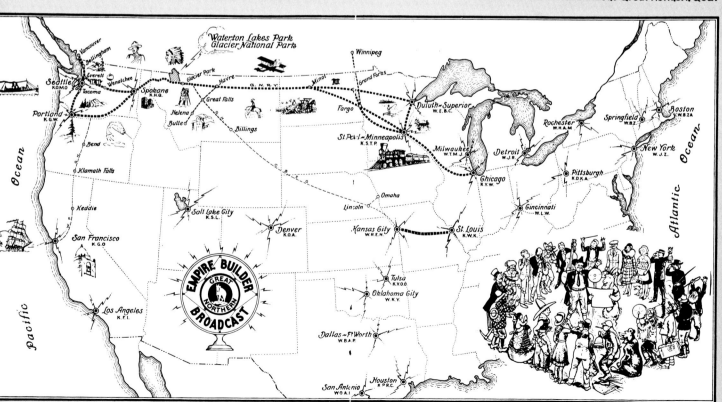

Close by the bank of the Mississippi River, the Great Northern Station in Minneapolis was completed in 1914, at a cost of $2,000,000. It is built about 2 stories above the level of the through tracks, and the track platforms are connected with the waiting room above by stairways and elevators.

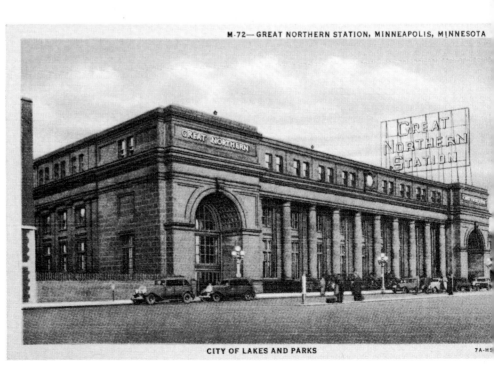

M-72— GREAT NORTHERN STATION, MINNEAPOLIS, MINNESOTA

CITY OF LAKES AND PARKS

7A-H9

Views of the Concourse and the interior front
entrance of the GN station in Minneapolis,
after the 1966 renovation.

Walt Grecula

Great Northern Railway

Charles R. Wood collection

The Builder waits for some head end work to be completed at Williston, North Dakota. On the station house track, a baggage and a refrigerator car are spotted for loading and a pick-up, possibly by No. 27 the Fast Mail.

The interior of heavyweight Pullmans changed very little in nearly thirty years. True, wood paneling and overlays became less fashionable, while lighter subdued grays, greens and tans came into fashion, and small partitions between sections, as in this car built for the 1929 Empire Builder, gave a little more privacy, but essentially the Pullmans were built to last for decades, and they differed only in detail.

Pullman Standard coach 938 was one of twelve similar coaches, all assigned to long distance service on the Empire Builder in 1937. They were good equipment for the late 1930's, and from the passengers' viewpoint, highly desirable. While neither lightweight nor streamlined, they were comfortable with reclining seats, a far step forward from the walk-over seats of earlier equipment. They seated 58, and in addition to the leg rests, individual lighting was provided and the windows were all hermetically sealed. A somber olive green on the outside, they were quite colorful inside. Heavy and stable, the ride on six wheeled trucks was superb.

It is 8:30 AM, May 17, 1940, and the 73″ drivers of Mountain type No. 2515, on the head end of the Empire Builder, have just started to turn, as the Builder pulls out of St. Paul to begin its 1,765 mile run to Seattle. With silvered smokebox and cylinder heads, the gleaming 4-8-2 shows little evidence of nearly two decades of service on the fast carded runs, and many regard the big class P-2's as the handsomest of all GN power.

W. R. McGee

Engine No. 2581 class S-2 gets out of Fargo with the Builder in November, 1938. The big high wheeled S-2's have been referred to as the "seven league boots of the Empire Builder", and indeed, the 80" drivers were only four inches short of seven feet in diameter. At speed, the big S-2's had more than adequate horsepower for the usual 1,000 ton Builder, but the big drivers did cause starting problems with a heavy train. Also, working up the long grade from Havre to Glacier [almost all of it 1%] every slight increase in gradient was noticeable in the cab as the engine slowed.

W. R. McGee

The Builder has crossed the bare high rolling plains of Western Montana, and now stops for water and oil at Shelby. From this point on, there is a steady ascending 1% grade and, with ten heavy weight cars tied to the tank of the big Northern, the engine crew of the Builder will need all the locomotive handling skill at their command to prevent the big 80" drivers from slipping.

GN stations ran the gamut from expensive ornate structures to simple bridge and building gang stations. At Shelby, Montana, a division point and communications hub, the simple wooden structure provided all of the functions of the most ornate stations for passenger service and local freight.

Walt Grecula

GN depot at
Great Falls, Montana

Walt Grecula

...an Townsend collection

The Havre—Great Falls local, with a Pullman from St. Paul [cut out of the westbound Empire
Builder] is ready to roll behind a venerable Pacific type No. 1423. Built by Baldwin in
1907, No. 1423 was one of the H-3s class converted to an oil burner and also fitted
with an outside bearing trailing truck. With a tractive effort of 42,860 lbs, the 69″ drivered
engine was well suited for its Havre—Great Falls assignment and easily capable of handling
the five to six cars normally assigned to this run.

Odyssey of the Empire Builder

W. R. McGee

On the second night out of Chicago, the Empire
Builder, behind an 80″ drivered Northern, raced
across North Dakota and into Eastern Montana,
chasing the green block signals that beckoned the
train on across the almost endless prairie. The sound
of the rapid sharp exhaust from the engine was
faintly audible back in the hushed Pullmans, and
the scream of the whistle drifted back shrilling its
warning and greeting as small towns, grain
elevators, standing boxcars and dimly lighted
stations flicked past the shaded windows. Nameless
deserted street corners, lighted by a high solitary
bulb, appeared and disappeared without a sign of life.
The low piercing beam of the headlight illuminated
both the track ahead and the wayside telegraph
poles, their banks of wires rising and falling like
ocean swells. Flickering flashing light, from the
firebox of the engine, dimly lighted wayside ditches
and clumps of strawlike grass, while the big
Pullmans gently swayed and dipped in response to
the pull of the locomotive and the tug of the broad
curves. The roadbed sang with a low solid rumble,
the wheels clicking like castanets across the rail
joints, and the rails adding their own high pitched
metallic notes. Occasionally a bridge over a stream
or a depression passed beneath the wheels of the
hurrying Empire Builder, adding the hollow rumble
of the deck and the thrumming steel of the
superstructure to the song. On through the night,
the prairie miles flowed by, bringing the high
country of the Rockies closer and leaving the big
cities of the Midwest further behind.

April, 1940 W. R. McGee

W. R. McGee

Near Spotted Robe, the westbound Empire Builder, behind S-2 class Northern 2588, passes through the Blackfoot Indian Reservation as it beats its way up the 1% approaching the Glacier National Park boundary. This country in summer is subjected to wind and heat that scorches the grasses on the east slope of the Rockies, while during the winter, which starts early at this 4,900' elevation, the thermometer plummets towards the bottom of the scale, and subzero winds whistle out of the north sweeping the fills and high areas bare and plugging the cuts with drifted snow.

W. R. McGee

In April, 1940, a white-faced Mountain type leads the eastbound Builder along the Pack River at Samuels, Idaho, in the scarcely 50 mile wide "Idaho Panhandle". Behind the Builder, looms the Cabinet Range of the Rocky Mountains.

Left: April 1941 and No. 2510 on the point of the eastbound Empire Builder has just climbed the 1% grade out of the Spokane River Valley. The 11 car Builder is heavy, and the big P-2 is working hard as it tops the grade and comes into Hillyard.

Lee Pickett

It is low tide along the shore of Puget Sound, as a fifteen car Empire Builder rounds the curve behind one of the handsome Mountains of the P-2 class. While the schedule was not overly fast, the heavy Builder overtaxed the capabilities of earlier Pacific types, even on this water grade route. The numerous stops required quick acceleration with a heavy train, and the fast light footed Pacifics lacked both the steam capacity and tractive effort to handle No.'s 1 and 2. The Mountains and Northerns were the only steam engines that could keep the Builder on time.

Above right: No. 2501 leads the 2nd section of the wartime Builder down out of the Cascades. A tie-up on the GN main has detoured trains over the NP. The odd shaped lens hood over the headlight and classification lamps on the engine were used early in World War II to cut down on extraneous light.

The eastbound Empire Builder, train No. 2, rolls along the Kootenai River near Libby, Montana in the spring of 1940. One of the most beautiful stretches of mountain scenery anywhere in the Northwest, it is unfortunately also one of the real trouble spots along the GN main. During the spring thaws, "frost boils" develop under the roadbed, the roadbed softens, and the track settles under the weight of a train. While usually not sufficient to derail equipment, the soft areas cause an undulating ride that is particularly noticeable in the cab, and slow orders are posted until section crews can refill and tamp down these areas. The melting snow, sliding off the mountains, carries with it rocks, trees and other debris, and the swift Kootenai often overflows its banks, washing out the main line.

W. R. Mc

The 1947 Streamlined Empire Builder

The 1947 Empire Builder follows behind E units between Minneapolis and St. Paul. Built by EMD, the E-7's, while lacking lugging power with a heavy train in mountainous country, were magnificent passenger power across the level districts of the GN—fully capable of 117 mph top speeds. The 1947 Builder scooped both the Northern Pacific and Milwaukee Road in transcontinental service, by many months, and both of these competitors scrambled frantically to match the equipment of the new Builder.

Four coaches were in the consist of each Empire Builder—one seating 60 for short distance passengers, and three 48 seat coaches for overnight and transcontinental passengers. The 48 seat "Day Nite" coaches featured deeply cushioned reclining seats with fold-out leg rests in the seat ahead.

Sleeping cars of the Empire Builder were the first to feature the duplex roomette, which accounted for the unusual staggered window arrangement on the exterior. Pullman-Standard had built one prototype just prior to World War II, and had tested the design thoroughly during the war, in exceptionally heavy service.

Great Northern Railway   5 photos

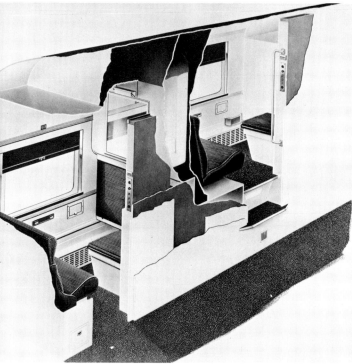

The dining car on the 1947 Empire Builder was painted in blues to match the Walter Loos Glacier Park wild flower reproductions on the panels between the tables. Copper trim in the diner gave an authentic touch of Montana, the largest copper producing state in the United States. A lighted portrait of James J. Hill faced into the car.

The coffee shop car of the Empire Builder contained seating for ten in the lounge, ten at the counter and a dormitory section for a twenty man crew further forward. Glass panels between the lounge and counter featured etchings of plants in Glacier Park—Bear Grass in this car.

Far left: A bulkhead in the observation car is decorated with a Charles M. Russell painting. Perhaps the most famous of all western artists, Russell was a genuine working cowboy. When his paintings began bringing as much as $30,000 each in eastern galleries, the state of Montana wisely started to collect them. Today, large collections are housed in the Montana State Capitol at Helena, at Great Falls and in the Buffalo Bill Museum at Cody, Wyoming.

Paintings of Blackfeet Indians [whose reservation forms the east boundary of the Glacier National Park] decorate panels between the windows of the observation car of the 1947 Empire Builder. The drapes were duplicates of Hudson's Bay blanket patterns, and a series of water color paintings by Charles M. Russell, world famous as the "Cowboy artist", graced the bulkheads.

February 7, 1947 and the brand new Empire Builder is christened in St. Paul by officers of the Great Northern Railway and dignitaries of the 1947 Winter Carnival.

February 23, 1947 and the eastbound Empire Builder is ready for its initial trip to Chicago. Mayor Devin of Seattle and Mr. Gavin, president of the Great Northern Railway break bottles of Puget Sound and Mississippi River water over the pilot, to symbolize the western and eastern terminus of the new Empire Builder.

The Empire Builder, on NP tracks July 10, 1948, is being detoured around
the Salmon Bay drawbridge in Seattle while the
broken GN span is being repaired

On a cold spring day in 1947, the Oriental Limited stops at Minot.

With pantograph raised, motor 5013, repainted in olive green and Omaha
orange to match the colors of the new Empire Builder
awaits an assignment at Appleyard

Diesel No. 354, brand new in 1947, appears on the head-end of the Oriental Limited in Minot. At this time, steam power, good efficient power was still plentiful on all divisions of the GN. Nonetheless, the diesels had shown themselves to be so much more efficient there was no question that the GN was dieselizing as rapidly as possible.

Far south of its usual route, the Builder heels to a curve along the Missouri River south of Great Falls, heading for NP tracks to take it into Spokane. It must have made quite a sight—a flash of Omaha orange and olive green—in an area usually served by the sombre colored, heavyweight equipment of the GN. This is May, 1948, and even the North Coast Limited, still in the process of being equipped with lightweight cars, was painted in dark green and olive.

Drifting down out of the Cascades, near Reiter [since eliminated by a line relocation], the 1947 edition of the Builder is on the last lap into Everett and Seattle. Typical are the morning mist and clouds that hang among the high peaks and drift down into the valleys. The climate of western Washington is mild and wet much of the year providing water power and accounting for the green look west of the Cascades.

Detoured in the spring of 1948 by a washout on the GN main line near Libby, the
Empire Builder emerges from Wolf Creek Canyon at Sieben, where it meets Extra
408 East. The Builder's lead unit grooves the siding switch, and 408's units hold the
main, idling just clear of the fouling point. The Builder slowly slips by, and then
stops at the far end of the siding, blocked until nearly 40 cars
of 408's 80 car train have cleared the switch.

The Mountain series Observation-Lounge cars, built in 1951 by American Car &
Foundry for the Mid Century edition of the Empire Builder, would have to rate very
high on any list of the most beautiful passenger equipment ever built. The striking
exterior color scheme of olive green and Omaha orange was striped in dulux gold,
and a pale gray stripe separated the black underbody from the side colors. The
taller windows in the observation end of the cars, were designed for better viewing
of the scenery. The names of these handsome, elegant cars—Appekunny Mountain,
St. Nicholas Mountain, Going-To-The-Sun Mountain, Cathedral Mountain and
Trempealeau Mountain—were selected from territory served by the Great Northern.
The interior decor was much more subdued than that of the 1947 observation cars,
with solid drapes, hidden valance lighting, and carved glass partitions that featured
the official flowers of the states and Canadian provinces served by the railway.

Great Northern Railway

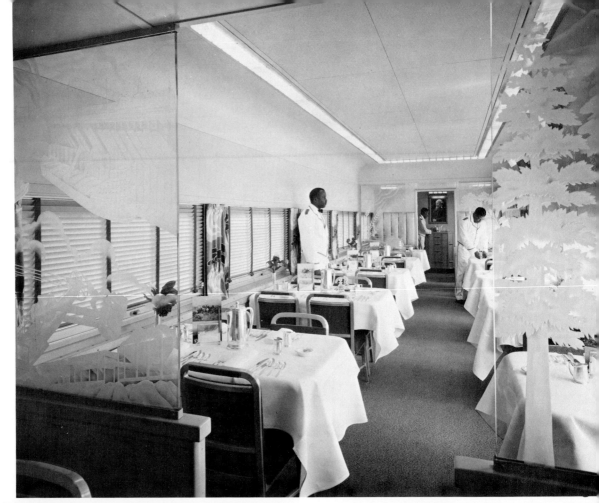

Great Northern Railway 5 photos

The dining car of the 1951 Empire Builder, although only four years newer than the diners constructed for the 1947 Builder, was far more elegant. One feature retained in both cars was the lighted portrait of James J. Hill at the entrance to the pantry section.

Of all the new equipment built by American Car & Foundry for the 1951 Builder, "The Ranch" [Coffee Shop-Lounge] car for coach passengers, was particularly outstanding. The ACF built diners were elegant in their simplicity, but "The Ranch" had as much effort expended on it as any car in the train. The wood panels, cedar beams, pinto leather seats, and authentic branding irons, all contributed to its western decor. An Eggenhoffer mural was behind the counter, and the "G Bar N" brand was registered in Helena, Montana.

Great Northern Railway
2 photos

The high peaks of the main range of the Rocky Mountains, reaching nearly two miles into the sky, form the back drop as riders from a nearby dude ranch watch a long and heavy Empire Builder nearing the summit of the Continental Divide. In the foreground, westerly flowing Bear Creek quietly meanders towards other waters that will eventually reach the Pacific.

The dome coaches of the 1955 Empire Builder achieved a level of popularity unmatched by any coach equipment ever put in service on the Great Northern. For perhaps the first time in railroad history, the coach was more popular than the Pullman.

Four diesel units lead a 14 car Builder away from Marias Pass after climbing the 1.8% eastbound grade. Now on the long 1% downgrade that leads to Havre, there is easy running. With long sweeping curves, and few grade crossings, the diesels of the Builder can start to unwind, and approach their speed limit of 79 mph.

Great Northern Railway

Three F units are on the point of the Builder as it drifts easily downgrade
along the southern boundary of Glacier National Park. Westbound, the Builder
needs only 3 F units climbing the 1% ruling grade to the summit of Marias
Pass, but eastbound, with miles·of l.8% to climb, another F unit is needed to
keep the Builder to schedule.

The Budd built dome coaches on the Empire Builder of 1955 proved to be so popular, that the Pullman passengers felt that they had not been benefitted by the addition of the new equipment. To correct this situation, in 1956, Great Northern added full length double-deck "Great Dome" cars. These beautiful cars seated 75 passengers, and in addition to their full length domes, had a lounge on their lower level where refreshments were served. The lower level lounge, decorated in the colorful art forms of the Pacific North Coast Indians, served as one of the most unusual "clubs" in America, but unfortunately, never achieved the popularity of the smaller more functional coach domes.

Conductor Claude Witt comes into Snohomish on the Appleyard Local in 1955. A steel ice-breaker has been added above the cupola of the caboose. The GN had added the ice-breakers to several cabooses to protect the dome cars from the icicles that form during the winter months in the tunnels between Seattle and Wenatchee. Crews were unimpressed with the innovation—fearing that any icicles broken loose would plunge into the caboose, and as the ice-breakers also caused the caboose to roll heavily, they were subsequently removed.

Great Northern Railway

Robert E.
Oestreich

Spokane Portland & Seattle Railway train No. 2—the eastbound Empire Builder connection—passes Stevenson, Washington, along the Columbia River. Leaving Portland at 3 PM, train No. 2 will cover the 380 miles to Spokane in seven hours, considerably faster than the Builder schedule out of Seattle, which takes 40 minutes longer to cover the 329 miles from Seattle to Spokane.

Left: The Empire Builder works its way up the long 1% eastbound grade along the Skykomish River. Ahead, the Cascades seem to present an impenetrable barrier to further progress.

The westbound Builder drifts downgrade past a pair of upper quadrant ABS signals on the dual main along the southern boundary of Glacier National Park. On the point of No. 31 are a pair of 3600 hp SDP-45's, purchased in late 1967. In the early fall, among these high peaks along the Continental Divide, the light fades rapidly into dusk and a trace of snow dusts the high ridge.

Burlington Northern

A sampling of GN passenger train memorabilia through the years

from the collections of Walt Grecula and Charles R. Wood.

Menu — 1939 Empire Builder

ROUTE OF THE EMPIRE BUILDER

RIDING BLACK HORSE—BLACKFEET BRAVE

Luggage Sticker — 1940's

GREAT NORTHERN RAILWAY

2772 — Great Northern Passenger

Postcard 1910

NATIONAL APPLE WEEK
OCTOBER 31st TO NOVEMBER 6th

CASE ORDER BY NUMBER AND WRITE YOUR SELECTION ON CHECK

*NUMBER ONE

Dinner

Choice of

TTON RADISHES   CELERY   YOUNG ONIONS

APPLE JUICE FRAPPE

SHRIMP COCKTAIL

BISQUE OF OYSTERS   SHRIMP COCKTAIL   CONSOMME

FRESH SEASONABLE FISH OR OYSTERS, BROILED OR FRIED

FRIED MILK FED CHICKEN ON TOAST, EGG NOODLES

GRILLED PORK CHOPS, APPLE FRITTERS

CHARCOAL BROILED SIRLOIN STEAK, G. N. SAUCE

ROAST LEG SPRING LAMB, MINT JELLY

CALLOPED POTATOES   STRINGLESS BEANS
OR
KED RUSSET POTATO   APPLE-BANANA SALAD   BAKED SQUASH

HOT TEA BISCUITS   ASSORTED COLD BREAD

WENATCHEE APPLE DUMPLING   ICE CREAM
LAYER CAKE

IMPORTED ROQUEFORT CHEESE
TOASTED WAFERS

FFEE   TEA   MILK   POSTUM

NUMBER TWO—PLATE DINNER

Choice of

QUE OF OYSTERS   APPLE JUICE   CONSOMME

FRESH FISH OR OYSTERS, BROILED OR FRIED

PORK CHOPS SAUTE, HOT APPLE SAUCE

BAKED INDIVIDUAL CHICKEN PIE, A LA G. N.

ROAST SPRING LAMB, AU JU'S

ALLOPED POTATOES   STRING BEANS OR SQUASH

APPLE-BANANA SALAD

HOT TEA BISCUITS   ASSORTED BREAD

FRESH BAKED PIE   ICE CREAM AND CAKE

FFEE   TEA   MILK   POSTUM

EASE WRITE ON MEAL CHECK "PLATE DINNER NO. 2," THEN YOUR
ICE OF SOUP, FISH OR MEAT, DESSERT AND BEVERAGE.

NUMBER THREE—PLATE DINNER

OICE OF ITEMS LISTED ON NO. 2 PLATE DINNER, OMITTING APPLE JUICE.
UP, CONSOMME, DESSERT.

EASE WRITE ON MEAL CHECK "DINNER NO. 3," THEN YOUR CHOICE OF
P, ENTREE OR MEAT AND BEVERAGE.

ECOND PORTION OF ANY ITEM, SERVED ON REQUEST, NO ADDITIONAL CHARGE

FOR THE LITTLE FOLKS

May we suggest Sieved Fresh Seasonable Vegetables cooked to order—
ume Juice, Tomato Juice, Orange Juice, Cup Custard, Jello, each fifteen cents.
A. W. DELEEN, General Superintendent, Dining Cars
St. Paul, Minn.

EAT WENATCHEE APPLES

A la Carte

FRUIT AND VEGETABLE JUICES 15 CENTS
APPLE, TOMATO, GRAPE, PRUNE, PINEAPPLE, ORANGE

RELISHES

RED RADISHES 15   SLICED TOMATOES 20

RIPE OR GREEN OLIVES 25   CELERY 20   YOUNG ONIONS 15   CUCUMBERS 20

THICK SOUP OR CONSOMME, CUP 15   TUREEN OF THICK SOUP 20
CRACKERS AND BUTTER WITH SOUP SERVICE

Fish—Seasonable 50

OYSTER STEW 50   FRIED OYSTERS 60

CREAMED SALMON ON TOAST EN CASSEROLE 50

GRILLED TO ORDER
SARDINES ON TOAST 50

SIRLOIN STEAK $1.00   TENDERLOIN STEAK $1.00   LAMB CHOP 50

HALF FRIED SPRING CHICKEN 65   HAM OR BACON AND EGGS 50
BREAD AND BUTTER WITH ABOVE SELECTIONS

POTATOES TO ORDER 10   SEASONABLE FRESH VEGETABLES 15

THE SALAD BOWL—TWENTY-FIVE CENTS PER PERSON
LETTUCE—TOMATOES—CUCUMBERS—RADISHES—GREEN PEPPERS
GREEN ONIONS, IF DESIRED

SPECIALS
Fresh Seasonable Fish, Cole Slaw, Hot Bread, Beverage 50
Baked Beans en Casserole, Hot Bread, Beverage 50
Baked Individual Chicken Pie, Hot Bread, Beverage 50
Country Sausage, Fried Apples 50

SALADS WITH DRESSING	SANDWICHES
Head Lettuce 25	Baked Ham or Cheese on Toast 25
Apple-Celery 35	Club House or Steak on Toast 50
Tropical Fruit 50	Chicken on Toast 35
Chicken en Mayonnaise 50	Salmon on Rye 25
Apple-Banana 35	Ham and Egg on Toast 35

CRACKERS AND BUTTER SERVED WITH ALL SALADS

CREAM CHEESE—CURRANT OR CRAB APPLE JELLY, TOASTED CRACKERS 35

PIES—VARIOUS—WITH CHEESE 20—A LA MODE 25   CHEESE AND TOASTED CRACKERS 20
ROQUEFORT, SWISS, CREAM, OR ENGLISH

BAKED WENATCHEE APPLE, CREAM 25

HOME MADE CAKE 15   SHERRY OR BRANDY DATE SUNDAE 45   ICE CREAM 15

WENATCHEE EATING APPLE 10   CHOCOLATE SUNDAE WITH CAKE 25

ICE CREAM WITH CAKE 25   PRESERVED FIGS 25   FRESH PLUMS IN SYRUP 25

BREAD AND BUTTER 10   PLAIN OR BUTTERED TOAST 10   RY-KRISP 10
NON-FATTENING

DRIP-O-LATOR SANKA COFFEE, POT 15

COFFEE, CHOCOLATE OR POSTUM, POT 15

BLACK OR GREEN TEA, POT 15

SWEET MILK OR BUTTERMILK 10   MALTED MILK 20

Hot Breads and Pies Baked on this Car daily

A service charge of twenty-five cents is made for each adult person
served outside of dining car.

m, Washington.

Advertising Card—1910

Timetable — 1922

The new interesting way to or from

California

is via the New

Oriental Limited

Ride in restful comfort on this luxuriously appointed *no-extra-fare* train. Delicious meals and perfect dining service. Attractive, one-way or all-year tourist round-trip fares. Choice of steamer or rail along the Pacific Coast to or from California.

J. H. Kenney, New England Passenger Agent
T. F. Carroll, City Passenger Agent
Shop 3, Little Bldg., 80 Boylston St.
Phone Liberty 1639, Boston, Mass.

 Great Northern

A Dependable Railway

PRINTED IN U. S. A.

Blotter — Oriental Limited 1920's

Through the **U·S·A·**

Via Seattle Gateway

The Very Best Way

Great Northern Railway

Route of the New Oriental Limited

Timetable — 1920's

1914 Pass

SAINT PAUL UNION STATION

Postcard 1920's

Great Northern Depot, Fargo, N. D.

Postcard 1925

SPEED SERVICE
GREAT
NORTHERN
A DEPENDABLE RAILWAY

Envelope Seal — 1926

Behind a P-2 class Mountain in the summer of 1940,
No. 27 out on the high plains of Montana reels off
the miles towards Shelby.

6. STEAM: FROM PRAIRIE TO TIDEWATER

Until the road pushed west beyond Minot in 1887, and then into the Rocky and Cascade Mountains in the early 1890's, GN motive power was not unlike the motive power of most railroads. The roster was dominated by the American Standard 4-4-0 type, which was similar to the William Crooks of 1862, and which in turn was basically a refinement of the little 4-4-0's of the 1840's and 1850's. The simple 4-4-0 was well within the servicing capabilities of the small, primitive railroad shops. Its operation and fundamentals were understood by enginemen as well as by mechanics; and in the event of a locomotive failure, it was often limped-in or "hay-wired" together to get it back to the engine shops. It could burn any type of fuel from cord wood to coal and could be watered from the nearest stream, by the bucketful if necessary. A typical consist behind an American Standard could be three to four light passenger cars or a dozen or so diminutive freight cars. The 4-4-0 was the prime mover of both freight and passengers from the Atlantic seaboard to the Mississippi; and it built the Central Pacific/Union Pacific from Omaha to Sacramento.

When pulling a light load in flat country and good weather, the 4-4-0 had adequate power. On grades it was necessary to double-head the little engines because the 15,000 lbs. or so of tractive effort could not take the load over a long grade single handed. When the GN pushed into the Rockies and then into the Cascades, the little 4-4-0 was completely outclassed by the demands being put upon it. Even double and triple-heading was only a temporary solution, as crew costs soared and engine failures became common.

Then too, the western expansion of the United States was getting into high gear, and the demand for transportation soared. By 1889, the GN (the Minneapolis, St. Paul & Manitoba) had increased the length of its main line by almost tenfold, from 283 miles to 2,770 miles, since James J. Hill became General Manager of its predecessor, the St. Paul & Pacific, in 1878. The road ran into Great Falls after turning south at Pacific Junction; and immigrants and freight continued to pour into the newly opened Dakota and Montana Territories. Yards became choked with freight that couldn't be moved out fast enough. The only solution to the growing problem was bigger and faster power that could move tonnage in increments of thousands — not hundreds — of tons.

The motive power roster was strengthened in 1887 by the new Mogul 2-6-0 type for freight service. The Mogul carried more weight on the low 55" drivers, which increased the tractive effort, and less weight on the two-wheel lead truck, which made it less stable at speed. Although somewhat slower over the road than the 4-4-0, it was a definite improvement over the American for heavier freight service. Built in five different sub-classes, the tractive effort ranged from 18,000 lbs. on the earliest models, (built by Rogers Locomotive Works), to nearly 25,000 lbs. on the later models (built by Brooks Works). By the time the last one was delivered in 1896, Moguls were being pushed to the limits of their power in the Cascades and the need for still more power was becoming critical — the road had more business than it could handle. Eventually the Moguls were put to work on the branch lines, and by 1940 only nine of the class D-5 were left, Nos. 453-461, in Spokane. By 1942, unsuitable for any further service, they too were dropped from the roster.

Brooks Works responded to the GN plea for more power with the Mastodon, a 4-8-0 that doubled the capacity of the 4-4-0. The 1891 models, class G-1, developed nearly

26,000 lbs. of tractive effort. The later G-2, G-3 (Rogers Locomotive Works), and G-4 classes developed just over 32,000 lbs. The last of the series, G-5, developed nearly 42,000 lbs. of tractive effort, making it briefly the most powerful locomotive in the world — that is if the fireman could keep up with its voracious demands for coal and water. The GN invested heavily in the G class, but its success was short lived. The slowness and complexity of the big G-5's doomed them to early replacement, although some remained in the Cascades for years as pushers. The lighter and simpler G-3 and G-4 soon found their way onto branch lines, where their light axle-loading and moderate speed were better suited to the service demands. In 1942, forty of them still were scattered about various divisions where there was a demand for a light footed yet comparatively powerful locomotive that was simple to repair and maintain. Worked lightly and at a slow pace, they were good engines; although in retrospect, perhaps their numbers, rather than their virtues, made them last as long as they did.

In the East, the Consolidation type was developing into a first rate engine, more powerful than the G-3 and G-4, simpler to maintain and fire than the G-5, and infinitely less complex. The road ordered large numbers of Consolidations, starting in 1892 with the F-1, which was designed by John Player and built by the Brooks Locomotive Works. It was at this time that the Belpaire firebox became a feature of GN locomotives. The Belpaire firebox had a flat crown sheet joined by short radius curves to flat side and roof sheets. The flat parallel plates eliminated the need to use crown bars to support and strengthen the crown sheet. With few exceptions (notably the P-2 and S-2 classes), the GN committed itself to the Belpaire firebox in the 1890's, and stayed with the unique design until the last GN steam locomotives (the famous 0-8

class) were built in the early 1930's. Only one other major railroad — the Pennsylvania — adopted the Belpaire as "standard", although in 1899 the Union Pacific did purchase one class of Brooks Works 4-8-0's that featured the Belpaire firebox. These engines, for all practical purposes, identical to the G class Mastodon widely used on the notorious 4% grades of the switchbacks in Stevens Pass, remained on the UP roster for nearly twenty-five years.

All sub-classes of the Consolidations were fitted with 55" drivers, with the exception of the Alco-built F-12 class (two engines), which was equipped with 52" drivers — real grass cutters. By far the most popular class of Consolidation was the F-8, with a tractive effort of 45,000 lbs. They were the main line work horses. By 1940, two thirds of the 66 F-8's still in service had been fitted with superheaters, mak-

ing them efficient power. Essentially, however, Consolidations were too small for heavy service over the 1,800 mile long main line; and yet in some cases they were too large to be good branch line power. Many of the older classes (other than the F-8's) were converted to switchers, helping to explain why nearly 16% of the 1940 steam roster was in eight-wheeled switching type. Many of these were used over rough mine trackage on the Mesabi Iron Range, where drag speed power was needed.

At about the same time the first of the Mastodons and Consolidations were delivered to the GN, the first of the popular 4-6-0 class E Ten Wheelers made their appearance. There were only two locomotives of the E-9 class built by Baldwin in 1892. These were crown bar boilered, while the twenty E-7's (Brooks built in 1893) and most succeeding sub-classes featured the Belpaire firebox. The progression of locomotive and sub-class numbers had little to do with the order in which they were manufactured. The E-7's were followed in order by E-13's, E-12's, E-10's, E-3's, E-8's and E-6's, E-14's and E-15's. The last of the E class, two locomotives built by Alco in 1915 with radial stayed boilers, were E-2's. Locomotives of the missing sub-classes did exist at one time; but they were few in number and not representative of the class. There were two E-1's built by Rogers in 1890. And in the same year, Rhode Island built four earlier E-2's — one of which became the only E-5. Two E-4's were built by Schenectady in 1889, and E-7 No. 959 was converted to the only E-11. The most locomotives in a sub-class were the forty-five E-14's, built by Baldwin in 1909/10. Essentially ten wheel versions of the Pacific class H-4's, they were rebuilt during the 1920's as Pacifics, class H-5 and class H-7. Driver size of the E's ranged from 55" to 63" to 73", with the lower wheel designed for branch or freight service and the higher wheel for passenger service. As trains became longer and heavier, the Ten Wheeler became inadequate for passenger service; and by 1942, only nineteen remained in service. By May, 1950, only No. 927 class E-6 was still on the roster.

In 1905, the Pacific type came to the GN, from Alco, as class H-1. So successful were these locomotives that large orders for the type followed from Baldwin and Lima, until by 1930 over 130 Pacifics were in service. The impressive H-4's built by Lima in 1914 were the last engines of the class to be built originally as Pacifics. The GN had found what to do with large numbers of Prairies and Ten Wheelers that were obsolete for main line service. In the 1920's they were rebuilt as Pacifics in the GN shops. Fifteen of the J class Prairies were stretched to become class H-6 Pacifics, the earlier-rebuilt E-14 Ten Wheelers became class H-5 Pacifics, and ten of the antiquated E-14 4-6-0's later entered the GN shops to emerge as class H-7 Pacifics, with Delta trailing trucks, large fireboxes, lengthened boilers, and super-heaters. In tractive effort (49,580 lbs.) they matched the power of the early New York Central Hudsons; but it is doubtful that they had the same long distance capability and sustained high speed. Some of the earlier upgraded engines went to the SP&S to fill a crying need there for more modern power; but as late as 1940, 96 Pacifics in classes H-2 through H-7 remained, comprising 12% of the roster.

The class J-1 Prairie 2-6-2, the class K-1 Atlantic 4-4-2, and the class L-1 Mallet 2-6-6-2, all Baldwin built, first arrived on the road in 1906. The GN became convinced that the Prairie was at least a partial answer to its fast freight problems and between 1906 and 1907 purchased 150 of them — on 69" drivers. It shared many parts in common with the basically similar 1906 Pacific, not an undesirable feature. The Prairie had not been developed as a fast road engine; it was noted instead for its flexibility on a short wheelbase and its ability to negotiate nearly any type of trackage. For this reason and because it had good tractive effort, digested many types of fuel and was about as stable while backing as while running forward, it was a favorite of logging railroads. The same flexibility that made it so popular with the loggers, however, scared the wits out of GN crews. As a center connected, symmetrically balanced engine, it was too flexible; at speed it developed violent nosing actions and undulations that threatened to throw the crew out of the cab. With proper guiding action from the lead truck or more stabilizing action from a bigger trailing truck, it might have been successful. While the motive power department pondered what to do with them, they were restricted to only a portion of their actual speed capability. By 1940, there wasn't one left on the GN roster.

While the Atlantic class K-1 did not suffer from the wild undulations of the class J, by the time they went into service, they were too small and underpowered for the type of trains the GN was beginning to handle. Fitted with 73″ drivers, they were not as fast as some contemporary versions of the Atlantic, but they were good steamers and stable at speed. They were fitted with a booster which raised the starting tractive effort to nearly 37,000 lbs. but the booster itself was a maintenance complication. On the head end of the name trains, they were prone to slip wildly, even at Wolf Point, Montana, on as flat a grade as could be found on the main; and once underway, they simply lacked the boiler horsepower to keep a heavy train to time. The SP&S acquired some of the class K's and even used them in light freight service, but on a water grade profile. By 1940, the only one left of the original ten was assigned to the Dakota Division.

A true Mallet compound, the L-1 class of 1906, was a modification of an 0-6-6-0 type demonstrated at the St. Louis Exposition in 1904 and used successfully on the Baltimore and Ohio. By contemporary standards a very complex piece of machinery, it had two engines that articulated under one large boiler, and was fitted with leading and trailing wheels to assist the tracking on the tortuous grades and curves of the Cascades. The wheels were small — only

55″ in diameter — but the tractive effort was something else. At almost 70,000 lbs., it was nearly twice as powerful as the 41,000 lbs. tractive effort of the F-7 Consolidations which, having supplanted the complex and unwieldly class G Mastodons, were the standard freight engines of the time. With a Consolidation leading and an L-1 pushing, they could by brute force get 1,300 tons up the 2.2% grade from Skykomish to Tye. In 1907, forty-five lighter class L-2's, fitted with the same boiler as the Baldwin Pacific of 1906, were delivered to the GN, and moved into the Rockies to assist the sorely pressed Consolidations on the 1.8% grades eastbound. Seventeen more L-1's were delivered in 1908; and the L-1's continued as both road and pusher engines in the Cascades. Push or pull, the L-1's and the lighter L-2's could serve either function, but both classes were the bane of the roundhouse forces, as their double machinery required constant service and attention. Mainly due to the small 55″ drivers, they suffered from lack of speed. They were also hampered by their voracious appetite for coal and water. In the 1920's, the GN shops converted the L-2's to 2-8-2 Mikado class 0-5's and the L-1's to Mikado class 0-6's.

Still on the search for bigger and bigger power, in 1910 the GN took delivery from Baldwin of a hybrid type of Mallet compound, a 2-6-8-0 class M-2 that looked like the shotgun marriage of a Mogul and an 0-8-0 switcher. This group of twenty-five locomotives rolled on 55″ drivers; but their tractive effort was upped to nearly 80,000 lbs. It was found necessary to work firemen in relays to keep these monsters hot, but they could pull, if slowly, and soon found their way onto the Iron Range where they established some notable records in pulling ore trains.

By 1911, the GN had the biggest roster of Mallet compounds in the country. While they were slow, complex and a maintenence headache, they had all the pull the GN could

use — when they were running that is. With a roster top heavy with Mallets, a pot pourri of Moguls, class G Twelve Wheelers, Consolidations, a vast group of Prairies intended to be fast freight locomotives and a few Pacifics that were really modern power — the GN found itself either with big power too slow for main line passenger service, or faster power too light for main line freight service. Double-heading on the more level districts was a common practice, but it was costly both in wear and tear on the equipment and for the crews.

What saved the day for the GN was the appearance of the class 0-1 Mikado. In this engine, the GN found what it really had been looking for all along. A simple machine, capable of a good turn of speed on 63" drivers, it had a wide deep firebox, (mounted over the trailing truck), that assured good steaming capacity, and it could pull. At 60,000 lbs. tractive effort, the 0-1 could nearly equal the tractive effort of the L-1 and could out pull the L-2, which only developed 55,000 lbs. of tractive effort. It also used less coal and water than the L-1 or L-2. While it could give a fireman a good work out, it wasn't a man killer. Eventually 150 of the 0-1's were purchased, followed by class after class of Mikados until by 1942, there were 264 Mikes, comprising 33% of the GN roster. They included the now venerable 0-1's, the 0-4's built by Baldwin, the nine heavy USRA types, and the 0-5's, 0-6's and 0-7's (that were rebuilds of the L-2's, the L-1's and some of the odd looking M-2's).

If any one GN engine were to be singled out as truly outstanding, it would have to be the 0-8, the most powerful Mike in the world, with a tractive effort rated at 78,000 lbs. Measuring 108' 11" over the coupler faces and a scant 3/8 of an inch less than 16' tall, the big 0-8 was a dray horse from a

power standpoint, and yet it rolled on 69" drivers that gave it a speed capability right up there with the S-1 and P-2. Built at Hillyard in 1932, the three 0-8's were so successful that the entire 0-7 class was rebuilt during and after World War II as 0-8's. The 0-8's were also the only non-articulated freight engines on the GN to be fitted with roller bearings.

One would have thought that after the first successful Mikados came along that the slow, complex Mallets would be dropped like hot potatoes. Not so. To the everlasting credit of the GN, it did not give up easily on a locomotive type merely because it had problems. The GN shops became real experts at rebuilding, modernizing, converting and working locomotive types up to their real potential. The 2-8-8-0 Mallet compound class N-1 of 1912, as first delivered, was as ugly a locomotive as could be found on any roster — even uglier than the big "Bull Moose" 2-8-8-0's of the Union Pacific. Part of this was due to the raised Belpaire firebox. Since the 2-8-8-0 did not have room between the frames for a big firebox, nor a trailing wheel truck to help support one, a huge firebox was built on top of the frame, practically on top of the last 63" drive wheel. The net result was that the N-1's (all 25 of them) emerged as the tallest locomotives yet built for the GN. The locomotive, 16' high to the top of the stack or cab, was so tall that the crew could look right back across the top of the tiny eight wheel tender for an almost unobstructed view of the whole train. The N-1 had a built-in capability for further development, however, that was lacking in the earlier L and M classes. With its big drivers and huge boiler and firebox, it developed a whopping 93,000 lbs. of tractive effort. In the mid 1920's, the GN shops simpled the engine and raised the tractive effort to 100,000 lbs. These rebuilt Mallets became class N-2. In the early 1940's, the entire class was completely rebuilt with new frames, roller bearings, and modern appliances to become class

N-3. The huge Vanderbilt tenders, applied in the 1920's, also were further modernized. What emerged were the most handsome and powerful 2-8-8-0's ever built. They could muscle tonnage at speed and show their heels to many passenger engines. They dragged ore off the Iron Range by the shipload; and during the war, they were often put on the point of 20 and 22 car "troopers."

In 1914, the GN took delivery on a passenger version of the 0-1 Mikado, fifteen class P-1 Mountain 4-8-2's. From the start, they were way too slow for passenger service on the heavy mountain grades, and they were quickly removed to spend their time in freight service on the very light grades between Whitefish and Troy, Montana. Nine years later, just after delivery of the Q-1 class 2-10-2's, the GN shops took the P-1's in hand and rebuilt the entire lot into Q-2 class 2-10-2's. They were actually somewhat lighter than the Q-1's, but to ease the burden on dispatchers who had great difficulty keeping the two classes separate, both classes were rated at the 76,000 lbs. of tractive effort of the Q-2's. The thirty class Q-1 Santa Fe's delivered by Baldwin in 1923, were good looking engines and well liked by the crews because they drew a higher rate of pay. The Q's however, were notorious rail pounders and

but by the 1940's the diesel was beginning to emerge, and the GN considered that more money spent on twenty-five year old steam engines was money thrown away.

At the same time the Q-1 class was delivered in 1923, Baldwin also delivered twenty-eight P-2 class Mountains for service on the Oriental Limited, the Fast Mail, the Glacier Park Limited, and later the Empire Builder. The P-2's were distinguished by their lack of the Belpaire firebox. Instead, they reverted to the conventional radial-stay firebox. Their general lines were very similar to the Q-1's, but the taller 73" drivers, shorter boilers, and smooth contoured firebox gave them a sleekness of line lacking in the freight engines. Originally the class was about equally divided between coal and oil burning types. The class also lacked roller bearings or boosters; but during World War II about half were equipped with roller bearings. Boosters applied to some raised the tractive effort from 55,000 lbs. to nearly 70,000 lbs. With both boosters and roller bearings, they were potent pieces of machinery that could double in freight or passenger service. The P-2's made many notable runs on the point of No. 27, the Fast Mail (billed as "the fastest long distance runs in the world"), the Empire Builder, and the famous Silk Trains. In August, 1924, No.

spent most of their working life slogging freight at 25 to 35 mph; although after World War II the Q-2's were modernized and their speed limit raised to 45 miles per hour. The GN learned the same lesson that the NP had in the late 1880's with ten coupled engines; that complex reciprocating machinery was extremely difficult to balance properly. Perhaps with taller drivers they could have been better balanced,

2517 (the Marathon) made the round trip between Seattle and St. Paul, a total run of 3,600 miles, in a running time nearly 2-1/2 hours faster than the diesel powered Western Star decades later. With only eight hours for servicing in St. Paul, average speed for the entire run was just over 45 mph, including stops for fuel, inspection, and crew changes. This run was made over the old route across Stevens

Pass — not via the new tunnel and easier eastbound grade. Between Cut Bank and Williston, and over the Breckenridge and Willmar Divisions, the silk special averaged over 50 mph — no mean running for 1924.

In regular service, however, the P-2's were limited to a maximum of 60 mph, out of consideration for passengers and machinery alike. Put into way freight service, and even switching after World War II, their record was remarkable for an engine that was never designed to double in freight service. Their only real shortcoming in very heavy, fast passenger service was that they lacked the boiler capacity of the later Northerns.

Superlatives come easily in a discussion of the relative merits of a road's motive power, but there are times when the superlatives fit the facts. A case in point is the GN R-1 and R-2 simple articulateds, the first Mallets built as simple engines for the Great Northern. Designed for heavy duty on the mountain grades, the first of the class R-1's (Nos. 2030-2033, built by Baldwin in 1925), were rated at 134,000 lbs. of tractive effort. Built in the GN shops in 1927/1928, Nos. 2034-2043 had their tractive effort increased slightly to 143,500 lbs. and their working pressure raised from 210 to 225 lbs. Also, due to tender changes, their overall length was about 7' longer than the earlier Baldwin-built R-1's. At Hillyard in 1929/1930, the GN built the real monsters of the R class, the R-2's that were rated at 153,000 lbs. of tractive effort. These immense 2-8-8-2's measured nearly 120' over the coupler faces. Between the fourteen locomotives of the R-1 class and the sixteen locomotives of the R-2 class, all of which remained in service into the 1950's, the GN had the biggest and, in terms of tractive effort, the most powerful simple articulateds in the world.

In the summer of 1929, the GN took delivery of its first Northern 4-8-4's, class S-1. The six locomotives (Montana types — the name didn't last long), built by Baldwin, featured the same 73" drivers as used on the P-2's. The big S-1's could exert nearly 69,000 lbs. tractive effort without a booster or roller bearings, about a 20% increase in power over the P-2's. Their much larger boiler could sustain the increased power demanded, while the P-2's became "short winded" under the same conditions. Not as handsome as the P-2's, the S-1's had a more squat appearance, due to the same size drivers under a much longer boiler. The cab also had a tremendous overhang beyond the 4 wheel trailing truck; and certainly the return to the Belpaire boiler was not an esthetic improvement. Their real asset was their ability to muscle fast freight. Designed for service west of Havre, up the long 1% grade to Marias Pass, their 73" drivers proved to be a handicap in passenger service elsewhere. They were hard on the rails and lacked a capacity for high speed running on the other divisions. The design was not repeated.

In late 1929, on the heels of the S-1's, came the fourteen engines of the S-2 class. Also built by Baldwin, the long, lean, racy S-2's reverted to the radial stay boiler — defined in the 1941 Kalmbach Locomotive Cyclopedia as "a boiler having a transversely arched crownsheet supported from the roof sheet by stays or staybolts set on lines that are the radii of the inner and outer sheets". Under this beautifully contoured boiler rolled 80" drivers — the tallest yet on a Northern. Tractive effort dropped to 58,000 lbs. — 10,000 lbs. less than the S-1 and slightly more than the P-2 class Mountains. Weighing only 420,000 lbs., (about 15 tons heavier than the P-2's), the S-2's were light for a Northern. Although they were limited by orders to 60 mph, the big 80" drivers could roll easily in the high 70's and even do better than 80 mph if they were pushed really hard. On the point of the Builder or No. 27 they had no peer. They had only one serious fault — they were extremely slippery in starting a heavy train, due to insufficient adhesion caused by the combination of their light weight and those big fragile-appearing 80" drivers. Engine crews soon learned, however, that with liberal sanding, setting the air, pulling out throttle, and then releasing the air, could give them enough added kick to start a heavy train. Once underway, careful throttle handling and judicious use of sanders kept matters under control. For nearly two decades they were — along with the P-2's — the pride of the motive power department. They finished their years in the 1950's as standby protection power. They also drew some freight assignments where their true capabilities were wasted. They were designed for speed, so coupling an S-2 to a freight was akin to putting "Man O' War" ahead of a lumber wagon.

The class Z Challengers were never fully accepted as Great Northern power. Six of the Z-6 4-6-6-4's, delivered to the NP by Alco in 1937, were assigned to the jointly owned SP&S. By 1940, with the rapidly growing demand for additional power, Nos. 4000-4001 had found their way to the GN, retaining their NP classification. By 1950, the GN, having acquired a number of Alco "covered wagons", had returned both of the Z's to the SP&S.

Studying the assignment roster of steam locomotives in 1940, it is interesting to see where the heaviest power was concentrated. On the Mesabi Division, which of course included the Iron Range, there were two M-2's assigned, fifteen N-2's and seven Q-2's, all of them real tonnage maulers.

The Dakota Division (Fargo to St. Cloud) drew a mere half dozen Q's, no Mallets of any kind, and the only K-1 on the roster. In this flat country, it was easy to get even a heavy train rolling with minimum power. In some cases, as one engineer remarked, "All you have to do is kick off the air, keep it pumped up for control and let 'em roll".

North from Fargo, up the Surrey cut-off to Minot on the Minot Division, big power was needed to cope with the sub-zero weather conditions often encountered so close to the Canadian border. In this area the GN stationed four R-1's, fifteen Q's, and a large roster of late model 0's, including eight 0-6's and four 0-7's. Extreme cold had a number of adverse effects on steam power: the boiler radiated much of its heat into the atmosphere; the wind

whistling across the barren prairie increased drag; steel rail became brittle and slippery; and every cut and draw plugged with loose snow that had to be pushed aside by the engine plow. Add to this the facts that the car axles in the journals grew so cold that the bare hand froze to the metal, and the journal grease was reduced to a taffy-like consistency that added drag, requiring 10% to 20% more power to get a train moving and to keep it moving. Under these conditions a big R-1 could be reduced to the pulling capacity of a heavy 0-8 class Mike. Passenger service added yet another problem — the heat needed for the cars was supplied by the train boiler, further reducing pulling power. In really severe conditions, it was necessary to double-head the Builder so that an extra, lighter engine could help keep up with the demand for heat in the cars.

The biggest concentrations of heavy power were on the Butte, Kalispell, and Cascade Divisions, where the complications of weather were compounded by altitude, mountain grades and curvature that sapped the tractive effort. Eight M-2's, six N-2's, ten Q's and fifteen 0-7's were included on the Butte Division.

On the Kalispell Division between Minot and Spokane — including the sub-divisions from Havre to Great Falls and from Shelby to Great Falls — there were assigned three N-2's, one R-1, sixteen R-2's, six S-1's and all three 0-8's as well as a number of 0-5's and 0-6's. In this Rocky Mountain country and on the formidable Plateau du Coteau du Missouri out of Minot, the combination of arctic weather, a .7% grade, and yet another 100 miles of 1% grade up to the ramparts of the Rockies themselves, could strain any engine.

Notwithstanding the electrics, the Cascade Division (old Spokane Division) was no picnic in the winter either. While eighteen class Z's and Y's had matters well under control on the electrified portion of the Division, the line from Seattle to Skykomish — with long stretches of 1% grade and 10 degree curves — called for R class engines. Between Seattle, Spokane and

Portland, nine R-1's, five Q-1's and two Q-2's were assigned. Further south on the Klamath Division there were four N-2's and two class Z-6's between Bend, Oregon and Bieber, California.

During World War II, when the electrics were being overwhelmed by the rising flood of tonnage, steam pushers were assigned from both Wenatchee and Skykomish up to the summit and through Cascade Tunnel. They went through Cascade Tunnel with the fires banked, and were of material help on the 2.2% grades, but getting them downgrade, running light, was something else again. Running light, a 500 ton engine built up momentum in a hurry To keep it under control, it was brought downgrade in reverse gear working against compression rather than by using the engine brakes. As engineer Bob Smith commented, "This was a little hard on the piston packing, but it was better than losing a driver tire due to overheated brakes". An R-1 was a big engine, but it looked even bigger down on the ties or laying on its side along the right-of-way.

The rough riding characteristics of many GN engines could be explained partly by the long cut-off valves used on most GN power. Steam was worked until the last possible moment to exert every bit of tractive effort out of the steam, and this contributed to the already heavy dynamic augment.

In the memories of many who are familiar with GN road power in the 1930's, 1940's and 1950's, its outstanding feature had to be its superb appearance. With the delivery of the P-2's, Great Northern power began to acquire the look we remember best — pump-heavy smokeboxes, the proud goat painted on the side sheets of the tender, and the beautiful glossy light-olive boilers. As it aged, this color both faded and began to pick up tones of light gray.

While much has been made of the so-called "Glacier Park color scheme", officially it never existed. The Kalispell Division, however, took great pride in the appearance of the locomotives assigned to the division, and many of the engines had the cab roof and/or window frames painted a mineral or oxide red, which was a standard GN color for work equipment and some freight equipment. The red, as initially applied, was subdued, and it became even more subdued as it aged with the effects of weathering and oil soot. The smokeboxes of the passenger power were painted a mixture of white and silver and became known as "whitefaces". The cylinder heads were either chromed or painted silver. Anyone who watched power being changed at Whitefish in the early 1940's will remember the color scheme well.

By contrast, most GN power on other divisions had the standard black roof with the smokeboxes either silvered or graphited. All GN engines had black running gear, tenders and appliances. While black was also standard for the cylinder saddles and domes, there was some variation of black with a band of green for the domes and green for the cylinder saddles. A few GN engines on display show silvered or whitened drivers and running boards; but in service this practice was so rare as to be non-existent.

It was company policy to build locomotives whenever possible in the company shops, as the Great Northern stated, ". . . for the purpose of stimulating industry in its own territory, augmenting the payrolls of the cities it serves, and affording year-around employment for as many of its shopmen as possible". In retrospect perhaps, GN steam power can be summed up as a tribute to the GN shops, for they alone built the biggest (the R-2) and the best (the 0-8 and the N-3) of their respective classes. Baldwin showed the way, but it was the GN shops themselves that built the really outstanding power, and perhaps this is why GN steam will be so long remembered.

Still, by the start of World War II the motive power and operating departments were ready for a change. The time had come when tractive power alone would not keep the railroad viable. In addition the road needed speed, standardization, and flexibility. No. 103, the FT road-diesel demonstrator of 1939, was a real eye opener.

2 photos Burlington Northern

American type No. 207, built by Rogers in 1887, and No. 103, built by
Baldwin in 1882, were typical of large numbers of 4-4-0's
operated by the GN in the late 1880's. Rebuilt by the shops many
times the little engines remained in service for nearly a half century.

American types: In 1922, Nos. 204 and 125 are at Devils Lake and No. 185 at Minot. Class B-20 [No. 204], built at Rhode Island in 1883, had new boilers applied in 1916/17. Oddly the boiler was designed to take 165 lbs. working pressure, but the reciprocating parts only 140 lbs. With a bare 13,000 lbs. of tractive effort, No. 125 class B-15, built by Schenectady in 1892, was reboilered in 1907 and scrapped in 1929. No. 185 class B-19, Brooks built in 1882/83, looks much huskier than when originally built. The visored headlight was quite common on older power fitted with electrified oil headlights. No. 290 class B-8, an oil burner, is at Everett in 1920. No. 192 class B-9, built in 1881, was among the last of the type to be scrapped.

Photographs J. Foster Adams collection, except as noted.

No. 226 class B-22 is shown first at Lester Prairie, and again leaving Minneapolis Station in June, 1922. Built by Rogers in 1889, the locomotives of class B-22 were all dismantled by the early 1930's. It is obvious that the engine has had excellent care. It gleams like satin from the smokebox to the tender flanks. In the early "roaring twenties", railroad heraldry or trademarks were very subdued on the locomotive or tender. No. 226 was identified simply with the road name painted on the tank without color or embellishment, GN lettered on the sand dome, and the engine number outlined with a metal frame on the side of the cab. Not until the advent of the P-2 class in 1923, did the rectangular Great Northern herald again appear, to be supplanted quickly by the Glacier Park Goat.

J. Foster Adams photo courtesy Mid-Continent Ry. Museum & Wisconsin State Historical Society

At York, North Dakota a branch line local waits on the house track for passengers from the Glacier Park Ltd. No. 351, an old class D-2 Mogul type, with the road name barely discernable on the tender flanks, is just a step away from the boneyard in this 1922 photo by J. Foster Adams. By 1930, even the later, but similar D-5 class was down to just 9 engines. Among them was No. 453, shown in these Wally Swanson photos at Vancouver, B.C. in 1940. No. 419, a class D-4 at Missoula in 1916, is from the collection of Harold K. Volrath.

Above: No. 609 class G-1 Twelve Wheeler, Brooks built in 1891, is on the North Dakota prairie with a stock car special in the 1920's. The G-1 class, the smallest and lightest of the Twelve Wheelers, had a tractive effort of 25,720 lbs.

Great Northern Railway

C. T. Felstead collection

No. 768 simmers at Minot in 1947, and No. 722 is spotted at Hillyard in 1946. The G-3 class Twelve Wheeler, built by Rogers Locomotive Works at the turn of the century, with a tractive effort of just over 32,000 lbs., was considerably more powerful than the G-1 class. These Twelve Wheelers, purchased in large numbers by the GN, were slow and easy on light track and structures. Thus they were well suited for branch line operations after being bumped off the main, and served long and well in this role.

A GN freight rounds the horseshoe curve near the station at Fielding [now Blacktail], Montana in 1899. The 4-8-0 Twelve Wheeler was built in 1898 by Brooks Locomotive Works.

Built in 1892 by Brooks, the class F-1 Consolidations—numbered in the 500 series—looked like stretched Moguls. With a tractive effort of 23,000 lbs., they were only slightly less powerful than the early G-1 class Twelve Wheelers. Pokey little teakettles, they survived for decades on the branches and secondary runs. Below, F-1 No. 511 burned coal in the Thirties. Above, the locomotive had been rebuilt with new cylinders and converted to oil, and at upper right with new numbers, it nears the end of its days.

Wally Swanson

H. K. Vollrath collection

The class F-5, built in 1901, with 47,000 lbs. of tractive effort rolled on 55 inch drivers. In later years, the F-5's burned oil and served on the main line, but in common with many smaller GN engines, they suffered from limited water capacity tenders.

The ten engines in the F-7 class were built by Cooke in 1901 with 45,000 lbs. of tractive effort. The first F-7, No. 1130, was sent to Korea in 1954 to help the war effort, and above, No. 1138 sits in the yards at Fargo in September, 1957.

No. 1195, one of the last of the F-8 class Consolidations to be equipped with a superheater, pauses for coal while working main line freights during World War II on the "Surrey Cutoff" between Fargo and Minot. Immediately behind the tender is an auxiliary water car, used to extend the operating range of the little 2-8-0 while working heavy drag freights.

At Sioux City, Iowa in 1953, F-8 class No. 1192 eases back with side rods just turning, to make a coupling many cars behind. This fundamental move required considerable skill in handling the throttle and the air. One to four mph is considered ideal coupling speed—above that damage results to lading and or equipment. On a grade, in the rain or at night—moving in response to lantern signals—this seemingly simple move was akin to eating bouillion with a fork. One error in judgment and the resulting boom of heavy cars coming together could rattle windows for blocks around.

The class F-12 Consolidations—No. 1326 shown at Butte in 1922 and No. 1327—were the lowest drivered Consolidations on the GN roster. Built for the Butte Anaconda & Pacific in 1907, the 52″ drivered engines could be readily identified by their lack of a Belpaire boiler.

1503.

A trio of E-3 class Ten Wheelers: No. 903 is spotted over the
ashpits at St. Paul in 1913; No. 907 is photographed at
Minneapolis in 1938; and No. 904 powers a branch line local at
Devils Lake in 1922. The E-3's, built by Rogers in 1889, with
73" drivers had a tractive effort of only 18,150 lbs.

Great Northern Railway

Bill Holt

A SOLID TRAINLOAD OF POTATOES AND ONIONS
SHIPPED BY O. J. ODEGARD
FROM
PRINCETON, MINNESOTA
SEPT. 20, 1937

Wayne C. Olsen collection

Built by Rogers in 1902, these E-6 class Ten Wheelers were modernized, trim and well kept. Husky for their size, the little shotgun stacked 4-6-0's were excellent branch line power in either passenger or freight service. Virtually unrestricted, due to the 152,000 lbs. total engine weight, the E-6's could work anywhere on the system, and at one time, double headed, they worked the hottest long distance mail run in the world—No. 27, St. Paul to Seattle. Above, No. 926 at Princeton, Minnesota heads a solid trainload of potatoes and onions bound for Minneapolis, in September, 1937. Both No. 926 below and No. 936 at upper left sit on turntables in the mid-West. At lower left, No. 925 waits on a weed grown siding near Leavenworth, Washington.

Great Northern Railway

The E-7's [950-969] were Brooks built in 1893. At upper left, Ten Wheeler No. 965 hustles out of Seattle past the roundhouse at Interbay in 1920. At lower left, No. 954 is at Tacoma in 1923. Twenty of the popular class E-8's [1053-1072] were delivered by Rogers in 1901-1903. Below, No. 1070 stands in the station in Seattle with her crew and conductor.

Burlington Northern

The E-8's were concurrent with the E-6's [1902], and were, with the E-6's, the last Ten Wheelers to be dropped from the roster. At upper right, No. 1055 comes barreling out of Vancouver, B. C. with the International Limited in 1920. Below, No. 1054 steams at Vancouver in 1908. At lower right, No. 1053, at Willmar in 1946, was scrapped the following year.

H. K. Vollrath collection

J. Foster Adams, collection of Dr. George Fischer

W. R. Swanson

Nos. 910 and 911 E-2 class, formerly Nos. 16 and 17 on the Willmar & Sioux Falls, featured radial stayed boilers. Built by Alco in 1915, the E-2's were the last of the Ten Wheelers.

No. 948 class E-13 is shown at Spokane in 1948. The E-13's of 1893 & 1896, like the E-12's of 1897 — both Baldwin built — had low 55" drivers.

H. K. Vollrath collection

No. 970 sits in the rain at Vancouver, B. C. in 1936. The two locomotives of the E-12 class Ten Wheelers were built originally for the Spokane Falls & Northern as Nos. 11 and 12. They became Nos. 970 and 971 after James J. Hill acquired the SF&N in 1898. The glossy light olive green color of their boilers was adopted for GN locomotives shortly thereafter.

E-14 class No. 1001 picks its way over the switches and crossings while leaving Portland on Christmas Day in 1921.

Foster Adams, Dr. G. Fischer collection

No. 1010 at Tacoma in 1923 was among the first of 45 E-14's built by Baldwin in 1909-1910.
The E-14's, ten wheeled versions of H-4 Pacifics, were rebuilt in the 1920's as
H-5's and H-7's.

H. K. Vollrath collection

Roberts collection; Oregon Historical Society

Twenty of these slim boilered E-15's were built by Baldwin in 1910 for passenger service. Left, No. 1076 at Devils Lake, Minnesota is as originally built, while No. 1089 above at Tacoma, displays the same headlight and tender lettering as E-14 No. 1010. Showing the locomotives' final configuration, No. 1082 (at the top of the page) charges through Chelan, Washington in 1932. Most of the E-15's were gone by the late 1930's, but Nos. 1090 and 1082 remained on the roster until 1949, used in freight service in their final years.

H-1 class Pacific No. 1404 waits at Devils Lake in 1922. Rogers built
in 1905, Nos. 1400-1405 were the first Pacifics on the system. So superior
in steaming, speed, reliability and overall performance were they
to other types such as the Prairie, Mogul and Ten Wheeler, that they
were ordered from Baldwin time after time. The next 20 ordered in 1906,
with spaced out front axles, were designated class H-2. They were soon
upgraded to class H-3. Included in this group are No. 1413 at Willmar in 1934
and No. 1408 at St. Paul in 1922—both photos from
the collection of Harold K. Vollrath.

It is 9:50 AM May, 1940, and train No. 235 daily, passes
Lippard, Montana—60 miles out of Havre—enroute to Great
Falls, Helena and Butte. Known locally as the "Havre to Butte
Stub", it provided service south of Havre for passengers from
No. 1—the Empire Builder. No. 1443 H-4 class Pacific is on the
smoky end. The H-4's, built by Baldwin in 1909, were the last
engines originally built as Pacifics.

W. R. McGee

HAVRE, GREAT FALLS, HELENA AND BUTTE.

Read Down   Read Up

27 Daily	1 Daily	Mls.	Table 56 Central Time	2 Daily	28 Daily
8 45	8 50	0	Lv St. Paul 1 🚗 Ar	10 30	6 30
9 18	9 25	11	" Minneapo-lis. 🚗 .... "	10 00	5 55
7 10	10 45	475	Ar Minot 2, 3 🚗 Lv	10 35	5 10
			Mountain Time		
3 20	8 00	905	Ar Havre 3, 4 Lv	11 30	5 45

221 Daily	235 Daily		Mountain Time	236 Daily	222 Daily
3 45	8 15	0	Lv Havre 3,4 .... Ar	10 55	11 10
f 3 57	—	8	" Assinniboine... "	—	f10 56
f 4 07	f 8 37	15	" Laredo........ "	—	f10 46
f 4 20	8 50	25	" Box Elder..... "	f10 22	f10 34
f 4 34	9 04	36	" Big Sandy..... "	10 09	10 20
f 4 42	—	41	" Verona........ "	—	f10 12
f 4 54	f 9 25	49	" Virgelle........ "	f 9 45	f 9 58
f 5 02	—	55	" Stranahan..... "	—	f 9 50
f 5 09	—	60	" Lippard........ "	—	f 9 42
f 5 17	f 9 52	66	" Chappell....... "	f 9 19	f 9 32
f 5 24	—	71	" Teton......... "	—	f 9 24
f 5 29	—	74	" Liscum........ "	—	f 9 18
5 36	10 17	79	" Fort Benton... "	8 54	9 10
f 5 46	—	84	" Kershaw....... "	—	f 9 01
f 5 55	—	89	" Tunis......... "	—	f 8 54
f 6 05	f10 41	94	" Carter........ "	f 8 28	f 8 45
f 6 14	f10 49	99	" Floweree...... "	f 8 20	f 8 38
f 6 29	f11 01	107	" Portage....... "	f 8 08	f 8 27
f 6 39	—	113	" Sheffels....... "	—	f 8 19
—	—	117	" Rainbow...... "	—	—
7 00	11 30	123	Ar Great Falls . 🚗 .Lv 8, 57, 58, 59, 60, 61	7 40	8 00

	11 45	123	Lv Great Falls...Ar	7 20	
	—	128	" Flood.........Lv	—	
	f12 10	137	" Ulm.......... "	—	
	—	144	" Riverdale..... "	—	
	12 34	152	" Cascade....... "	6 28	
	f12 48	160	" Hardy........ "	f 6 14	
			(Elev. 3,358 ft.)		
	f 1 02	168	" Mid Canon.... "	f 6 00	
	1 14	175	" Craig......... "	f 5 48	
	1 27	183	" Wolf Creek.... "	5 35	
	f 1 45	192	" Sieben........ "	f 5 17	
	f 2 05	204	" Silver City.... "	f 4 57	
	—	208	" Gearing....... "	—	
	—	213	" Iron.......... "	—	
	2 35	221	Ar Helena......Lv	4 25	
	2 45	221	Lv Helena.......Ar	4 15	
	—	226	" Four Range...Lv	—	
	—	230	" Montana City. "	—	
	3 12	236	" Clancy....... "	3 43	
	3 14	237	" Alhambra H. S. "	3 41	
	—	241	" Jefferson..... "	—	
	f 3 29	243	" Corbin........ "	3 29	
	—	247	" Wickes....... "	—	
	—	248	" Portal........ "	—	
	—	249	" Amazon....... "	—	
	3 57	255	" Boulder H. S.. "	2 59	
	—	260	" Fuller......... "	—	
	4 12	263	" Basin......... "	2 45	
	—	267	" Bernice....... "	—	
	f 4 38	275	" Elk Park...... "	f 2 24	
	—	280	" Trask......... "	—	
	—	284	" Woodville..... "	—	
			(Elev. 6,358 ft.)		
	—	289	" Mountain Jct.. "	—	
	5 15	293	Ar Butte. 🚗 ...Lv 8, 57, 64	1 45	

LOW COST TRAVEL

$2.47 One-Way
$4.45 Round-Trip
60 Day Limit
Havre to Great Falls
● ●

$4.44 One-Way
$8.00 Round-Trip
60 Day Limit
Havre to Helena
● ●

$5.90 One-Way
$10.65 Round-Trip
60 Day Limit
Havre to Butte
● ●

Fares apply in either direction.

LOW COST TRAVEL

$1.97 One-Way
$3.55 Round-Trip
60 Day Limit
Great Falls to Helena
● ●

$3.44 One-Way
$6.20 Round-Trip
60 Day Limit
Great Falls to Butte
● ●

$1.47 One-Way
$2.65 Round-Trip
60 Day Limit
Helena to Butte
● ●

Fares apply in either direction.

No. 1450 class H-4 at Kelly Lake, Minnesota in 1952 displays the rods,
conduits, piping and assorted appliances hung on the outside of the
locomotive that became a hallmark of GN power in later years. By contrast
No. 1490 class H-5 at Minot in 1923 is remarkably clean lined.
No. 1490 had just been rebuilt in the GN shops from E-14 No. 1022. It was
renumbered as No. 1354 at a later date.

Daily except Sunday from Glasgow and Williston to Havre, Train No. 223 behind engine No. 1364 arrives at Havre 5 PM May 2, 1940. Typical "accomodations" equipment follow the Pacific—head end car, baggage car, and an elderly truss road braced coach carrying the markers. Unusual, however, are the two express refrigerators cut into the middle of the train. Below, No. 1361 at Portland in 1950—as well as No. 1364—had been rebuilt from Ten Wheelers into H-5's by the GN shops.

Until the introduction of the Vanderbilt type, GN locomotive tenders were characterized by a boxy and often cluttered appearance. Equipped with a steam operated coal pusher and resembling a rolling grape arbor, the outside braced versions were functional, but almost entirely lacking in esthetics..

No. 1531 class J-1 at St. Paul in 1922 was among the first 50 Prairies built by Baldwin in 1906. The J's proved to be powerful moderate speed freight engines with almost 38,000 lbs. tractive effort. However, they were very unstable in the service for which they had been designed—fast dual service passenger/freight engines. A number of them were "sold" to the SP&S, and by the mid-1930's, only one—No. 1559—was left on the Dakota Division. Fifteen of the 2-6-2's were rebuilt into Pacifics class H-6 by the GN shops. No. 1722 was rebuilt from a J-1 class engine in 1926. No. 1713 was a rebuild of No. 1552, one of 100 J-2's built by Baldwin in 1907.

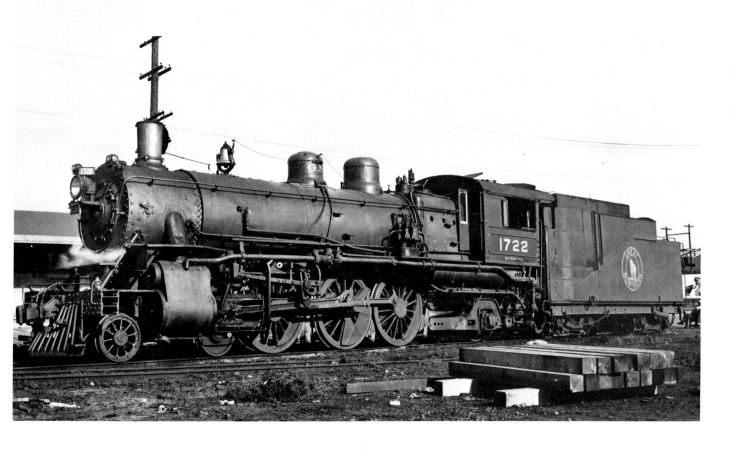

W. R. McGee

With No. 1379 class H-7s Pacific carrying the markers, No. 27, the Fast Mail hustles out of Libby, Montana in the spring of 1941. Between Whitefish and Troy, over the 3rd subdivision of the Kalispell Division, four of the fast 4-6-2's [1379-1382] were regularly assigned to No. 27 and No. 28. With 15 regular and 73 conditional stops in the 530 miles between Havre and Spokane, No. 27 was the fastest train—between stops—of any scheduled GN passenger train.

Great Northern Railway

With almost 50,000 lbs. of tractive effort, 73″ drivers, superheater, enlarged tank and modern appliances, the ten H-7's built by the GN in 1926 and 1927 from E-14 class Ten Wheelers, were the biggest and the best of the Pacifics. Often used on first class trains over the more level divisions, they released P-2's for service elsewhere. No. 1375 is shown above just after completion of its conversion from E-14 No. 1033, and below at St. Paul in 1946 after further modernization.

C. T. Felstead collection

C. T. Felstead collection

Built in 1906 by Baldwin to power the Oriental Limited across the nearly level Montana prairie, the K class Atlantics—even when modified extensively and fitted with a booster equipped trailing truck—were always lacking in power. They were a maintenance headache, and the 73" drivers effectively prevented any real turn of speed. They worked out their years on plug runs and in commuter service where neither speed nor power were needed. [Above] No. 1705, with a delta trailing truck, is at Superior, Wisc. in 1935. [Below] No. 1702 at Minneapolis in the same year.

Class A-8 light switcher No. 71, built by Rogers in 1900, was one of two
surviving members of the class in 1930. With only 24,550 lbs. of tractive effort,
the A-8's were simply too light to warrant further rebuilding.

Coal burning "hand bomber" No. 6 class A-9 switcher was the first locomotive
on which Alfred Strandrud [left] pulled the throttle.

Strandrud Family

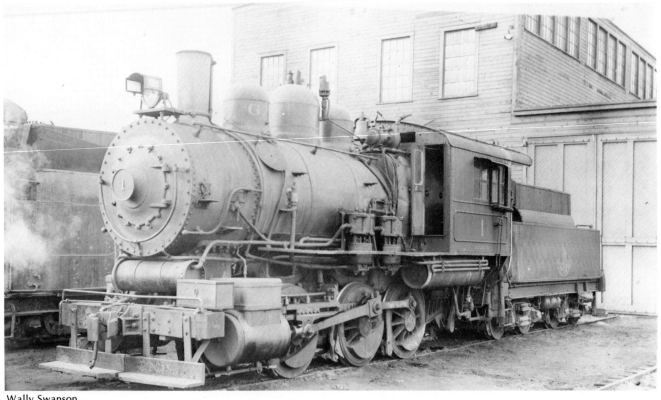

Wally Swanson

GN No. 1 class A-9 oil burning switcher is at Klamath Falls, Oregon in 1938. Coal. burning class A-9 No. 16, at Tacoma in 1951, is close to the end of its working days. The A-9 class was built between 1906 and 1909 by GN, Baldwin and Rogers.

No. 98 class A-10 at Minneapolis was built by Brooks in 1899-1900. No. 30 class A-11 switcher was built by Lima in 1917 with a radial stayed boiler. With a tractive effort of just under 30,000 lbs., the A-11's were the most modern and powerful of the GN 0-6-0's.

C.T. Felstead collection

Arch bar trucks on the tender of C-1 class switcher No. 829 at Minneapolis in July, 1952 are an anachronism in the 1950's, but there is no violation of ICC rulings since this engine is not designed for road service much less interchange. The open ventilators and running board door would indicate the weather is warm, yet a vestige of winter operation remains—the partially enclosed bay window on the side of the cab.

Engine No. 850 shuffles cars at Minot. Formerly a Consolidation type, it was converted to an 8 wheel switcher by the road in 1925. The care lavished on the engine is evident. Every part of the boiler, tank and cab gleam, the domes shine like mirrors, and even the driving wheels are clean. The GN was never one to waste locomotives if they could be modified, rebuilt or restored, and few ever reached the age where they were not useable in some way.

Class C-3 switcher No. 896 at Seattle in 1940 is a rebuild of an F-9 class Consolidation.

Casey Adams

Wally Swanson

Wally Swanson

No. 1909, in the second group of class L-1's built by Baldwin in 1908, was designed for pusher service in the Cascades, and could handle 800 tons on the 2.2% grades. The second Mallet type to have been built in the U.S. [the first being an 0-6-6-0 put into operation on the Baltimore & Ohio in 1904], the L-1's were the first Mallet type in this country to be fitted with leading and trailing wheels. They epitomized the "maximum ton miles, minimum train miles" philosophy of James J. Hill, for with no increase in fuel consumption or additional crew costs, the slow ponderous sloggers could do 20% more work than a Consolidation type. The lighter L-2 class, built in 1907, was moved to the heavy grades in the Rocky Mountains in 1908, with the delivery of the additional L-1's for road service on the Cascade Division. The competing Northern Pacific, faced with nearly identical operating problems through Stampede Pass, was so impressed by the performance of the 2-6-6-2's in the Cascades, that they ordered six of them [class Z] in 1907. So far as can be determined, these were the only locomotives on the NP with Belpaire boilers.

Night scenes are a particular favorite with rail artist
Howard Fogg. Here, a 2-6-6-2, used in helper service in the
Rockies, sits under a bright full moon.

Courtesy of Miner Enterprises

Overleaf: A 2-6-6-2, cut in a few cars ahead of the caboose,
pushed with all its 70,000 lbs. tractive effort against a tonnage
train in the Montana Rockies. These engines were
replaced by 2-10-2's in 1923.

Mallory Hope Ferrell

427

Dr. George Fischer collection

The first group of L-1's [Nos. 1800-1804], built by Baldwin in 1906, is ready for delivery from Pennsylvania to the Cascades.

Also brand new, class M-1 No. 2000 at Minneapolis in 1910 has just been converted by Baldwin from 2-8-0 Consolidation No. 1254, built in 1907.

Philip C. Johnson

Virtually a rolling antique, and far removed from main line service, No. 1951, an M-2 class 2-6-8-0, is shown on the Kettle Falls Branch, north of Spokane, Washington in 1947. Constructed by Baldwin in 1910 as a compound Mallet, No. 1951 was simpled by the GN shops in 1926. Notoriously slow, poorly counter-balanced, and trailing a 10,000 gallon tender that will barely get the old hog from one water plug to the next without having to cut off the train and run for more, it is a striking example of why the railroads dieselized as quickly as possible following World War II.

Soot begrimed class M-2 No. 1972 is in ore train service at Butte, Montana in 1941.

Wally Swanson

Wally Swanson

W. R. McGee

Class M-3 No. 1973, overhauled at Dale St. shops in St. Paul in 1951, was used on the iron range. Simpled in the 1920's—and later fitted with a Vanderbilt tender, sport cab and modernized "bandstand", its appearance belies its age of 40 years.

Headed for Great Falls, Great Northern Extra 1984, with 44 cars behind a 2-6-8-0 articulated, is about to enter Basin Tunnel on June 3, 1939. Located along the Continental Divide just a few miles from Elk Park, Montana, Basin Tunnel, at an elevation of 5,339' is the highest tunnel on the GN.

Collections of Harold K. Vollrath, Dr. George Fischer and C. T. Felstead

With a long drag of high cars, a coal burning O-1 class Mikado crests an acceleration grade on the Willmar Division. Much of the train is still hanging over the slight grade, and the old 2-8-2 is working hard, sanding the rails as she goes, to keep her feet from slipping. While older GN and NP steam power both were characterized by high mounted, off centered headlights, no one could mistake this engine for other than GN. The distinguishing features are all there—high Vanderbilt tank, Belpaire boiler and the high mounted headlight.

At left three eras of 0-1's are represented in No. 3108 in 1916 at Eddystone, Pa., No. 3086 in 1922 at Minot and No. 3002 in 1946 at Minneapolis. Note differences in the headlight, cab, tender, herald, pilot, and particularly the ash pans under the firebox.

Just outside of Minneapolis, No. 3104 one of two GN engines [both O-1 class Mikados] equipped with Elesco feedwater heaters, is photographed with a long cut of new boxcars built in the St. Cloud shops. The picture was used in the 1941 timetable, with smoke and speedlines airbrushed in to give the impression of blinding speed—hardly possible with a 32 year old engine on 63" drivers. It must have been warm that day in the cab of No. 3104—the roof ventilators are propped open, the cab door is open and the fireman appears a little bored waiting for the photographer to finish his work.

C. T. Felstead collection

On older power such as No. 3035, the rectangular tank was standard, but at Minneapolis in 1937, No. 3035 class O-1 Mikado has acquired the look of heavy GN power with the addition of a huge Vanderbilt tank.

With the purchase of the Willmar & Sioux Falls by the Great Northern, ex-South Dakota Central No. 18, at Willmar in April, 1931, became No. 3149, the sole member of the O-2 class.

Great Northern Railway

Harold K. Vollrath collection

W. R. McGee

Train No. 697, with 80 cars of apples from the Okanogan Valley, heads for Appleyard in October, 1946. After passing the station at Stayman, the train nears Winesap, Washington, about 26 miles north of Wenatchee. Nearby are the famous Beebe Orchards—one of the biggest apple producers in the United States.

The nine engines of the O-3 class, USRA types built by Alco in 1919/20, were considerably less powerful than engines of the O-1 class. From the collection of Harold K. Vollrath, No. 3205 at Superior in 1935, is pretty much as delivered to the GN. Nos. 3201 and 3207 at Kelly Lake, from the collection of C. T. Felstead, were used on the Iron Range. They have been fitted with a switching style pilot and double air pumps, thereby gaining more of a GN look, but the radial stayed boiler is unmistakeable. These engines are not typical of GN Mikados.

Locomotive No. 3306 class O-5 Mike at Seattle, was built from a class L-2
Mallet by the GN shops in the mid 1920's. The forty five O-5's were
similar, with a major identification feature the extremely heavy driver
tires—due to increasing the driver diameter from 55" to 63". No. 3254,
at Minneapolis in 1953, was one of the O-4 class that was later fitted with a
large Vanderbilt tender to replace its "blockhouse" styled tender.

Right: The turbo generator of No. 3368 sings its high pitched tune as the big
2-8-2 class O-6 Mikado simmers on the GN main, eight miles from the
Canadian border at Eureka, Montana, in November, 1948. Built by the GN
shops in 1926, from the early 1906 L-1 class 2-6-6-2's, it is
the personification of heavy GN power.

R. McGee

Above: Train No. 689, consisting of just eight cars, comes storming down the main, west of Bonners Ferry, Idaho. The old wooden reefers are beginning to sway and roll, as No. 3355 accelerates to the 50 mph speed limit. It is still nearly ninety miles into Spokane, and the crew is "trying to get home for Saturday nite", September, 1950.

Philip C. Johnson

With brute strength, No. 3393 urges 6,100 tons and 97 cars into motion at Wagner,
Montana, up on the "High Line"—that long stretch of Great Northern track
close to the Canadian border between Glacier Park and Williston, North
Dakota. After taking water, the hogger kicked off the air, and pulled open the
throttle and sanders. With a mighty explosive whoosh from the stack, the
drivers of the O-8 class Mike began to turn, and then cannonading furiously,
the drag moved out of town in September, 1952.

W. R. McGee

Displaying metal flags as 2nd 436, engine No. 3399 roars around the big curve at
MP 1343, about nine miles west of Libby along the Kootenai River. The train
[3310 tons], consisting of 63 loaded cars and 0 empties, is only a few signal
blocks behind 1st 436. Engineer Schradi and the head end brakeman, looking
over the photographer, are unable to understand his hand signals for smoke.

Rebuilt from an O-7 into an O-8, No. 3391 displays the chunky, yet fast lines,
that made the O-8's probably the handsomest heavy Mikes every built.

Above: N-1 class, 2-8-8-0 compound, as built by Baldwin in 1912, was modernized, modified and rebuilt by the GN shops many times. No. 2020 was simpled by the GN shops into an N-2 in 1926, and the final rebuilding of the entire N-2 class was done in 1940/41. New boilers, roller bearings and new appliances were fitted to the 25 locomotives, and they became, collectively, class N-3. As originally built, the N-1's were not bad looking locomotives, but the tiny tanks made them look like a St. Bernard towing a wagon. In later years, they received large Vanderbilt tanks, more in keeping with their size and water consumption.

Above right: N-2 class No. 2020 is at Great Falls, Montana in 1934. Fitted during rebuilding with 21,500 gal. tenders and converted to burn oil, the N-2's tractive effort increased to 100,000 lbs. at 72.5% of the designed working pressure of 210 lbs.

Right: N-3 No. 2020 at Spokane in the 1950's spent nearly as much time on subsidiary SP&S rails as it did on the Cascade Division of the GN. The SP&S invariably found itself power short during harvest season—particularly on the Oregon Trunk's rough operating profile.

W. R. McGee

Ed Mueller collection

First 436, with 81 loads and 14 empties [4520 tons], works its way east along the Kootenai in the spring of 1941. Engine No. 2019, a modernized N-3 class 2-8-8-0, is making fairly easy work of the heavy train. During extensive modernization at Hillyard, the front edge of the cab of No. 2019 was slanted forward, giving the big articulated a distinctive appearance. This same "styling" was also incorporated in some Pacifics that were rebuilt at the Hillyard shops.

Ed Mueller collection

At Klamath Falls, Oregon, in 1950, an N-3 class, No. 2002 awaits an assignment north to Bend, Oregon and the SP&S. The big N-3, originally built in 1912 and one of the most unesthetic Mallets ever to appear on the GN, is here a beautiful and efficient piece of machinery—simpled, with new frame, new boiler and appliances, and fitted with roller bearings and all the appurtenances common to modern GN power. Capable of sustained speed on the level districts, it could outwork a Challenger in mountainous terrain.

Left: Running as an extra westbound, No. 2009, class N-2, at Browning, Montana in 1934, is beginning to acquire some of the lines and form that will appear in the vastly modernized N-3's of the 1940's.

447

P-1 class No. 1754 is at Missoula, Montana in this 1916 photo
from the collection of Harold K. Vollrath. Q-2 class No. 2182
at Willmar, Minnesota in 1953, was one of the 15 Q-2's built
by the GN shops in 1928 from the 63" drivered class P-1
Mountains built by Lima in 1914. The unusual trailing truck
under the cab of No. 2182 was a Lima design known as the
Austin truck and applied to the original P-1 class of 1914.
Powerful and slow, both classes were true "freight hogs" in
every sense of the word. They were popular with engine crews
because they were good steamers and also because they
carried a higher pay scale than, for example,
Mikes and Consolidations.

Engine No. 2179, a 2-10-2, pounds its way — literally — along NP
track in South Tacoma. Engines of the big Q class always
suffered from poor counterbalancing, and were notorious track
pounders. Eventually all of the 2-10-2's were prohibited from
using this NP track, due to broken rails at speeds above 35
mph. In some areas of GN light rail, they were either
prohibited or restricted down to 20 mph, and even on the
heavy duty GN main line, they were restricted to 45 mph.

W. R. McGee

C. T. Felstead

The resemblance of the Q-1 class 2-10-2 built by Baldwin in
1923, to the class P-2 Mountain delivered the same year, is
obvious. Although the two classes had many parts in common,
the most striking differences were the Belpaire boiler and the
63" rather than 73" drivers on the Q-1, No. 2115.

In the roundhouse at Hillyard, a pair of 2-10-2's are
"stored serviceable" in 1951. Even without the neatly
lettered G.N. on the sides of the sand dome, they would
be recognized immediately as heavy GN power. Their flat
pump heavy faces were hallmarks of modern GN steam.

Ed Mueller collection

Dr. Philip R. Hastings

The P-2's roll the Silk!

Mountain class P-2 No. 2517 [the Marathon] is taking on oil and water at New Rockford,
North Dakota after bringing in a Silk Train from Seattle in September, 1925. Citizens gathered
when news that the Marathon was arriving came over the telegraph, and they
watched while the crew hurriedly serviced her before she continued towards Fargo and St. Paul
with $5,000,000 worth of raw silk aboard. It was to be a record breaking round-trip,
with stops only for crew changes and to take on fuel and water—3,567 miles in 99 hours and
55 minutes. At upper left, a cargo of raw silk from Japan is unloaded at the docks in Seattle.

Great Northern Railway

Engine No. 2521 poses for what is probably one of the last photographs made of the P-2 class. Pilot deck mounted air pumps with shields, pilot mounted footboards for switchmen, twin sealed beam headlights inside the old headlight casing, engine number boards and mechanical lubricators are some of the modern touches that have appeared.

Everett Herald

Builder crews change at Fargo—Dakota Division—in the late 1930's. Ahead, almost due northwest, lies the longest and straightest piece of track on the Great Northern. Also known as the Fargo-Minot "Surrey Cutoff", the nearly 224 miles of tangent was built in 1911, and was shorter by 28 miles than the Minot-Grand Forks-Fargo transcontinental route.

Casey Adams

During the era of steam, the motive power department was not one to engage in unnecessary frills. For years, the basic philosophy had been to buy the biggest motive power available [or build it in the shops], to improve the track and structures to hold this power, to pull the longest trains possible with the least number of engines and to maintain this motive power—in so far as possible—to eliminate breakdowns. Roller bearings, boosters, improved methods of cross counterbalancing, high horsepower/high speed freight locomotives, streamlining and stream styling were all looked upon with a skeptical eye. The road did experiment briefly with a casing around the stack on several of the Mountain types, in the early 1940's, to try to lift the smoke higher, away from the cab. The smoke, restricting visibility, could be a nuisance at best and a hazard at worst. The tests were inconclusive, and No. 2519 was refitted with its original stack at the shops in Minot.

P-2 class Mountain at Hillyard

Watercolor by Mike Pearsall

The veteran hogger, on Mountain type No. 2524, looks back for the highball after completing station work at Priest River, Idaho, in September, 1950. Just a few short years before, No. 2524 was assigned to the fast runs across this division on the point of the Builder and the Fast Mail, but in this scene, it is being used to power a local freight. Yet, the boiler, cab and flanks of the tender still gleam in green and gloss black, and the proud red and white herald of the GN clearly decorates the side sheets of the oil bunker.

Assigned to local freight work, No. 2524 waits in the hole at Newport, Washington, along the Clark Fork of the Columbia, as an eastbound fast freight passes through town after slowing to pick up orders. As the freight accelerates once again, the crew, on the back platform of the caboose, read the orders, and a brakeman of the local stands ready to throw the switch to let the local out onto the main again once the caboose has cleared the points.

W. R. McGee

Great Northern Railway

458

Below: A travel worn and stained S-1 steams quietly on the ready track at Minot. Pulled off the Builder and Fast Mail by diesels, the tall drivered Northern is showing evidence of its reduced status.

Casey Adams

Above left: Extra 2551 West, with a string of 124 empty reefers [3100 tons] charges down the main between a pair of upper quadrant semaphores, in April, 1941. On 73″ drivers, the long and low slung Northern was one of six in the S-1 class [2550-2555], originally designed to handle the Builder and No. 27. Road tests and experience showed, however, that they were also superb heavy freight locomotives. Powerful, fast, free steaming and trailing a huge water bottom tender [22,000 gallons of water and 5,800 gallons of oil] that permitted them to run by many water plugs, even when working hard—they were popular with the engine crews.

Left: The S-1 class was the first Northern type in service on the GN, and the only Northern built with a Belpaire firebox. Shown at Minot, every line of No. 2555 suggests power—the 73″ drivers, the big boiler and heavy main rods. The smokebox mounted air pumps, the low mounted headlight [not far above the boiler tube pilot], the squat low stack and the massive trailing truck—all added to the long engine's impression of power. Excelling in heavy expedited freight service, the capabilities of the S-1 class were never exceeded by the later, and more numerous S-2 class.

Wiped down and polished from boiler tube pilot to driving wheels and tender trucks, Northern 2576 waits for the return of the presidential party at Ephrata, Washington, 120 miles from Spokane. Ground breaking ceremonies are taking place at the site of Grand Coulee Dam during the first term of President Franklin D. Roosevelt. Flying extra flags, the big 4-8-4 holds the main, and nothing will move east or west of Ephrata until the Presidential Special has cleared the old Spokane Division.

Great Northern Railway

Telegraph poles flick past the cab windows like closely spaced fence posts as Northern 2585 crowds the 60 mile per hour speed limit coming up out of the Spokane River Valley with 2nd No. 4, a Christmas mail extra. The exhaust of the big Northern is one sustained roar, while behind the Vanderbilt tank, an express reefer does a jig in response to the swaying of the big engine, working hard on the 1% eastbound grade to Hillyard.

Shining and cold, in the clutter of an engine terminal, a Northern of the S-2 class is posed for a press photo. Although No. 2581 is five years old, there is hardly a visible mark or stain. Picture this same engine on the fast track leading down in long sweeping curves along the eastern slope of the Rockies, past Browning, Meriwether, Cut Bank, and out onto the rolling plains. With smoke drifting back over the cars, the hurried clatter of the trucks, the long boiler nosing around the curves and down the tangents, it whipped the Builder through hamlets too small to remember. The cry of the whistle still seems to be out there somewhere, as twilight comes and the last light of day gleams on the silvery railheads.

Pulling a GN freight up the west slope of the Rocky Mountains, Engine No. 2032, a class
R-1 articulated, is posed on the horseshoe curve at Blacktail. About two thirds of
the way back in the train, another R-1 is cut in to assist in starting the long heavy
freight train up the 1.8% grade to the summit. Acting on the whistle signal of the
lead engine, the helper engine pushes against the train to bunch the slack and avoid
a break-in-two, and the road engine begins to pull. Working together, the two
mighty steam engines, with exhausts crashing, move the thousands
of tons up the mountain grade.

Class R-1 No. 2031 leaves Minot in 1946 with a westbound drag. Of the 14 engines that comprised the R-1 class, only the first four [2030-33] were built by Baldwin in 1925. Nos. 2034-43 were all built in Hillyard in 1927/28 with the boilers supplied by Puget Sound Machinery Depot. In 1929/30 the 16 locomotives of the slightly larger R-2 class were also built at Hillyard with PSMD boilers. All of the R-2's and four of the R-1's received new boilers from Alco in 1947/48. Interestingly, the original Baldwin built R-1's were never reboilered, but were retired from active service in 1951, while a number of the remaining R-1's remained serviceable until the middle 1950's.

Z-6 class No. 4000 shown at Spokane in 1947, enjoyed a short life on the GN. The Z-6's appeared on the GN equipment roster of 1942, and while fine modern machines, they simply were not designed to work system wide on the GN. As "orphans" they operated in the GN's "backyard" mainly between Spokane and terminals on the SP&S along the Columbia, and on occasion in the Deschutes Canyon and as far south as Bend. By 1950 they were no longer on the GN roster, having been sold to the SP&S.

Left: 16' to the top of the squat stack, 11' wide over the cab handrails, and 119' long — the R-2's weighed just over 1,000,000 lbs. With a maximum designed working pressure of 240 lbs., they were rated at 146,000 lbs. tractive effort at 76.5% of working pressure or 153,000 lbs. at 80% of working pressure. Although both the GN and Baldwin built R-1's were designed with a 210 lb. maximum boiler pressure, the GN built R-1's were rated identically with the R-2's, while the Baldwin built R-1's [with less total weight] were rated at 127,500 lbs. at 76.5% or 134,200 lbs. at 80% of designed working pressure. The R-2 was 5' to 10' longer than an R-1, depending on whether the R-1 was Baldwin or GN built. The R-2's also had an elongated Delta trailing truck, solid center lead wheels and skirting under the cab, which was set further back on the frame than on the R-1's. High speeds were beyond their design capabilities, and a speed limit of 35 mph was in force during their entire working life, which spanned a quarter of a century. These mountain levelers were designed with one thought in mind — to pull thousands of tons into motion and to keep it moving. At this they excelled.

Eastbound time freight No. 82 crosses Fort
Wright Bridge over the Spokane River at Spokane.

7. THE DIESELS: OMAHA ORANGE, BIG SKY BLUE AND CASCADE GREEN

The GN was among the first of the Northwest carriers to recognize the merits and economies inherent in diesel operation. Although it was not widely recognized at the time, the diesel era really began in the early 1920's, when the little gas-electric railcars or "doodlebugs" moved onto branch lines from the Dakotas to British Columbia. There, the early Americans, Ten Wheelers, and Moguls, which required a full crew, had become too costly a means of transporting the few passengers and the small consignments of local freight. Some of the first models were highly erratic and many was the time that gas-electrics had to be towed back into the terminal. But as improvements and modifications were made, the new engines became as reliable as the steam power and far less expensive to operate. Some of the later, more powerful models were not only capable of propelling themselves and a rider coach, but a freight car or two as well.

In 1926, the GN invested in the first true diesel or "Oil-Electric-Locomotive" in the Northwest, No. 5100, built by Alco-GE-Ingersoll Rand. It was used in the Twin City terminals of St. Paul and Minneapolis, where it proved that diesel switching engines were practical and less costly than steam switchers.

By 1938 the GN was firmly sold on the diesel switcher. The railroad ordered twenty-eight 600 and 1,000 horsepower units from Electro Motive Corporation, planning to use them throughout the system. In 1940/41, an order for seventeen additional switching types was placed, including two 360 hp mini-switchers from GE, two 1,000 hp switchers from Baldwin (for service in Minneapolis and St. Paul), and fourteen from EMD.

Even more significant was the order placed for three EMD FT A-B road units, one FT A-B-A for service on Walton Hill (Marias Pass), and a four unit A-B-B-A for service from Interbay to Skykomish. This order was a direct result of the capabilities demonstrated by the prototype four unit FT diesel No. 103. Not only did No. 103, with its 228,000 lb. tractive effort, out pull and out perform the biggest power on the GN (the N-3 articulated and the massive R-1's and R-2's) in the Rockies and Cascades, but it was seemingly tireless. Its 90% availability impressed the Motive Power and Operations Departments of the GN as no other locomotive had. Pull it off a hard run on the Iron Range, perform a quick inspection, replenish the tanks with diesel oil and — like a heavy truck that needed minimal servicing — it was ready to go again. There was no fire to clean, no boiler to wash out, no detailed inspection to perform, and no leaking flues or loose machinery. If the next assignment was light passenger, the two semi-permanently coupled A-B sets could be uncoupled, one set could go on its way while the second set was available for either another passenger assignment or a lighter freight assignment.

Each unit of the 4 unit freighter was powered by a V-16 cylinder diesel engine that developed 1,350 hp, or about 57,000 lbs. of tractive effort. Gearing could be ordered to suit, and with low gearing (up to 65 mph maximum), each unit was as powerful as a light Mikado. With high speed gearing, the unit had a maximum speed of about 89 mph. Most FT's ordered for freight work were geared to a maximum of 65 mph; while the passenger units, which came along after World War II, were ordered for an 89 mph maximum (although they were capable of speeds in the low 90's).

The utility value of the new power must have been obvious. Not only were the FT diesels available "off the shelf", but with options and modifications they could be suited to more specialized services. No longer would there be a need for specialized, custom-built engines for each purpose — to handle ore drags, battle mountains, power the Builder, work the branch lines, or power the passenger and freight runs across the flatter districts. Only the axle ratios needed to be varied to suit the FT's for a multitude of assignments. And with identical parts available in company shops, heavy repairs could be handled by trained company personnel or the entire unit could be sent to the manufacturers for overhaul and refurbishing. In addition, the dynamic braking offered would obviate many of the train handling problems coming downgrade. With enough FT's on hand, any assignment could be handled from St. Paul to Seattle.

In addition, by eliminating water tanks, ash pits, coaling towers and all the other equipment necessary to steam operation, the GN saved on capital expenditure, structure maintenance; taxes on these structures, and the cost of the labor force necessary to operate and maintain them. The savings were even more striking in regard to crew costs. If diesels could be run in multiple units of four, then there was no reason why they could not be run as six or seven or even more units under the control of one crew in the lead unit cab. Operating as multiple units, helpers could virtually be eliminated, except in the most hazardous districts, where mid- or rear-train helpers were necessary to ease coupler strain on long freights and to help the dynamic braking power keep the tonnage under control on long downgrades.

The GN switched to diesels as rapidly as the builders could deliver the power and company forces could be trained to operate and maintain them. At one time the GN was the biggest operator of the FT type in the United States, with 96 of them in service. Only the short

supply of engines prevented a more rapid conversion of the entire system. If the FT had been more readily available for purchase during World War II, it is very doubtful that the twenty-two 0-7's would have been upgraded into 0-8's. Moreover, if the diesel type had been available in quantity immediately after the war, it is unlikely that any steam power would have undergone heavy repairs or rebuilding to more modern standards. The tradition of steam had been built up over a hundred years of railroad operation; but the diesel, with its economic savings, performance and availability, created a virtual revolution in railroad motive power in less than a decade. In fact, diesel was the force that saved the railroads from virtual extinction.

There was no doubt that the existing steam freight power needed replacement as quickly as possible, and that the passenger service on the Empire Builder (with lightweight equipment on order), the Oriental Limited, the Fast Mail and lesser trains needed new power as well. In 1945, the GN took delivery on the first of a series of EMD E-7-A's that were eventually destined to power the Empire Builder of 1947. These 2,000 hp passenger units — striking in their new livery of orange and green — were fast units designed with a speed capability in excess of 100 mph. To break them in, they were assigned to the Fast Mail (train Nos. 27 and 28) and continued in this service for some months. With their quick acceleration, easy riding qualities and stability at speed, they could whip the comparatively light and fast mail trains to schedule easily, making up time if necessary.

Although the GN had not owned or operated big passenger units like these before, there seemed to be plenty of experience to draw upon from the subsidiary Burlington which had been operating EMD diesel passenger units since the 1930's. Overlooked, however, was the fact that the Burlington was a "granger" railroad with an almost

469

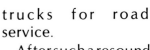

table top profile on its main lines out of Chicago as far west as Denver at the foot of the Rockies. The GN, on the other hand, had long grades in the Rocky Mountains and Cascades and miles of 1% ruling grade on the western approach to the Rockies. The E-7-A's, with their 2,000 hp and high gearing, were ideal as passenger power. But with a heavy load on a grade, and the speed dropped below 30 mph for sustained periods, the traction motors would start over-heating.

As in the operation of straight electric power, heat in the traction motors limited the amount of heavy tractive effort that could be sustained for long periods. Over-heating for a prolonged period would burn out the insulation and very quickly fuse the entire motor into a pile of useless copper windings. Traction motor problems began to plague the Empire Builder on the mountain grades in 1947, when it became longer and heavier with the extra coaches added for Seattle and Portland. It became necessary to take the E-7-A's out of the service for which they had been designed and replace them with the more versatile and lower geared 1,500 hp F-3's, F-5's and F-7's, classified by the GN as P-3's, P-5's and P-7's in passenger service.

By May, 1950 the GN had 183 diesel locomotives in service, with delivery expected on 119 more during the rest of 1950 and 1951. Of the 119 on order, only 20 were Alco products — half of which were yard switchers. Also in 1950, the GN placed their first order for the GP-7, after having had considerable success with the NW-5 series of 1946 (the predecessor of the GP series) and, prior to that, the NW-3 of 1939. Both the NW-3 and NW-5 were basically elongated 1,000 hp yard switchers with train heat equipment and FT type trucks for road service.

After such a resounding success with their smoothly contoured F series, which by now far and away dominated the diesel rosters of the United States, EMD surprised the railroads by touting what to some looked like a pair of skinny cracker boxes mounted on wheels with a cab sandwiched in between. The GP-7 (General Purpose Locomotive), however, was an immediate success; for it was equally efficient on the main line, on the branch, or even in the yard. Visibility for the crew was far better during backing moves, and the diesel's engines were readily accessible for servicing through doors along the sides of the hoods. The later GP-9, with better dynamic braking and with 1750 horsepower, was as functional as its slightly less powerful brother, (1,500 hp). The Great Northern ordered a total of fifty-six GP-7's and seventy-nine GP-9's.

Also purchased for specialized service were twenty-three (6 motor) SD-7's and twenty-seven SD-9's. These units, riding on 6 wheel trucks, could negotiate very light trackage, get down and lug all day if necessary below 10 mph, and never overheat a traction motor. Many were used as hump engines where their low crawling speed was ideal for pushing long cuts of cars up the hump and then kicking them a few at a time down into the yard.

From the purchase of the first NW-3 in 1939 through the last GP-20 (high hoods) to be delivered, the GN operated the GP's and SD's long nose forward for better crew protection in case of collision, particularly at grade crossings. In the early 1960's, with the delivery of the low nosed 2,250 hp turbocharged GP-30's, the GN began to operate short nose forward, because the increased forward visibility was a greater safety feature for the crew than the protection of the long hood. The GN purchased seventeen of the GP-30's and then came back again with an order for twenty-four 2,500 hp GP-35's. The horsepower race was on, and with it a return to the 6-wheel truck, which better utilized the increased horsepower.

The horsepower race was precipitated by the Alco Century series starting with the C424 (2,400 hp) in 1965, which was followed by the 2,500 hp C425 and finally the 3,600 hp C636. GE, too, had jumped on the high horsepower bandwagon with their U-25-B (2,500 hp), U-28-B (2,800 hp), and U-30-B (3,00 hp) — all mounted on 4 wheel trucks. The companion models, U-25-C, U-28-C and U-33-C, all rode on 6 wheel trucks.

GN ignored the high horsepower Alco Century series; for while Alco products had enjoyed a brief spell of popularity on the GN, maintenance problems forced their early demise. The GN bought its last Alcos (RS-3's) in 1953. Two of these and one RS-2, along with two four-unit sets of FA "covered wagons" purchased in the late 1940's, were sent to the subsidiary SP&S, which owned more Alcos (79 of them) than the GN, NP and CB&Q combined. The biggest user of Alco products in the Northwest, the SP&S seemingly had little trouble with them.

However, the GN did not ignore the new GE units, purchasing fifteen of the U-33-C's, six of the U-28-B's, and twenty-four of the U-25-B's. Still, out of a total fleet of 527 freight locomotives and 61 passenger locomotives in 1970 (just before merger), the GN owned only 45 locomotives which were built by manufacturers other than EMD — and these were the 45 GE units just mentioned.

Obviously standardization was not the only reason the GN stuck with EMD. Through the years, EMD locomotives had given little serious trouble. The shop forces were more familiar with EMD's products, and how to maintain and overhaul them; and engine crews preferred EMD products because of the familiar control stands. Even a seemingly minor EMD feature, such as individually controlled cab heaters for engineer and fireman, was important if the fireman preferred a relatively warm cab while the engineer preferred a cooler cab to help keep him alert in the early morning darkness.

As far as the GN was concerned, the horsepower race — and the dominance of EMD engines — reached its climax in 1966 with the purchase from EMD of a total of fourteen SDP-40 (3,000 hp) and SDP-45 (3,600 hp) locomotives for passenger service and forty-one SD-45 and F-45 cowl units for freight service. The F-45 cowl units were based in Havre, Montana, because the fully enclosed diesels were easier for both the engine crew and shop forces to check and service in the sub-zero temperatures common to the area. Accumulations of snow and ice on the exposed running boards of earlier models made it difficult to open and close the access panels. And walking along the icy, exposed gangway was extremely hazardous, especially when the train was moving. In the milder climates, where there was little problem with snow and ice, the SD (exposed gangway) models were preferred because the visibility from the cab of an SD or SDP model was considerably better. The fireman or engineer merely had to glance out the rear facing window to see if everything was running "all black" behind the engine units; and it was also easier for the head-end brakeman riding a trailing unit to check both the engine ahead and the cars behind. The engineer or fireman of an F-45 cowl unit had to lean far out of the cab to look back along the train, and at night, due to restricted clearances alongside many wayside structures, this could be very dangerous.

In retrospect, it was not at all surprising that the diesel also swept away the electrics in the mid-1950's. The beautiful Y class, chunky Z class, and monstrous W class were simply out of step with the new general operating concept of the road. The only real reason for their being kept in service was the 8 mile long Cascade Tunnel, where diesels could not work a heavy train upgrade through the tunnel without choking on their own exhaust gasses, as each succeeding unit picked up the overheated, exhaust-laden air of the units ahead. Even if the engines could have stood the strain, the crews could not tolerate the noxious oil fumes without being overcome.

The solution to this smoke problem was worked out by the Engineering and Electrical departments of the GN. It was decided that diesels could work through the tunnel if thousands of cubic feet of fresh air could be forced by huge fans from the east end downgrade through the tunnel and exhausted into open air at the west portal. The cooling air would carry away much of the super heated exhaust from the tunnel roof so that trailing units would not overheat and automatically cut out. Also fresh air passing by the crew in the

leading cab would eliminate any chance of their being overcome by fumes as the units ground upgrade at a steady 17 mph. During trial runs, and in actual practice, the ventilation system has worked well; although

the crews in the rear end helpers, a mile or so back, are somewhat less than charmed by the amount of exhaust smoke they are subjected to. Cascade Tunnel can be cleared in about 30 minutes. The new 7 mile long Flathead Tunnel in Montana, with two fans at the tunnel entrance over twice as powerful as the two 800 hp units in tunnel 15, can be cleared in something less than 18 minutes.

With the advent of tunnel ventilation, the electrics disappeared almost overnight. Engine crews still miss them, particularly for their extremely powerful regenerative braking that could hold back half again as much tonnage as they could pull. During the days of electric operation, it was a rare circumstance when the brakes were used at all, since the regenerative braking could and did keep thousands of tons under near perfect control on the 2.2% grades. By comparison, the diesels' dynamic braking holds back about one half of what they can pull. This is one of the reasons helpers are used coming down Stevens Pass.

The diesels of the late 60's and 70's, as different in performance, color, appearance, and size from the earlier models as the later Northerns and Mikados were from the early American Standards, still march upgrade in the Cascades and the Rockies at a steady 17 to 22 mph, not because they lack the horsepower, but out of deference to the strain drawbars will take. Helpers are still common to keep the slack bunched and to equalize the strain on drawbars of mile long 6,000-ton-plus freights. Out of Cashmere and Skykomish, freights wait for their helpers to couple in behind the caboose before the throttle is notched out; and the crew in the caboose ride the helper engines as a standard safety practice.

Many engineers will not bid for service on the "hill" (across the summits of the Cascades or Rockies), even though their seniority entitles them to it. The "hill crews" are a highly select group of engineers; and many of the firemen are also qualified engineers. Bringing a 6,000 ton train up and down the segments of 2.2% and 1.8% grades requires constant alertness to keep the slack either all bunched or all stretched out. A condition halfway between is an open invitation to a broken coupler or worse. Engine crews who have had the experience of a break-in-two on the mountain grades have no desire to repeat the experience. Digging a broken coupler and/or drawhead out of the dirt and snow between the rails and then replacing the heavy parts is exhausting, frustrating labor and can result in hours of delay.

In the past decade or so, much in railroading has changed. The cars are larger and they accelerate and roll more easily on their roller bearings. The big six wheel truck engines can ride as smoothly as a Pullman. Train orders have largely disappeared, replaced by the green and red indication of CTC signals set by a dispatcher hundreds of miles away. Train radios

in the cab and the caboose provide instant communications between crew members a mile apart. Trains communicate between themselves over the same radios and train location is measured not in blocks but in feet. Colors too have changed. The beautiful orange and olive was simplified in the early 1960's; and then in 1967/68, Big Sky Blue came into vogue for a brief period. Since merger into the BN in 1970, most GN units (as well as NP and SP&S) have been repainted in the now familiar Cascade Green and black, with huge white stylized engine numbers painted on the long diesel hood. The BN symbol has replaced the goat, the NP monad, and the SP&S red football as well. Largely the system that James J. Hill visualized and fought for, the BN today is the longest railroad in the land, powering freights from all points of the compass, reaching from the Gulf to Canada and from the Great Lakes to the Pacific.

G.E. No. 2, an experimental Steam/Turbine/Electric, tested on the Spokane Division about 1943, was theoretically capable of handling 125 cars at speeds up to 75 miles per hour. The huge unit burned out its generators while under test on the GN, and was returned to the G.E. shops in Erie, Pa., where it was scrapped as being too costly to repair.

No. 5100 was the first diesel purchased by the Great Northern in 1926. A "one-only", the 600 horsepower locomotive was a joint venture of Alco—Ingersoll Rand—GE.

Listed in the January, 1942 Great Northern Railway List of Equipment as an 0-4-4-4-4-4-4-0 type, No. 5900 was one of two semi-permanently coupled 3 unit diesels. The GN had a total of seven FT locomotives, all of them semi-permanently coupled as 2, 3 and 4 unit locomotives. All performed valuable work for the GN during World War II, particularly in the Marias Pass area—helping keep this strategic bottleneck open. Lack of ventilation in tunnel 15 (Cascade) kept them out of the Stevens Pass area. The FT's proved so useful, and so tireless, that the GN was completely convinced that the entire main line should be dieselized as quickly as possible following World War II.

Burlington Northern

Diesel-electric switcher No. 5300, at Minot in 1940, was one of two 900 horsepower switchers delivered to the GN in 1939. The Electro-motive built switcher was similar, in weight and tractive effort, to the class C-1 steam switchers built by Baldwin in 1918. Each locomotive weighed about 115 tons and exerted about 58,000 lbs. tractive effort. Beyond this point, however, there was very little similarity. Compared to the steam switcher, the diesel was available for service over 90% of the time, burned less than half as much fuel, required less maintenance and could pay for itself through the savings in five years. In addition it did not require a coaling or water tower, an ash pit, a water treatment plant, nor a 70 ton tender to carry fuel and water. It was more comfortable for the crew, in both summer and winter, and the better visibility vastly improved safety for the switching crews. Nevertheless, the diesel was not, at first, welcomed with open arms. Historically, steam power was railroad power, and traditions give way slowly and grudgingly, but a new generation of railroad men was coming onto the scene, and in just over a decade, steam was abandoned and the diesels powered the railroads.

No. 5332, a Baldwin 1,000 hp switcher built just prior to World War II is shown in the black color scheme as originally applied to all GN diesels. No. 24, a 1,200 hp switcher, was built by Baldwin—Lima—Hamilton—Westinghouse in 1953.

Great Northern Railway

Jim Vyverberg

Philip C. Johnson

Eastbound along the Kootenai River, No. 28 the Fast Mail, passes milepost 1344 in April, 1952. The usual assortment of heavyweight, lightweight, older and newer equipment, that characterized the Fast Mail, streams around the curve behind the F-3 diesels.

Motor car No. 2322, built by Brill—Westinghouse in 1927, was rebuilt by the GN in 1946 to power the Great Falls—Havre "Baby Streamliner". Listed as trains 237-238, the little streamliner provided Great Falls residents a connection with the Empire Builder.

With its lightweight coach, Motor 2300 is spotted for loading at Whitefish, in 1948. Running as train 246, it made three round trips per day between Whitefish, Columbia Falls and Kalispell. Perhaps better known as a "gas-electric", 2300 had a 220 hp gasoline engine that powered the generator—visible through the first door opening. The generator, in turn, supplied the direct current to the traction motors on the lead truck. As of 1950, the GN still had 30 of these "Motors" in service.

479

Extra 423 East slowly follows steam powered SP&S train No. 2 across the
Spokane River Bridge in 1950.

No. 187 at Seattle and No. 194 at Fargo were a part of a 1946
order to EMD for 10 NW-5's. Listed by the railroad as class RS-
2, the 1,000 hp road switchers were the predecessors of the
ubiquitous GP series.

W. C. Whittaker

NW-3 No. 179 at St. Paul in 1948, was one of the first road service switching types purchased by the GN in 1939-42. The NW-3's were fitted with a train heat boiler for light passenger train service, and this accounts for the unusual shape of the elongated cab.

W. C. Whittaker

Extra 182 East—a work train—is doing maintenance work in front of the ornate station at Palouse, Washington in June, 1947. The station and tracks, constructed by the Spokane, Coeur d'Alene and Palouse Railway, were acquired by the GN in the 1920's.

Philip C. Johnson

At Interbay roundhouse, switcher 124 idles out of stall No. 19 towards the turntable and its daily assignment in the yard.

Delivered to the road in 1944, this 1,000 horsepower Alco RS-1 road switcher at Minot, was one of the first of the road service diesels built for the GN by Alco.

Casey Adams

John M. Budd, President of the Great Northern from 1951 until its merger with the Burlington Northern, began his career in railway operations and advanced to a division superintendency. He entered the Military Railway Service in 1942—serving in Algeria, Italy, France and Germany—and upon returning to the GN became Assistant General Manager Lines East. In 1947, he was elected President of the Chicago & Eastern Illinois Railroad with headquarters in Chicago. Mr. Budd returned to the GN as Vice President of Operations, in 1949, and in May, 1951, was elected President—a position also held some years previously by his father, Ralph Budd.

Kim Forman

Ed Mueller collection

Behind a trio of F-7's, an ore drag at Wrenshall, Minnesota (just a few miles west of
Superior, Wisconsin) heads for the ore docks at Allouez in 1959.

Business Car A-26 was rebuilt from a standard heavyweight observation, after World
War II. Steel framed with wood posts and painted in streamliner colors in the
1950's, it was scrapped after new lightweight business cars were built.

Stan Styles

Alco S-2 switchers No. 2 and No. 4 at Spokane in 1955, were built for the railroad in 1950. Rated at 1,000 hp, the 10 switchers of this class were ordered from Alco under A.F.E. (authorization for expenditure) number 78313.

High above the Spokane River, engine No. 1 crosses the trestle with a load for Fort George Wright, in March, 1951.

Dr. Philip R. Hastings

Alco 183 trundles across an old trestle about 8 miles out of Moscow, Idaho in May, 1947. The trestle was built by the Spokane, Coeur d'Alene and Palouse Railway, a heavy interurban line, purchased by the GN in order to gain entry into the rich agricultural areas south and east of Spokane, and thereby compete directly with the NP and Milwaukee that dominated the traffic in this area.

Philip C. Johnson

A diesel powered freight works its way past Mt. Index up the I% towards Skykomish. With many of the 10 degree curves removed, the grade and heavy train are all in a days work for the 6,000 horsepower freighter. Many of the veteran hoggers were not sorry to see the steam go, although they were sorry to see the enormously powerful, clean, and virtually trouble free electrics go from the "Hill".

The Cascadian, No. 6 eastbound, comes into Spokane past St. Luke's Hospital and the UP yards, in the late afternoon, July, 1950. The open-end platform observation car is thought to have come from the Oriental Limited, and rebuilt into a Parlor/Cafe/Observation car. Diesel 227 is on the head-end, where just a year before S-2's, bumped from main line passenger/mail service, were powering the Cascadian between Wenatchee and Spokane.

A rider coach, carrying the rear markers, and seven cars of mail, bound for Seattle, follow the three unit diesel across the Spokane River towards the SP&S Junction at Fort Wright. No. 27 has just left Spokane, and the vestibule door on the coach is still open, while on the end of the roof, a gyrating red Mars light is faintly visible. At sunset, long shadows have dimmed much of the landscape, and No. 27 is off the timecard by several hours, but fast track is ahead. The speed limit has been raised to 79 miles per hour with the advent of diesel operation, and coach passengers will be getting a fast ride once No. 27 clears the interlocking at the SP&S Junction.

Dr. Philip R. Hastings

Dr. Philip R. Hastings

Dr. Philip R. Hastir

With speed down to a fast walk, the eastbound Western Star eases across the deck truss bridge, located almost directly over Spokane Falls. Ahead is the GN station on Havermale Island. Crossing this bridge was quite a treat for the passengers. From the car windows or vestibule, no portion of the bridge deck was visible on the far side. The view was straight down into the rushing waters of the Spokane River, only a few feet from the precipitous drop of the main falls.

Casey Adams

In a painting by the dean of American railroad illustrator's, Howard Fogg, a diesel powered GN freight tops the Montana Rockies in 1957. This painting was one of a series of calendar illustrations for the Union Tank Car Company.

Built by EMD in 1950, Nos. 307A and 307B, F-7 type locomotives rated at 1,500 hp, were classed by the railroad as F-3-7's. The F-7B units were fitted with a train heat generator, and in 1950 five of the F-7B's were numbered 500B-505B, for use as B units between two E-7A's. In 1952 F's used in freight service were geared for 65 mph, while passenger F units — classed by the railroad as P-3's, P-5's (rebuilds of the 3's) and P-7's — were geared for 89 mph. The GN did so much rebuilding in their own shops that a quick visual identification of a certain class became increasingly difficult as the locomotives became older. Late model stainless steel grills for example were applied to earlier models when they were rebuilt, giving an early F-3 or P-3 the external appearance of a late F-7. Tractive effort of the F series, both passenger and freight, ranged right around 60,000 lbs— somewhat higher than this for late models and lower for early models.

Train 23, the "Badger" powered by E-7 No. 512
between Minneapolis and St. Paul, March 14, 1970.

Ed Traficante

Charles R. Wood

Dr. Philip R. Hastings

Powered by an Alco RS-3, extra 223 South hustles down the Colville River Valley, enroute to Hillyard from Kettle Falls on the 3rd Subdivision of the Cascade Division. Kettle Falls, once one of the most spectacular sights along the Columbia River, has long since been inundated by the waters of man made Roosevelt Lake, backed up behind Coulee Dam. Gone also now are the Alco RS-3's, with their smoky exhaust and peculiar burbling sound.

Never really popular with the GN, a pair of Alco road switchers ride the turntable at Interbay. The GN preferred EMD products, and the Alco's were sold to the subsidiary SP&S as quickly as possible.

Great Northern Railway

An E-7, bumped out of service on the Empire Builder by the more versatile
F units, is refueled at Interbay. In this mid 1950's scene, the E's were
running out of Seattle on the Internationals to Vancouver,
B.C. With their 2,000 horsepower and fast gearing, they could easily run
at speeds in excess of 100 mph. Below 30 mph however, on sustained grades
and pulling hard, their traction motors could overheat. On the water
level grades to and from Vancouver, this was not a problem, but regrettably,
the numerous grade crossings on this subdivision effectively
restricted their real speed capabilities.

An E-7 powers train 236, the Butte/Havre local, near Silver City, Montana in 1952. The heavyweight steel equipment has been modernized and repainted to blend better with the lightweight streamlined equipment.

W.R. McGee

The four units and 80 cars of Extra 408 East pull by the Empire Builder at Sieben, Montana. Far to the north, slides and washouts along the Kootenai River have put the GN main line out of service. At Sieben, the passing track will hold only 43 cars, so the dispatcher has put the fast running No. 1 into the hole, and Extra 408 East growls by on its way to Great Falls in the spring of 1948.

The placid waters of the Spokane River above the Falls reflect the buildings of downtown Spokane and the famous clock tower of the GN/SP&S station, built in 1902 on Havermale Island. Of all the structures on the island, only the tower was saved, and became the focal point of Expo '74. Today the tower remains as a monument to the railroad industry, and its role in the development of Spokane and the Pacific Northwest.

June, 1951 Dr. Philip R. Hastings

Read Down	SEATTLE-EVERETT-BELLINGHAM-VANCOUVER			Read Up	
Streamlined Internationals				Streamlined Internationals	
360 Daily	358 Daily	Miles	**TABLE 11** Pacific Standard Time	357 Daily	359 Daily
2 45	8 00	0	Lv **Seattle♦ 10, 12** Ar	11 05	4 45
63 15	8 30	18	" Edmonds	φ10 30	4 12
3 36	8 53	33	" **Everett 10** "	10 10	•3 45
—	—	41	" Marysville	—	—
—	—	48	" English	—	—
—	f 9 29	57	" Stanwood	9 29	—
4 28	9 47	70	" **Mount Vernon** "	9 13	2 55
	9 53	74	" Burlington	f 9 05	
5 10	10 29	98	" **Bellingham** "	8 30	2 16
	f10 43	107	" Ferndale		
5 38	10 57	120	" **Blaine, Wash**	8 01	1 46
			U. S.-Canadian Boundary		
5 46	11 06	123	" White Rock, B. C. "	7 52	1 33
	f11 12	128	" Crescent Beach		
6 18	11 38	144	" **New Westminster**	7 23	1 05
6 40	11 59	156	Ar **Vancouver, B. C.** Lv	7 00	12 45

The southbound International at New Westminster, B.C. grinds around the tight curve on the approach to the Fraser River Bridge. Speed over the draw bridge is strictly limited to 10 mph, and the approaches are controlled by absolute stop signals.

Stan Styles

Above:
At Burlington, Washington, a pair of Alco hood units lead a freight north towards the Canadian border, in the 1950's. It was then still GN practice to run hood units with the long hood forward, as a protection to the crew. With the advent of newer power, such as the GP-30, it quickly became the practice to run with the short nose forward. Increased visibility over the short nose was more a safety factor than the longer hood.

Above right:
On the south side of the Spokane River Valley, across from the GN main, an RS-3 Alco, bound for Moscow, Idaho, is making easy work out of the 1% grade as it leads a southbound local freight upgrade out of the valley on the old Spokane, Coeur d' Alene and Palouse electric line.

Right:
With class lamps and indicator boards lighted, Alco Road Switcher 217 idles on the ready track at Interbay roundhouse, Seattle in the late summer of 1966. Alco power was not widely used on the GN. Only 25 of the 631 diesel units on the roster in 1965 were Alco built, and 10 of these were yard switchers.

Dr. Philip R. Hastings

Dr. Philip R. Hastings

North of Spokane, on the Kettle Falls Branch, a three unit Alco FA
freighter eases back through the siding switch at the Northwest
Magnesite plant. At the same site, the trio of Alco covered wagons
sets out four hopper cars. Even with the fine control possible using diesel
freighters, this move required careful handling and a deft touch on the
air brakes, lest the hopper cars became a part of the plant structure.
Alco freighters, not overly popular with the motive power department,
after a brief stint in main line service on the Cascade Division, worked
the Kettle Falls Branch for some years.

It is high water in the late spring of 1952, at the confluence of
the Yaak and Kootenai Rivers in Western Montana, almost to
the Idaho line. The waters of the Yaak River, flowing down
from the Purcell Mountains, have met the Kootenai, whose
banks are overflowing, as an Alco powered Livestock Extra
moves east.
Great Northern Railway

Great Northern GP-7's, numbered from 600 to 655, were built by
EMD in 1950, 1951 and 1953. No. 611 is at Seattle in 1955, and No.
626 is at Burlington, Washington in 1968. Nos. 600 601 and 602 are
shown cutting off the Cascadian at Skykomish in the 1950's. The
Cascadian did not require 3 units, but these GP's will take a
westward freight back to Seattle from Skykomish.

Stan Styles

In eastern British Columbia on
the Kettle Falls — Nelson B.C.
branch, a pair of GP-9's do the
local switching at Salmo.

Dr. Philip R. Hastings

Out of Willmar, Minnesota, train No. 419 — behind four GP-20's — is about to cross over the rails of the Illinois Central at Wren Jct., Iowa. Interesting is the restrictive — rather than stop — indication of the GN block type signal. The position of the lower quadrant IC signals also indicate a restrictive rather than a stop signal, even with the lead unit of the GN freight fouling the IC main.

GP-9's with three different color schemes and two different brake systems: Nos. 724 and 690, in gold striped olive and orange at Seattle in 1962, clearly show the familiar dynamic brake bulges along the top edge of the hood. Without dynamic braking are No. 678, a battle scarred veteran in the simplified olive and orange at Burlington in 1967, and No. 734 at Vancouver in 1969 repainted in Big Sky Blue with a side panel added to carry the trademark and goat logo.

Stan Styles

Freshly washed, as befits the occasion, GP-7 No. 604 pulls the
short consist of the last eastbound Cascadian along the
Skykomish River near Monroe in August, 1959.

SD-7 No. 550 at Minot in May, 1968, and BN SD-7 No. 6007 (formerly GN 557)
at Spokane in July, 1971 were rated at 1,500 hp, while the later SD-9 No. 599
shown in the lower photograph at Waneta, B.C. in September, 1967 was rated
at 1,750 hp. Both the 23 SD-7's and 27 SD-9's, built for the GN, made excellent
drag or branch line power, as well as "hump" locomotives. The six wheel
trucks reduced the axle loading, while the lower gear ratio made it possible
for them to work hour after hour at drag speeds without overheating
their traction motors.

Ted Bronstein

The whine of dynamic braking fills the air, as four F's and a GP-9 lead a long eastbound freight down the 1% between Fairchild and Fort Wright, on the First Subdivision of the Cascade Division. Ahead, beyond milepost 1481.7, another long curve swings to the right past Fort George Wright (junction with the SP&S), and the freight continues on across the long bridge into Spokane.

Above right: A trio of brand new GP-30's pose for their official photograph, before entering service. The color scheme of olive green and Omaha orange with gold striping—so striking on the earlier F models—was superceded by this simplified scheme, which unfortunately did not particularly enhance the car-like styling of the GP-30. Seventeen GP-30's were purchased by the GN, but larger orders for EMD locomotives did not follow until the introduction of the GP-35.

The "prairie skyscraper" town of Conrad lies between Great Falls and Shelby in the wheat raising belt of north central Montana. Five GP series diesels move out with a full trainload of wheat for the markets of the world.

The 3,600 horsepower SD-45's, purchased by the GN in 1966 to power the Empire Builder and the Western Star, were repainted, two years later, in the new GN color scheme of Big Sky Blue, white and dark gray. Engine crews like these big locomotives: they ride well on the 6 wheel trucks; the noise level is low; visibility over the low nose is excellent; and typical of diesel units with narrow hoods, the visibility to the rear is also good, enabling the crew to observe the train while rounding curves without having to lean far out of the cab.

It is late summer, and in the pre-dawn light, a brace of SD-45's hustle west across Montana with 5,000 tons of wheat. With diesel power, roller bearings, CTC and train radio, the long freight is making time that would have put the steam powered Builder to shame.

The afternoon Portland-Seattle train makes a station stop in Tacoma. Tacoma's Union
Station, serving the GN, NP and UP, opened its doors for the first time on May 1, 1911.
It was designed by Reed and Stem of St. Paul, the same architectural firm that designed
Grand Central Station in New York City and King Street Station in Seattle. Present plans
by BNL Development Corporation, a BN subsidiary, call for complete renovation
of the old station in a project known as "Depot Galleria", which also includes new
construction of retail services on 20 acres of railroad property adjacent to the station.

No. 27, the westbound Western Star/Fast Mail, has drawn a pair of 3,000 hp SDP-40's for power. During a late afternoon stop at Wenatchee in 1969, No. 27's engine crews are changing while the train is being inspected and head-end work is being done.
Stan Styles

The southbound Seattle-Portland "Pool Train", on a trestle with an SDP-40 leading, skims over the freshly plowed field of a truck farm just south of Kent in June, 1967.
Robert E. Oestreich

U-25B No. 2505 leads a quartet of modern high horsepower diesels across the rolling prairie out of Minot. Rated at 2,500 hp, 24 of the U-25B's were purchased from General Electric in 1960 and 1965.

Stan Styles

No. 3034 at Havre and No. 3022 at Whitefish were among the 24 GP-35's ordered from EMD in 1964/65. Rated at 2,500 hp, the GP-35's were the first of the "second generation" diesels purchased from EMD.

Stan Styles

No. 2527 was one of five G.E. built 2,800 hp U-28B's delivered in 1966.

Just minutes out of Butte, Train 236 tops the Continental Divide at Elk Park, Montana over track constructed by the Montana Central Railway. RDC No. 2350 went into service on July 30, 1956 as Trains 42-43 between Great Falls and Billings, and Trains 235-236 between Great Falls and Butte. The RDC's, assigned to this run, made the round trip between Butte and Great Falls during the day, and at night, made an additional round trip between Butte and Billings, a total of 810 miles every 24 hours. July 5, 1959, Trains 42-43 were discontinued, and on November 6, 1961, Trains 235-236 were also discontinued. The RDC then operated for a time as Trains 3-4 between Great Falls and Shelby, connecting there with the eastbound Empire Builder.

Charles R. Wood

A freight, bound for Seattle's Interbay yard, rumbles across bridge No. 4 at Salmon Bay. A landmark in Northwest Seattle for at least 60 years, the huge bascule bridge, close to the entrance of the Hiram Chittenden Locks connecting Puget Sound and Lake Union, is a key link on the Great Northern (now BN) between Seattle and Everett.

The lead units of the Builder thump across the rail joints on the Salmon Bay drawbridge, just north of Interbay yard, in Seattle. Eastbound, the Builder is under CTC control by the operator at Interbay.

Charles R. Wood

Great Northern Railway   5 photos

March, 1966, the greatest snowstorm in 104 years closed the line on the Surrey Cutoff between Minot and Fargo for 8 days.

520

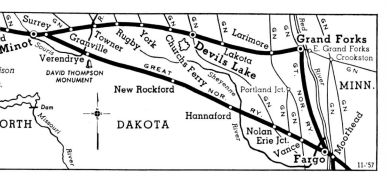

Observation, business or official private car? Probably car B 2 was all of these at various times. In this 1961 scene at Wenatchee, car B 2, all 74'1" of it, is listed as "Rail Detector". Actually it is serving as the crew car for the rail detector car, spotted just ahead on the same siding.

The long wooden pullman green baggage car on six wheel trucks, is loaded with a myriad of roof smoke jacks, ventilators, steps, springs, grab-irons and safety chains. This car has been out of main line service for some years, and the neatly stencilled gold letters on the lower right corner now read "System Elect'l Crew No. 8 Lines West".

Walt Grecula

Built after World War II, the beautiful station serving Sauk Center, Minnesota, is a credit to both the railroad and the community. Mrs. Rachel Moore, a homesteader, laid out the townsite in 1863 and opened its first store. Located about 115 miles northwest of St. Paul at the head of the Lake Park Region of Minnesota (which comprises nearly one-third of the more than 10,000 lakes in Minnesota), Sauk Center leaped into national prominence when it was reported to be the locale of Sinclair Lewis' famous novel "Main Street, U.S.A.".

Special heavy-duty bulkhead end flatcars are required to move aluminum ingots from the Anaconda Aluminum Company smelter in Columbia Falls, Montana. The ingots on the flat car, shown here, weigh 8,800 lbs. each, and the total load on each car is nearly 90 tons.

Dawn at Wolf Point, Montana—once a steamboat landing on the Missouri River—and wheat flows from the elevator into covered hoppers of the Great Northern. The Great Northern is now a part of the 24,000 mile Burlington Northern system, the longest rail line in the United States, and the major grain carrier of the entire Western Hemisphere.

Pete Volkert, Burlington Northern

One of the largest grain carriers in the world, the GN moved enormous quantities of wheat from Washington, Montana, the Dakotas and Minnesota. In 1971, the BN (successor to the GN) hauled over one billion tons of grain, a large share coming from Montana's Golden Triangle—encompassing an area roughly defined by Havre, Great Falls and Shelby. All interstate shipments of grain are subject to inspection, and at Hillyard, government inspectors take samples of grain to determine the protein, moisture and weight content, and to determine whether any foreign objects are present. From this sampling, the class of the grain is determined and the price that it will bring.

Great Northern Railway

At the Scott Paper Company's unloading facility in Everett, a 100 ton capacity chip car is inclined at a 45 degree angle to unload the wood chips. These cars were specially built for wood chip service, and may be seen in long cuts on many of the BN trains in the Pacific Northwest.

Great Northern Railway

The signals of the Union Pacific at UP Junction are in the foreground, as Spokane Portland & Seattle Alco 4244 pushes a long cut of cars back down the main line just beyond Tacoma's Union Station. Climbing the grade, a long Union Pacific freight, its heavily laden cars creaking, groaning and protesting at the side thrusts imposed upon the couplings and running gear, heads toward the old NP "Prairie Line". The unusual UP operation is due to a burned out trestle on the GN-NP-UP main line south of Tacoma.

Above right: After the merger of the Great Northern, Northern Pacific, Chicago Burlington & Quincy, and Spokane Portland & Seattle Railway in 1970, as the Burlington Northern, many strange appearing combinations of equipment and colors began to appear. Green, Orange, Sky Blue, Vermillion, Black, Gold—it seemed as if the entire spectrum had been included. At Tacoma, Willard Wilkinson caught a GN-NP nose to tail lash-up of F units with a green and yellow NP buggy coupled behind. Newspapers in the Northwest had poked a little fun at the new name, Burlington Northern, but the one real regret of many, was the elimination of the GN Goat—Rocky. The logo was world famous, and immediately recognizable even by those who didn't understand English.

W. Wilkinson

Robert E. Oestreich

Behind an SDP-40 and three F units, the Empire Builder approaches
the west portal of Cascade Tunnel in June, 1969. Behind is the 2.2%
grade, stretching 17 miles back to Skykomish. Ahead lies the
nearly 8 mile long tunnel—and then—downgrade into Central
Washington and east.

A westward freight whines downgrade through the fresh snow and early darkness of a winter day in the Rockies. The long freight crossing Nimrod Bridge, 14 miles below the summit of Marias Pass, is still under the firm hand of dynamic braking, and the slack is bunched tight against the trailing diesel unit.

Tom Hoff

Out on the high plains of the Dakotas, a drag leaves Minot, behind a trio of
GP-20's. Long a GN practice, until the advent of the low nose GP-30's, GN
hood diesels were operated long hood forward as protection to the crew.
Visibility was somewhat restricted, but the crew was much better protected in
case of a grade crossing incident. Crews today prefer the infinitely better
visibility of the low hood short nose diesels.

U-33C No. 2541, at Wenatchee in 1969, was one of 24 of this
3,300 hp class delivered by GE in 1968 and 1969.

The Canadian flag snaps in the wind as the Winnipeg Limited stops at the customs and immigration station at Emerson Jct., Manitoba. Train No. 7 has left GN rails and is now on the CNR for the last lap of the run into Winnipeg (Canada's fourth largest city, and the western headquarters for both the Canadian National and the Canadian Pacific), some 65 miles to the north. Foreground track connects with the NP line south to Pembina, N.D. At St. Cloud, Minnesota the passenger station is viewed from the vestibule of the sleeper Invya Pass, assigned to train No. 7. EMD E-7-A No. 510, on the point of No. 7 was part of the 1947 delivery of six similar passenger diesels built for service on the GN. Geared for speeds in excess of 100 mph, few of the E-7's had the opportunity to demonstrate their capability. While assigned to the Builder, they were found to be lacking in power on heavy grades, and soon found their way onto the head end of lighter trains such as the Winnipeg Limited and the Seattle/Vancouver Internationals. Viewed through the train shed at Winnipeg Union Station, No. 510 has just been cut off the Winnipeg Limited after its 7:50 AM arrival from Minneapolis—12 hours and 504 miles to the south. The slow schedule did little to create demand and the service was dropped following the formation of Amtrak in 1971.

Dr. Philip R. Hastings

The WINNIPEG LIMITED
BETWEEN ST. PAUL-MINNEAPOLIS-WINNIPEG
Detailed Schedule on Page 7, Tables 2 and 3

Read Down				Read Up
	7 Daily	Central Standard Time	**8** Daily	
. . . . . .	7 55	Lv St. Paul . . . . Ar	7 30	. . . . .
. . . . . .	8 15	Ar Minneapolis Lv	7 05	. . . . .
. . . . . .	8 30	Lv Minneapolis . . . . Ar	7 00	. . . . .
. . . . . .	9 40	Ar St. Cloud Lv	5 40	. . . . .
. . . . . .	9 45	Lv St. Cloud . . . . Ar	5 35	. . . . .
. . . . . .	10 38	" Sauk Centre Lv	4 39	. . . . .
. . . . . .	11 03	" Alexandria . . . . "	4 06	. . . . .
. . . . . .	11 57	" Fergus Falls . . . . "	3 09	. . . . .
. . . . . .	12 43	" Barnesville . . . . "	2 30	. . . . .
. . . . . .	1 12	Lv Moorhead . . . . "	1 58	. . . . .
. . . . . .	1 15	Ar Fargo Lv	1 55	. . . . .
. . . . . .	1 25	Lv Fargo . . . . Ar	1 45	. . . . .
. . . . . .	f 2 07	Lv Hillsboro Lv	f12 58	. . . . .
. . . . . .	2 47	Ar Grand Forks Lv	12 17	. . . . .
. . . . . .	3 10	Lv Grand Forks . . . . Ar	11 59	. . . . .
. . . . . .	3 44	" Crookston Passenger Sta. . Lv	11 26	. . . . .
. . . . . .	4 25	" Warren . . . . "	10 44	. . . . .
. . . . . .	7 50	Ar Winnipeg Lv	7 30	. . . . .

A GN freight approaches a short tunnel at Libby Dam site in 1968. The construction of the dam overhead and the rockwork on the banks, has necessitated a change in the track location to some 60' riverward from the original alignment. The total railroad relocation of 60 miles between Stryker and Jennings, Montana included the building of the seven mile long Flathead Tunnel (second only to Cascade Tunnel in the western hemisphere). Drilling on the tunnel was started September 30, 1966. It was "holed through" in June, 1968 and completed and put into service in October, 1970.

U.S. Army Corps of Engineers

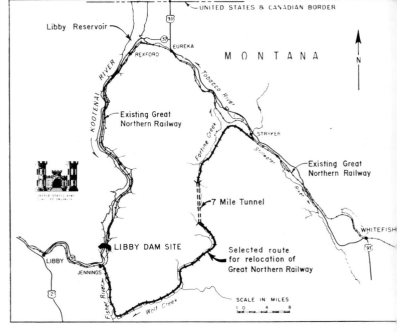

The first Chairman of the Board of Directors of the new Burlington Northern, John M. Budd, officiates at the formal dedication of Flathead Tunnel near Stryker, Montana on November 7, 1970. The north portal of the tunnel is the site of the twin 2,000 horsepower ventilating fans used to clear diesel exhaust gases from the tunnel. Experience with Cascade Tunnel ventilation led to the tripling of the horsepower of the fans. As a result, Flathead Tunnel can be ventilated in 18 minutes as compared to 28 minutes to clear Cascade Tunnel.

Libby Dam on the Kootenai River was completed in 1971. The concrete gravity type dam—420' high and 3,056' across the crest—produces 420,000 KW with an ultimate capacity of 840,000 KW. Designed as both a power producing and flood control dam, flood storage was started in 1972. The reservoir pool is 90 miles long and stretches nearly 42 miles into Canada with 83% of the storage within the USA.

The first train crosses the new GN main line between Stryker and Jennings, Montana. The new line, with sixty miles of new railroad construction and the new seven mile long Flathead Tunnel, was shorter by some 15 miles than the old line. It eliminated 71 curves, and reduced maximum curvature from 4 degrees 24 minutes to 2 degrees 24 minutes. However, the ruling grade westbound increased from .25% to 1% and increased eastbound from .7% to 1%, with .46% in the tunnel east to west. Interestingly, the relocation of the road along the Fisher River, south of Jennings, follows much of the 1890 alignment that had been abandoned because of 1.5% grades over Haskell Pass.

Just west of Skykomish, between Index and Reiter, the main line of the Great Northern crosses the Skykomish River over bridge 1750.9 in the spring of 1965. The bridge was part of a multi-million dollar project designed to eliminate the 10 degree curves that had slowed operations on the steady 1% grade since the building of the line in the late 1890's.
Phil Kohl

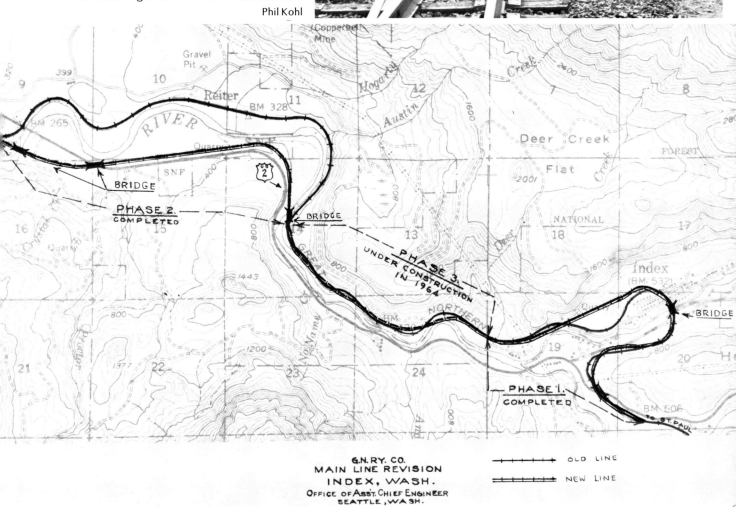

G.N. RY. CO.
MAIN LINE REVISION
INDEX, WASH.
OFFICE OF ASST. CHIEF ENGINEER
SEATTLE, WASH.

OLD LINE
NEW LINE

535

A GN freight, powered by brand new U-33C's, crosses the Skykomish River above Sunset Falls in 1969.

Great Northern Railway

The first rays of sunshine light the cab of SD-40 No. 887 — leading four other units, 101 cars, and 3 helper units — on train No. 78 eastbound at Skykomish in September, 1975. Moments before, engineer Bob Smith had spoken into the radio, "The air is released on the helper, we have a clear block". Helpers have bunched the slack tight, the road engines begin to pull, and the 5,772 tons of the 5,900′ long train slowly moves out on the main. Below, No. 78 climbs the 2.2% towards Cascade Tunnel.

Charles R. Wood

The Fireman's view of the approach to the West Portal of Cascade Tunnel. Freight train speed, eastbound through the tunnel, is restricted to 17 mph, and once inside the bore, the ride seems interminable — consuming nearly half an hour. Enginemen in the lead unit hardly notice the multiple diesels' exhaust gas and steady roar, but the crew of a helper on the "hind end" behind the caboose get the full benefit of the smoke and gas. The ride becomes a game of watching the numbered lighted safety bays — 21 of them — 1,200 to 2,400 feet apart. The block signals are spaced two miles apart, with an additional tunnel door signal close to the east entrance. Westbound, in the afternoon of a bright day, once inside, it is possible to see the opposite portal. It appears as a tiny bright dot, almost like a distant star on a clear night.

Charles R. Wood

Fireman David Vincent is out on the front platform of 887 as train No. 78 eases to a stop on the 2.2% descending grade at Berne. Meeting No. 77 grinding upgrade, the fireman and engineer both look over the running gear of the opposing train for any sign of dragging or hot equipment, because even at low speed, any failure within the confines of tunnel No. 15, or anywhere else on this mountain grade, can cause serious trouble.
Charles R. Wood

Above: A BN work train advances on new trackage laid along Sarpy, Beaver, Bear and Horse Creeks into the low sulphur coal reserve area of Montana's Big Horn Country.

Burlington Northern

Left above: Late in the afternoon of April 30, 1971, one year after the merger of the Great Northern into the BN and the day before Amtrak took over the operation, the last Burlington Northern eastbound Empire Builder crosses a bridge near Sunset Falls.

Robert E. Oestreich

Left: Ending 42 years of continuous service, the last westbound Empire Builder rumbles over the bridge at Salmon Bay, headed for Seattle's King Street Station early on the sunny morning of May 2, 1971.

Robert E. Oestreich

The pillars of the new BN bridge, crossing Latah Creek, rise 190' in the air to the "weathered steel" box girder spans, some of which are 160' long. The impressive new structure, practically maintenance free, will help route the railroad around the city center of Spokane to BN's preferred route connecting at Lyons, Washington.

Burlington Northern

On August 24, 1972, a Burlington Northern unit train, with 10,000 tons of low sulfur coal, pulls out of the newly opened strip mine at Decker, Montana bound for Havanna, Ill. where the 105 cars of Montana coal will be mixed with eastern coal and barged to Commonwealth Edison generating plants in the Chicago area. Not far from here, close to the Wyoming border, General Custer and the 7th Cavalry were decimated by the Sioux in the battle of the Little Bighorn in 1876.

Spokane Mayor David Rogers takes his turn driving the "gold spike" on December 6, 1972, completing the new 4,240' Latah Creek Bridge. To the far right is Rod Lindsay, Chairman of the Expo board. Standing between the two is Robert M. Downing, Vice Chairman and Chief Operating Officer of the Burlington Northern. The line improvement project at Spokane cost more than $16 million, and includes 7 miles of new track and 11 new bridges.

Viewed from Windy Point Tunnel, where GN steam and electric
powered trains once fought their way to Tye, a westbound
BN freight emerges from the "new" Cascade Tunnel,
in the summer of 1977. Included as one of the units is a Southern
Pacific SD45T-2 "tunnel motor".

Mike Pearsall

Appendix
CABOOSES

The most distinguishing features on GN cabooses, whether the plywood sheathed cars of the early '40s, the little dinky transfer cabooses or the imposing Hutchinson Branch "Hutch caboose", were the bright vermilion paint and the huge "goat" symbols on the sides. Highly visible in the daytime, they were made more visible at night by the addition of reflective strips applied to the corners and along the bottom of each side.

Photos: Top, Charles R. Wood.
Left, E. Traficante.
Right, PFM collection.

Caboose X137, one of the earliest GN 8 wheel types, has been assigned to a wire-stringing gang in Stevens Pass in 1927. It is considerably larger and quite different than the road caboose below. Caboose 90777, a 25 footer built in 1924, shows off the squarish lines and details that were to distinguish GN cabooses for several decades. The handsome 90777 also features one of the big GN heralds that came into use in the mid-twenties. Conjecture among GN employees at the time was that the facial expression of "Old Bill" was inspired by the visage of James J. Hill.

Great Northern Railway

Cabooses X375 and X1, in the top
and bottom photos, are modernized
versions of the standard 25' road
cabooses built between 1914 and 1930.
End rails have been changed to the
square GN design, new lower steps
have been added and hand grabs have
been striped in black and white.
The cupola side windows, now double,
fill nearly the entire side of the cupola;
while the end windows have been
made smaller with safety bars added inside.
Caboose X1 was assigned to the Pacific
Coast R. R. when it was acquired by
the GN in 1951. While several railroads
used cabooses of GN design, only the
Pacific Coast had its name appear on the
sides. Caboose X124, in the center photo,
is a standard 30 footer of the 1941 series,
like most built with tongue and
groove siding. A few, such as the
famous Ambroid GN model,
were plywood sheathed.

upper & center Dr. Philip Hastin
lower Charles R. Wood collectic

546

Steel sheathed cabooses X1 through X30 were built by the GN St. Cloud shops in 1958, following extensive testing of the similar No. X130. Some of the series rode on express trucks, making them the best riding cabooses of all GN models and the most suitable for high speed service. Still, these big 32' buggys were not as popular with the crews as the earlier wood sheathed cabooses because of the increased interior noise level. In 1960, for the first time in decades, the GN turned to an outside supplier and purchased cabooses from International Car Division of Morrison International Corp. X111, a 30' caboose built in 1967 and finished in Big Sky Blue, is typical of the extended vision cabooses supplied to the road. The earlier models were vermillion with either a black or aluminum roof, while the later blue versions were finished only with an aluminum roof and a new simpler all-white herald.

ROSTER OF MOTIVE POWER

NUMBER & CLASS	BUILDER	DATE BUILT & WHEEL ARRANGEMENT	CYL. DIMENSIONS & DRIVER DIA.	WEIGHT ON DRIVERS	NOTES
1-3 (ST. P&P)	SMITH & JACK	1861 4-4-0	No Data		Named Wm. Crooks, E. Rice, Minnesota
4-7 (ST. P&P)	D. COOKE	1866-67 4-4-0	No Data		Named Itasca, Anoka, St. Paul, & St. Cloud #5 to GN as #4
8-11 (ST. P&P)	MASON	1867-69 4-4-0	No Data		Named G.L. Becker, F.R. Delano, Jared Benson, Jud Rice 10-11 to GN as #5-6
12-15 (ST. P&P)	COOKE	1868-69 4-4-0	No Data		Named Wayzata, Willmar, Litchfield, H. Trott 12-15 to GN as #7-10
3	BROOKS	1879 0-4-0	No data		Ex-ST. P. M&M first 51
14-16	BROOKS	1881 0-4-0	do		Ex-ST. P. M&M 87-89
17-20	ROGERS	1882 0-4-0	do		Ex-ST. P. M&M 90-93
13 A-1	ROGERS	1879 0-6-0	16x20'' 49''	——	
47 A-3	ROGERS	1890 0-6-0	17x24'' 55''	90000	
48 A-3	ROGERS	1891 0-6-0	17x24'' 55''	67050	
27-29 A-4	BROOKS	1882 0-6-0	do		
32-33 A-5	BROOKS	1896 0-6-0	18x24'' 49''	87300	Formerly D-5
34-35 A-5	ROGERS	1887 0-6-0			
36 A-5	BROOKS	1887 0-6-0			
37-46 A-5	ROGERS	1888 0-6-0			
58-59 A-6	BROOKS	1899 0-6-0	18x26'' 49''	109400	
378-379 A-6	BROOKS	1899 0-6-0			
60-61 A-7	BROOKS	1893 0-6-0	19x26'' 49''	114700	
62-69 A-7	BROOKS	1895-8 0-6-0			
70-72 A-8	ROGERS	1900 0-6-0	do		
1 A-9	G.N. RY.	1908 0-6-0	19x26'' 49''	135000	
2-11 A-9	BALDWIN	1907 0-6-0	19x26'' 52''	135000	Nos. 2, 6, 8 & 10 — 49'' drivers
12 A-9	G.N. RY.	1908 0-6-0	19x26'' 49''	135000	
14-26 A-9	G.N. RY.	1906 0-6-0	19x26'' 52''	135000	Nos. 22 & 25 built 1908 — 49'' drivers
49-51 A-9	G.N. RY.	1908 0-6-0	19x26'' 49''		
52-55 A-9	BALDWIN	1907 0-6-0	do		
56-57 A-9	G.N. RY.	1908 0-6-0	do		
73-85 A-9	ROGERS	1903 0-6-0	do		
86-88 A-9	ROGERS	1905 0-6-0	do		
89-94 A-9	BALDWIN	1907 0-6-0	do		
380-399 A-9	BALDWIN	1912 0-6-0	do		
95-97 A-10	BROOKS	1898 0-6-0	19x28'' 49''	137000	
98-99 A-10	BROOKS	1900 0-6-0			
240 B-1	COOKE	1866 4-4-0			Ex-ST. P&P #16
241-242 B-3	PITTSBURGH	1872 4-4-0	16x24'' 63''	43700	Ex-ST. P&P #18-19
243	BALDWIN	1871 4-4-0	No Data		Ex NP 20 to GN AS #20
244	PITTSBURGH	1870 4-4-0			Ex ST. P&P #17 ''Chippewa''
248 B-3	PITTSBURGH	1872 4-4-0	16x24'' 63''	46000	
245 B-4	BALDWIN	1879 4-4-0	16x24'' 63''	44450	
249-252 B-4	BALDWIN	1879 4-4-0	do		
265-266 B-5	ROGERS	1878 4-4-0	16x24'' 55''	41600	
232-237 B-6	ROGERS	1890 4-4-0	17x24'' 63''	56000	
139 B-7	ROME	1890 4-4-0	17x24'' 63''	49000	
288-289 B-8	PITTSBURGH	1880 4-4-0	17x24'' 55''	48000	
290 B-8	PITTSBURGH	1880 4-4-0	17x24'' 63''	48000	
291-293 B-8	PITTSBURGH	1880 4-4-0	17x24'' 55''	48000	
187-196 B-9	PITTSBURGH	1881 4-4-0	17x24'' 63''	492000	
270-282 B-10	BALDWIN	1880 4-4-0	17x24'' 63''	44650	
141-142 B-11	BALDWIN	1890 4-4-0	17x24'' 63''	52000	
144 B-12	ROGERS	1882 4-4-0	No Data		
100-113 B-13	BALDWIN	1882 4-4-0	17x24'' 63''	49150	
118-124 B-14	BALDWIN	1882 4-4-0	17x24'' 63''	45450	Nos. 118-120 built 1880
125-129 B-15	SCHENECTADY	1882 4-4-0	17x24'' 63''	57400	
130-131 B-15	SCHENECTADY	1882 4-4-0	17x24'' 64''	49450	
132-134 B-15	SCHENECTADY	1882 4-4-0	17x24'' 63''	57400	
135-138 B-16	RHODE ISLAND	1882 4-4-0	17x24'' 63''	55650	
145-149 B-17	GRANT	1882 4-4-0	? 63''	43650	
150-151 B-18	BROOKS	1882 4-4-0	No Data		
152-186 B-19	BROOKS	1882 4-4-0	? 63''	52500''	
197-206 B-20	RHODE ISLAND	1883 4-4-0	17x24'' 63''	49200	
207-225 B-21	ROGERS	1887 4-4-0	18x24'' 63''	60300	
226-230 B-22	ROGERS	1889 4-4-0	do		
231 B-23	BALDWIN	1893 4-4-0	18x24'' 63''	56100	
810-849 C-1	BALDWIN	1918 0-8-0	26x28'' 55''	232600	
850-869 C-2	BROOKS	1901 0-8-0			Built from F-6
875-899 C-3	BROOKS	1903 0-8-0			Built from F-9
780 C-4	BALDWIN	1908 0-8-0			Built from M-2
781-782 C-4	ROGERS	1902 & 3 0-8-0			Built from F-8
477-480 D-1	BALDWIN	1889 2-6-0	18x24'' 55''	77000	
300-324 D-2	ROGERS	1887 2-6-0	19x24'' 55''	78200	
325-340 D-2	ROGERS	1888 2-6-0			
341-349 D-2	ROGERS	1889 2-6-0			

NUMBER & CLASS	BUILDER	DATE BUILT & WHEEL ARRANGEMENT	CYL. DIMENSIONS & DRIVER DIA.	WEIGHT ON DRIVERS	NOTES
432 D-3	BALDWIN	1901 2-6-0	18x24'' 55''	106500	
400-426 D-4	BROOKS	1895 2-6-0	19x24'' 55''	108000	Nos. 400-404 built 1893
450-476 D-5	BROOKS	1896 2-6-0	19x26'' 55''	114000	
430 D-6	SCHENECTADY	1902 2-6-0	19x24'' 55''	101800	
431 D-6	SCHENECTADY	1906 2-6-0	19x24'' 55''	126900	
992-993 E-1	ROGERS	1890 4-6-0	18x24'' 55''	74000	
900-909 E-3	ROGERS	1899 4-6-0	18x26'' 73''	112000	
910 E-2	ALCO	1915 4-6-0	18x24'' 63''	96000	
911 E-2	ALCO	1915 4-6-0	18x24'' 61''	97500	
298-299 E-4	SCHENECTADY	1889 4-6-0	18x24'' 55''	77000	
925-939 E-6	ROGERS	1902 4-6-0	19x26'' 63''	120000	
950 E-7	BROOKS	1893 4-6-0	18x26'' 73''	110000	
951-969 E-7	BROOKS	1893 4-6-0	19x26'' 73''	110000	
1053-1062 E-8	ROGERS	1901 4-6-0	19x28'' 73''	134000	
1063-1069 E-8	ROGERS	1903 4-6-0			
1070-1072 E-8	ROGERS	1901 4-6-0			
998-999 E-9	BALDWIN	1892 4-6-0	20x24'' 69''	103300	
1000-1001 E-10	BROOKS	1898 4-6-0	20x30'' 63''	130000	
1002-1005 E-10s	BROOKS	1898 4-6-0	do		
1006 E-10	BROOKS	1898 4-6-0			
1007 E-10s	BROOKS	1898 4-6-0			
970-971 E-12	BALDWIN	1897 4-6-0	19x24'' 55''	93850	
948-949 E-13	BALDWIN	1893 & 6 4-6-0	19x26'' 55''	85000	
1008-1032 E-14	BALDWIN	1909 4-6-0	22½x30'' 73''	150000	Built to H-5
1033-1042 E-14	BALDWIN	1910 4-6-0			Built to H-7
1073-1092 E-15	BALDWIN	1910 4-6-0	22x28'' 73''	134000	
500-507 F-1	BROOKS	1892 2-8-0	19x26'' 55''	120000	
508 F-1s	BROOKS	1892 2-8-0	22x26'' 55''	120000	
509-543 F-1	BROOKS	1892 2-8-0			
544 F-1s	BROOKS	1892 2-8-0			
545-565 F-1	BROOKS	1892 2-8-0			
595-599 F-2	BALDWIN	1892 2-8-0	19x26'' 55''	130000	
701 F-3	BROOKS	1898 2-8-0	19x32'' 55''	160000	Formerly 4-8-0
1094 F-4	BALDWIN	1896 2-8-0	19x24'' 47''	113300	
1095-1099 F-5	ROGERS	1901 2-8-0	20x32'' 55''	179000	
1100-1104 F-5s	ROGERS	1901 2-8-0	23½x32'' 55''	179000	
1105-1109 F-5	ROGERS	1901 2-8-0			
1110-1114 F-6s	BROOKS	1901 2-8-0	23½x32'' 55''	178000	Built to C-2 (0-8-0)
1115 F-6	BROOKS	1901 2-8-0	20x32'' 55''	178000	Built to C-2
1116 F-6s	BROOKS	1901 2-8-0	21x32'' 55''	178000	Built to C-2
1117 F-6s	BROOKS	1901 2-8-0	23½x32'' 55''	178000	Built to C-2
1118 F-6	BROOKS	1901 2-8-0			
1119-1120 F-6s	BROOKS	1901 2-8-0	23½x32'' 55''	178000	Built to C-2
1121 F-6	BROOKS	1901 2-8-0			
1122-1124 F-6s	BROOKS	1901 2-8-0	23½x32'' 55''	178000	Built to C-2
1125-1126 F-6	BROOKS	1901 2-8-0			
1127-1129 F-6s	BROOKS	1901 2-8-0	23½x32'' 55''	178000	Built to C-2
1130-1133 F-7s					
1136 & 1138 F-7s	COOKE	1901 2-8-0	23½x32'' 55''	174000	
1134-1135 F-7s					
1137 & 1139 F-7	COOKE	1901 2-8-0	20x32'' 55''	174000	
1140 & 1142	ROGERS	1902 2-8-0	20x32'' 55''	180000	
1144-1145					
1149 F-8					
1141 & 1143					
1146-1148 F-8s	ROGERS	1902 2-8-0	23½x32'' 55''	180000	
1150-1153 F-8	ROGERS	1901 2-8-0			
1154-1155 F-8s	ROGERS	1901 & 2 2-8-0			
1156-1162					
1167 & 1169 F-8	ROGERS	1902			
1163-1166 F-8s	ROGERS	1902			
1168 & 1170 F-8s	ROGERS	1902 & 3			
1171					
1174-1180					
1182-1183					
1186-1187					
1189-1190					
1192-1193					
1195-1196 F-8s	ROGERS	1903 2-8-0			
1172-1173					
1181					
1184-1185					
1188 & 1191					
1194					
1197-1199 F-8	ROGERS	1903 2-8-0			

NUMBER & CLASS	BUILDER	DATE BUILT & WHEEL ARRANGEMENT	CYL. DIMENSIONS & DRIVER DIA.	WEIGHT ON DRIVERS	NOTES
1200-1214 F-8 1215-1219	ROGERS	1905 2-8-0			
1221-1253 F-8	BALDWIN	1907 2-8-0			
1220 F-8s	BALDWIN	1907 2-8-0			
1254-1264 F-8	BALDWIN	1908 2-8-0			
1300-1306 F-9	BROOKS	1903 2-8-0	20x32'' 55''	180000	Built to C-3 (0-8-0)
1307 F-9s	BROOKS	1903 2-8-0	23½x32'' 55''	180000	Built to C-3 (0-8-0)
1308-1310 F-9	BROOKS	1903 2-8-0			Built to C-3 (0-8-0)
1311-1312 F-9s	BROOKS	1903 2-8-0			Built to C-3 (0-8-0)
1313 & 1315 F-9	BROOKS	1903 2-8-0			Built to C-3 (0-8-0)
1314 & 1316 F-9s	BROOKS	1903 2-8-0			Built to C-3 (0-8-0)
1317-1324 F-9	BROOKS	1903 2-8-0			Built to C-3 (0-8-0)
806 F-10	BROOKS	1898 2-8-0	21x34'' 55''	197100	Built from G-5
590-591 F-11	ALCO	1912 2-8-0	20x24'' 52''	123000	Ex W&SF 14-15
1326-1327 F-12	ALCO	1907 2-8-0	21x28'' 52''	167000	Ex BA&P 26-27
600-608 G-1	BROOKS	1891 4-8-0	20x26'' 55''	132000	
609 G-1	BROOKS	1891 4-8-0	20x24'' 55''	132000	
610-615 G-1	BROOKS	1891 4-8-0	20x26'' 55''	132000	
700-719 G-2 720-721 723-733	BROOKS	1898 4-8-0	19x32'' 55''	142000	
735-769 G-3	ROGERS	1899-1900 4-8-0	19x32'' 55''	148000	
722 & 734 G-3s	ROGERS	1899 4-8-0	25¼x32'' 55''	148000	
770-779 G-4	BROOKS	1900 4-8-0	19x32'' 55''	150000	
800-807 G-5	BROOKS	1898 4-8-0	21x34'' 55''	172000	
1400-1405 H-1 1406 1410-1413 1415-1416 1420 1432 & 1435	ROGERS	1905 4-6-2	21x28'' 73''	139000	
1438 H-2 1407-1409 1414 1417-1419 1426-1429 1431 & 1434 1436-1437	BALDWIN	1906 4-6-2	22x30'' 69''	151000	
1439-1440 H-2s 1421 & 1423	BALDWIN	1906 4-6-2	23½x30'' 69''	151000	
1425 H-3	BALDWIN	1906 4-6-2			do
1430 & 1433 H-3	BALDWIN	1907 4-6-2			
1441-1448 H-4	BALDWIN	1909 4-6-2	23½x30'' 73''	152000	
1449 H-4	BALDWIN	1909 4-6-2	23½x26'' 73''	152000	
1450-1460 H-4	BALDWIN	1909 4-6-2	23½x30'' 73''	152000	
1461-1485 H-4	LIMA	1914 4-6-2	23½x30'' 73''	150750	
1350-1374 H-5	BALDWIN	1909 4-6-2			Built from E-14
1486-1495 H-5	BALDWIN	1909 4-6-2	23½x30'' 73''	164600	
1710-1717 H-6	BALDWIN	1906-7 4-6-2	23½x30'' 69''	161580	Built from J-1, J-2
1375-1384 H-7 1500	BALDWIN	1910 4-6-2			Built from E-14
1502-1513 J-1 1501	BALDWIN	1906 2-6-2	22x30'' 69'.	151000	Built to H-6 Some—not all
1514 & 1524 J-1s 1515-1523	BALDWIN	1906 2-6-2	23½x30'' 69''	151000	do
1525-1530 J-1	BALDWIN	1906 2-6-2			do
1531 & 1537 J-1s 1532	BALDWIN	1906 2-6-2			do
1536 & 1538 J-1	BALDWIN	1906 2-6-2			do
1539 & 1549 J-1s	BALDWIN	1906 2-6-2			do
1540-1548 J-1 1550-1552	BALDWIN	1906 2-6-2			do
1554-1556 J-2s 1533	BALDWIN	1907 2-6-2	23½x30'' 69''	151000	do
1557-1558 J-2 1559 & 1565	BALDWIN	1907 2-6-2	22x30'' 69''	151000	do
1566 & 1573 J-2s 1560-1564	BALDWIN	1907 2-6-2			do
1567-1572 J-2 1574-1581	BALDWIN	1907 2-6-2			do
1584-1589 J-2 1582-1583 1590	BALDWIN	1907 2-6-2			do
1594-1598 J-2s 1591-1593	BALDWIN	1907 2-6-2			do
1599-1612 J-2 1613 & 1615	BALDWIN	1907 2-6-2			do
1622 & 1624 J-2s 1614 1616-1621	BALDWIN	1907 2-6-2			

NUMBER & CLASS	BUILDER	DATE BUILT & WHEEL ARRANGEMENT	CYL. DIMENSIONS & DRIVER DIA.	WEIGHT ON DRIVERS	NOTES
1623 & 1625 J-2 1626 & 1631	BALDWIN	1907 2-6-2			
1637-1638 J-2s 1627-1630 1632-1636	BALDWIN	1907 2-6-2			
1639-1648 J-2	BALDWIN	1907 2-6-2			
1649 J-2s 1700	BALDWIN	1907 2-6-2			
1702 & 1704 K-1 1701 & 1701	BALDWIN	1906 4-4-2	21x26'' 73''	124500	
1705-1709 K-1s	BALDWIN	1906 4-4-2	do		
1900 L-1	BALDWIN	1906 2-6-6-2	21½ &33x32'' 55''	316000	Rebuilt to 0-6
1901 L-1	BALDWIN	1906 2-6-6-2	24 & 33x32'' 55''	316000	do
1904-1907 L-1	BALDWIN	1906-8 2-6-6-2	21½ & 33x32'' 55''	316000	do
1909-1920 L-1	BALDWIN	1908 2-6-6-2	do		do
1922-1924 L-1	BALDWIN	1908 2-6-6-2	do		do
1902-1903 L-1s	BALDWIN	1906 2-6-6-2	24 & 33x32'' 55''	316000	do
1908 & 1921 L-1s 1800-1813	BALDWIN	1906 & 8 2-6-6-2	do		do Nos. 1800-1804 built 1908
1817-1821 L-2 1823 1827-1841	BALDWIN	1907 2-6-6-2	20 & 31x30'' 55''	316000	do
1843-1844 L-2 1814-1816 1822 & 1842	BALDWIN	1907 2-6-6-2			do
1824-1826 L-2s	BALDWIN	1907 2-6-6-2	do		do
1950-1984 M-1	BALDWIN	1910 2-6-8-0	23 & 35x32'' 55''	350000	
1999 M-2	BALDWIN	1908 2-6-8-0	20 & 33x32'' 55''	350000	
2000-2024 N-1	BALDWIN	1912 2-8-8-0	28 & 42x32'' 63''	420000	N-1's originally compounded, later converted to simple and re-classed as N-2 (1934) further upgraded in 1939-41 and changed to N-3
3000-3019 0-1	BALDWIN	1911 2-8-2	28x32'' 63''	220000	
3020-3069 0-1	BALDWIN	1913 2-8-2			
3070-3094 0-1	BALDWIN	1916 2-8-2	28x32'' 63''	229000	
3095-3099 0-1	BALDWIN	1917 2-8-2			
3100-3148 0-1	BALDWIN	1918 2-8-2			
3149 0-2	ALCO	1915 2-8-2	20x28'' 52''	128000	Ex W&SF #18
3200-3203 0-3	ALCO	1919 2-8-2	27x32'' 63''	239000	
3204-3208 0-3	ALCO	1920 2-8-2			Ex EP&SW 390-394
3210-3254 0-4	ALCO	1920 2-8-2	28x32'' 63''	242800	
3300-3344 0-5	BALDWIN	1907-8 2-8-2	25x30'' 63''	214500	Built from L-2
3350-3371 0-6	BALDWIN	1906-8 2-8-2			Built from L-1
3375-3396 0-7	BALDWIN	1910	31x32''	268000	Built from M-2 2-6-8-0
3397-3399 0-8	G.N. RY.	1932	29x32''	280000	All 0-7's rebuilt 1944-46 and changed to 0-8 with 28X32 cly. and 325000 wt. on dr.
1750-1764 P-1	LIMA	1914 4-8-2	28x32'' 63''	220000	Built to Q-2
2500-2527 P-2	BALDWIN	1923 4-8-2	29x28'' 73''	238000	
2100-2129 Q-1	BALDWIN	1923 2-10-2	31x32'' 63''	342490	
2175-2189 Q-2	LIMA	1914 2-10-2			Built from P-1
2030-2033 R-1	BALDWIN	1925 2-8-8-2	(4)28x32'' 63''	594940*	wt. of engine
2034-2035 R-1	BALDWIN	1927 2-8-8-2			
2036-2043 R-1	BALDWIN	1928 2-8-8-2			
2044-2053 R-2	G. N. RY.	1929 2-8-8-2	(4)28x32'' 63''	630750*	
2054-2059 R-2	G. N. RY.	1930 2-8-8-2			
2550-2555 S-1	BALDWIN	1929 4-8-4	28x30'' 80''	273700	
2575-2588 S-2	BALDWIN	1930 4-8-4	29x29'' 80''	420900*	
4000-4001 Z-6	ALCO	1937 4-6-6-4	23x32'' 69''	624500	To SP&S-903-904

ROSTER OF ELECTRIC LOCOMOTIVES

ROAD NUMBER	FORMER NUMBER	CLASS	WHEEL ARRANGEMENT	BUILDER	BUILDER NUMBER	DATE BUILT	DISPOSITION
5000-5003 1st	same	none	B + B	ALCO-GE	45286-9/2892-5	2-3/09	Ret. 4/27
A5000, B5000*	5000, 5001 2nd	Z-1	1-D-1	BALD.-WEST.	60325, 60365	12/27, 1/28	Ret. 1956
A5002, B5002*	5002, 5003 2nd	Z-1	1-D-1	BALD.-WEST.	60627, 60633	9/28	Ret. 1956
A5004, B5004*	5004, 5005	Z-1	1-D-1	BALD.-WEST.	59168, 59276	4, 6/26	Ret. 1956
A5006, B5006*	5006, 5007	Z-1	1-D-1	BALD.-WEST.	59381, 59382	8/26	Ret. 1956
A5008, B5008*	5008, 5009	Z-1	1-D-1	BALD.-WEST.	60443, 60444	3/28	Ret. 1956
5010, 5011	same	Y-1	1-C+C-1	ALCO-GE	67022, 3/10160, 1	10/27	5011 burned & rebuilt with streamline body
5012, 5013	same	Y-1	1-C+C-1	ALCO-GE	67542, 3/10537, 8	?/28	Ft. cabs-Y-1A — 5010, 5012-17 sold to
5014-5017	same	Y-1	1-C+C-1	ALCO-GE	68272-5/11149-52	3/30	P.R.R. 8/56, all scrapped 1962.
5018, 5019	same	W-1	4-D+D-4	GE	28448, 28449	5/47	5019 scrapped — 5018 sold to U.P. for conversion to coal turbine

ROSTER OF ELECTRIC LOCOMOTIVES (SC&P)

ROAD NUMBER	FORMER NUMBER	ORIGINAL NUMBER	WEIGHT	BUILDER	BUILDER NUMBER	DATE BUILT	
500	M4	B2	45 ton	BALD.-WEST.	27927	4/06	360hp
501	M99	same	46 ton	BALD.-WEST.	31244	7/07	360hp — (500-503 were 600 volt D.C.)
502	same	same	51 ton	BALD.-WEST.	37513	2/12	steeple cab; 500hp
503	M1	A1	52 ton	BALD.-WEST.	27735	3/06	500hp
603	M3	B1	50 ton	BALD.-WEST.	27823	3/06	RB to operate on 6600 volt or 11000 volt A.C.
604	M2	A2	50 ton	BALD.-WEST.	27926	4/06	RB to operate on 6600 volt or 11000 volt A.C.
605	M5	C1	50 ton	BALD.-WEST.	27885	4/06	
606	M6	C2	50 ton	BALD.-WEST.	27928	4/06	(603-606, 701-704,706 were 6600 volt A.C.
701	M7	same	73 ton	BALD.-WEST.	31371	7/07	1160hp
702	M8	same	73 ton	BALD.-WEST.	31372	7/07	1160hp
703	M9	same	73 ton	BALD.-WEST.	31423	8/07	1160hp
704	M10	same	73 ton	BALD.-WEST.	34397	3/10	1160hp
705				-----------------NO RECORD OF THIS LOCOMOTIVE-----------------			
706	M11	*same	73 ton	BALD.-WEST.	34398	3/10	1160hp

ROSTER OF GAS & DIESEL MOTOR CARS

ROAD NUMBER	TYPE	BUILDER	ORDER OR BLD. NUMBER	DATE BUILT	
2300, 2301 1st	G/E	ST. L-GE	GE 3741, 3742	2, 1/13	
2302, 2303 1st	—	ST. L	?	?/13	Trailers for 2300, 2301 1st
2300-2303 2nd	G/E	ST. L-EMC	1395/142-145	4/26	2302, 2303 2nd RB with two engines
2304	?	See note		?/22	Built by Flandrau Motor Truck
2305	G/M	MACK	60006	2/22	Retired in 1937
2306	G/M	See note	19027	?/22	Built by Four Wheel Drive Auto Company
2307	G/M	WHITE	?	?/22	To Montana Western 20 in 3/29
2308	G/M	BRILL	21514	?/22	Retired in 4/37
2309	G/E	ST. L-EMC	1352/113	5/25	RB to coach 572, then scrapped
2310	G/E	ST. L-EMC	1360/114	5/25	Scrapped in 7/53
2311	G/E	ST. L-EMC	1360/115	5/25	RB to rail detector car, then scrapped
2312	G/E	ST. L-EMC	1360/116	5/25	RB to coach 568, engine used in 2302
2313	G/E	ST. L-EMC	1368C/130	6/25	To Montana Western 31 in 1/40
2314	G/E	BRILL-WEST.	22216	11/25	RB to coach 600 then scrapped
2315, 2316	G/E	ST. L-EMC	1395A/146, 7	7, 6/26	RB to D/E, then scrapped in 6/58
2317-2319	G/E	ST. L-EMC	1411/176-178	11/26	RB to D/E, then scrapped 1957-59
2320, 2321	G/E	ST. L-EMC	1410/179, 180	11/26	Scrapped in 10/57
2322	G/E	BRILL-WEST.	22481	3/27	RB to D/E, then scrapped 10/57
2323	G/E	ST. L-EMC	1423/206	3/27	RB to D/E, then scrapped 12/59
2324	G/E	ST. L-EMC	1458/246	1/28	RB to D/E, then scrapped 7/59
2325	G/E	BRILL-WEST.	22627	4/28	RB to D/E, then scrapped 7/59
2326-2330	G/E	BRILL-WEST.	22657	6/28	RB to D/E, then scrapped 6/56-12/59
2331	G/E	BRILL-WEST.	22764	6/29	RB to D/E, then scrapped in 7/59
2332-2335	G/E	ST. L-EMC	1504/405-408	8/29	RB to D/E, then scrapped 7-12/59
2336	G/E	ST. L-EMC	1505/409	8/29	RB to D/E, then scrapped in 12/59
2337	G/E	ST. L-MACK	1506/162006	9/29	RB to Tower Car X2804, R# X838
2338	G/E	ST. L-EMC	1531/443	7/30	RB to D/E, then scrapped 7/59
2339	G/E	BRILL	22850	10/30	RB to D/E, then scrapped 8/57
2340	D/E	ST. L-WEST.	1532/6147	10/30	Scrapped 4/49
2341	D/E	STD. STL.-WEST.	?	?/30	Ex BAR 5 2nd, Acq. 11/33, nee WEMCO 20 Demo
2350 1st	—	4 WHL DRIVE AUTO	?	?/22	Trailer for 2306
2350 2nd	D/M	BUDD	6302	7/56	RDC3
2351	—	BRILL	21929	?/24	Trailer for 2308
2400	?	BRILL	?	?/06	Ex SC&P 74, R# SC&P 90

ROSTER OF DIESEL LOCOMOTIVES

ROAD NUMBER	BLD. & MODEL	WEIGHT	BLD. NUMBER	DATE BLT.	FORMER NUMBER	LATER NUMBER
1-6	ALCO S2	247,000	77021-77026	2/50		
7-10	ALCO S2	247,000	77460-77463	4/50		
11-13	EMD SW7	248,000	10869-10871	6/50		BN 143-145
14-16	EMD SW9	248,000	A114-A116	12/50		BN 146-148
17-23	EMD SW9	247,000	13297-13303	5/51		BN 149-155
24-28	BALD. S12	240,000	75818-75822	2/53		
29-33	EMD SW1200	248,000	22481-22485	4, 5/57		BN 162-166
50, 51	GE 44 ton	89,000	12910, 12911	9/40	5200, 5201	
75, 76	EMD SW1	203,000	859,860	2/39	5101, 5102 2nd	
77-79	EMD SW1	203,000	1380-1382	9/41	5103-5105	BN 77, —, —
80-82	EMD SW1	198,000	10118-10120	1/50		BN 80-82
83	EMD SW1	198,000	11025	1/50		BN 83
98, 99	EMD SW8	233,000	13304, 13305	6, 8/51		BN 98, 99
100	EMD NW (SW1200)	249,000	647	1/38 (2/55)	5300	BN 106
101	EMD NW1 (SW8)	232,000	777	1/38 (6/53)	5301	BN 101
102-109	EMD NW2	251,000	861-868	2-5/39	5302-5309	BN 450-457
110, 111	EMD NW 2	251,000	883, 884	5/39	5310, 5311	BN 458, —
112-123	EMD NW2	251,000	939-950	6-8/39	5312-5323	BN 459-470
124-131	EMD NW2	251,000	1370-1377	7-8/41	5324-5331	BN 471-478
132, 133	BALD. VO1000	240,000	64211, 64212	10/41	5332, 5333	
134-136	EMD NW2	251,000	1711-1713	8, 9, 9/42	5334-5336	BN 479-481
137, 138	BALD. VO1000	241,000	69785, 70109	11, 12/43	5337, 5338	
139-144	BALD. VO1000	241,000	71942-71947	8/44		

145-150	EMD NW2	249,000	2475-2480	8-9/45		BN 482-487
151-162	EMD NW2	247,000	7786-7797	7-11/49		BN 488-499
163-170	EMD SW7	248,000	9569-9576	3/50		BN 135-142
175, 176	EMD NW3	214,000	869, 870	11/39	5400, 5401	
177-179	EMD NW3	214,000	890-892	9/40, 4, 12/41	5402-5404	
180, 181	EMD NW3	214,000	1719, 1720	3/42	5405, 5406	
182-184	ALCO RS1	245,000	72922-72924	9, 9, 11/44		
185	ALCO RS1	245,000	71433	10/44		
186-195	EMD NW5	216,000	3479-3488	12/46		BN 986-995
197-199	ALCO RS3	250,000	78043-78045	5/50		225-227 2nd
200A, 200B	EMD FTA, FTB	233,000	1385, 1387	10/41	5600A, 5600B	253A, 253B
200-203 1st	ALCO RS2	248,000	75145-75148	6/47		
204 1st	ALCO RS2	248,000	75259	7/47		
205-207 1st	ALCO RS2	248,000	75262-75264	8/47		
208-211 1st	ALCO RS2	248,000	76997-77000	8/49		
200-209 2nd	EMD SW1500	260,000	33202-33211	9-10/67		BN 300-309
212-214	ALCO RS2	248,000	77197-77199	9/49		
215-217	ALCO RS2	248,000	77400-77402	9/49		
218, 219	ALCO RS2	248,000	77893, 77894	1/50		
220-224	ALCO RS3	250,000	78046-78050	5/50		
225-227 1st	EMD F3A	254,000	3489-3491	11/46		271A, B 1st, 275A 2nd
228-231 1st	EMD F3A	254,000	4355-4358	10/47		360A, C, 361A, C
225-227 2nd	ALCO RS3	250,000	78043-78045	5/50	197-199	
228-232 2nd	ALCO RS3	250,000	80497-80501	6/53		
247A, B, 248A, B	EMD FTA	233,000	2921-2924	3-4/45	304A, C, 305A, C	
249A, B	EMD FTA	233,000	3493, 1383	10/45, 10/41	300A 2nd, 254A	
250A, B, 251A, B	EMD FTA, FTB	233,000	1221A, B, 1222A, B	5, 5, 6, 6/41	5700A, B, 5701A, B	375A, B, 376A, B
252A, 252B	EMD FTA, FTB	233,000	3492, 3498	10/45		418A, B 2nd
253A, 253B	EMD FTA, FTB	233,000	1385, 1387	10/41	200A, 200B	
254A, 254B	EMD FTA, FTB	233,000	1383, 3499	10/41, 10/45	300A 1st, —	249B, 418C 2nd
255A, 255B	EMD FTA, FTB	233,000	1384, 3500	10/41, 10/45	300C 1st, —	
256A-258A	FTA	233,000	3495-3497	10/45		
256B-258B	FTB	233,000	3501, 3503	10/45		
259A, 259B	F3A	235,000	4341, 4342	10/47		
260A, 261A	F3A	248,000	4334, 4335	10/47		366A, 367A
260B, 261B	F3B	248,000	4336, 4337	10/47		366B, 367B
262A, B, 263A, B	F3A	231,000	4343-4346	9/47		
264A, B, 265A, B	F3A	231,000	4826-4829	10/48		470A, D, 472A, D
266A, 267A	F3A	248,000	4830, 4831	10/48		368A, 369A
266B, 267B	F3B	248,000	4832, 4833	10/48		368B, 369B
268A-270A	F7A	249,000	9563-9565	6/50		370A, 367C, 368C
268B-270B	F7B	249,000	9566-9568	6/50		370B-372B
271A, 271B 1st	F3A	254,000	3489, 3490	11/46	225, 226 1st	359A, 359C
271A, 271B 2nd	F7A	242,000	16096-16097	4/52		BN 600, 602
272A, 272B	F7A	242,000	10081, 10082	4/49	EMD 801, 802	474A, 474D
273A, B, 274A, B	F7A	242,000	11063-11066	10/50		BN 604, 6, 8, 10
275A, 275B 1st	F7A	250,000	11071, 11072	10/50		363A, 363C
275A 2nd	F3A	254,000	3491	11/46	227 1st	366C
275A, B 3rd	F3A	243,000	4679, 4680	12/47	356A, 357A	BN 612, 614
276A, B 1st	FA1	250,000	77015, 77016	4/50		
276A, B 2nd	F7A, F3A	243,000	11076, 4831	10/50, 10/48	365C, 369A	BN 616, 618
277A, 277B	FA2	250,000	78268, 78269	11/50		
278A, 279A	FA2	258,000	78270, 78271	11/50	ALCO 1602A, D	
278B, 279B	FA2	258,000	78202, 78203	11/50	ALCO 1602B, C	
280A, 281A	F7A	252,000	16092, 16093	6/52		369C, 370C
280B, 281B	F7B	252,000	16094, 16095	6/52		373B, 374B
300A, C 1st	FTA	233,000	1383, 1384	10/41	5900A, C	254A, 255A
300A, C 2nd	FTA	233,000	3493, 3494	10/45		249A, 418D 2nd
300B	FTB	233,000	1386	10/41	5900B	401C
301A, C-303A, C	FTA	233,000	2915-2920	3/45		401, 403, 405A, D
301B-303B	FTB	233,000	2925-2927	3/45		401, 403, 405B
304A, C, 305A, C	FTA	233,000	2921-2924	3-4/45		247A, B, 248A, B
304B, 305B	FTB	233,000	2928, 2929	3-4/45		403C, 405C
306A, 306C	F3A	230,000	4821, 4822	10/48		458A, 458D
306B	F3B	230,000	4825	10/48		458B
307A, C-309A, C	F7A	241,000	11079-11084	10/50		BN 620-630 even
307B-309B	F7B	240,000	11087-11089	10/50		BN 621, 625, 629
310A, 310C	ALCO FA1	251,000	77017, 78118	4/50		
310B	ALCO FB1	249,000	78129	4/50		
311A, C-317A, C	EMD F7A	247,000	16071-16084	3-4/52		BN 632-658 even
311B-313B	EMD F7B	247,000	16085-16087	3-4/52		BN 633, 637, 641
314B-316B	EMD F7B	247,000	16088-16090	4/52		BN 645, 649, 653
317B	F7B	247,000	16091	4/52		BN 657
320-325	SDP40	369,000	31592-31597	5/66		BN 9850-9855
326-333	SDP45	395,000	33041-33048	6-8/67		BN 9856-9863
350A-354A	F3A	245,000	4673-4677	11-12/47		
355A	F3A	245,000	4678	12/47		BN 9700
356A, 357A	F3A	245,000	4679, 4680	12/47		275A, B 3rd
358A	F3A	245,000	4681	12/47		
350B-353B	F3B	250,000	4691-4694	11/47		BN 9701-07 odd
354B, 355B	F3B	250,000	4695, 4696	11, 12/47		
356B-358B	F3B	250,000	4734-4736	12/47		BN 9711, —, 9713
359A, 359C	F3A	254,000	3489, 3490	11/46	271A, 271B 1st	BN —, 9710
359B	F3B	250,000	9558	6/50	500B 2nd	
350C-357C	F3A	245,000	4682-4689	11-12/47		

ROAD NUMBER	BLD. & MODEL	WEIGHT	BLD. NUMBER	DATE BLT.	FORMER NUMBER	LATER NUMBER
358C	F3A	245,000	4690	12/47		BN 9708
360A, C, 361A, C	F3A	253,000	4355-4358	10/47	228-231 1st	BN 9712, —, 14, 16
360B, 361B	F3B	252,000	9559, 9560	6/50	501B, 502B 2nd	BN 9717, 9719
362A, 362C	F3A	253,000	4834, 4835	10/48	375C, 376C	
362B, 363B	F3B	252,000	9561, 9562	6/50	503B, 504B 2nd	BN —, 9721
363A, 363C	F7A	250,000	11071, 11072	10/50	275A, 275B 1st	BN —, 9724
364A, 364C	F7A	248,000	11073, 11074	10/50	(379A, C)	BN 9726, 9728
365A, 365C	F7A	253,000	11075, 11076	10/50	(380A, C)	—, 276A 2nd
364B, 365B	(F7B	255,000	11077, 11078	10/50	379B, 380B 1st)	BN 9723, 9725
366A, 367A	F3A	248,000	4334, 4335	10/47	260A, 261A	BN 9732, —
366B, 367B	F3A	248,000	4336, 4337	10/47	260B, 261B	
366C, 368A	F3A	254; 248,000	3491, 4830	11/46, 10/48	275A 2nd, 266A	
367C, 368C	F7A	249,000	9564, 9565	6/50	269A, 270A	BN 9736, —
368B, 369B	F3B	248,000	4832, 4833	10/48	266B, 267B	BN 9729, 9733
369A	F3A	248,000	4831	10/48	267A	276B 2nd
369C	F7A	249,000	16092	6/52	280A	BN 9740
370A, 370C	F7A	250,000	9563, 16093	6/50, 6/52	268A, 281A	BN 9742, 9744
370B-372B	F7B	249,000	9566-9568	6/50	268B-270B	BN 9735, 37, 39
373B, 374B	F7B	252,000	16094, 16095	6/52	280B, 281B	BN 9741, 9743
375A, 375B	FTA, FTB	233,000	1221A, 1221B	5/41	250A, 250B	250A, 250B
376A, 376B	FTA, FTB	233,000	1222A, 1222B	6/41	251A, 251B	251A, 251B
375C, 376C	F3A	253,000	4834, 4835	10/48		362A, 362C
(379A, 379C)	F7A	248,000	11073, 11074	10/50		364A, 364C
(379B, 380B 1st)	F7B	255,000	11077, 11078	10/50		364B, 365B
(380A, 380C)	F7A	253,000	11075, 11076	10/50		365A, 365C
380B, 381B 2nd	F7B	232,000	17277, 1959	8/52, 8/44	460B, 460C	BN 9709, 9715
382B, 383B	F7B	245; 230,000	17859, 17863	1/53	462B, 462C	BN 9727, 9745
384B, 385B	F7B	247; 230,000	17860, 17864	1/53	464B, 464C	BN 9747, 9749
400-407	SD45	366,000	31598-31605	5/66		BN 6430-6437
408-417	SD45	366,000	32988-32997	4/67		BN 6438-6447
418-426	SD45	382,000	33785-33793	7/68		BN 6448-6456
427-432	F45	385,000	34736-34741	5/69		BN 6600-6605
433-440	F45	386,000	35110-35117	7-9/69		BN 6606-6613
(441-452)	F45	386,000	36341-36352	7-8/70		BN 6614-6625
400A, 400D	FTA	234,000	1585, 1586	12/43		
400B, 400C	FTB	225,000	1587, 1762	12/43		
401A, 401D	FTA	234,000	2915, 2916	3/45	301A, 301C	
401B, 401C	FTB	225,000	2925, 1386	3/45, 10/41	301B, 300B	
402A, D, 404A, D	FTA	234,000	1721-1724	1/44		
402B, C, 404B, C	FTB	225,000	1725-1728	1/44		
403A, D, 405A, D	FTA	234,000	2917-2920	3/45	302A, C, 303A, C	
403B, 405B	FTB	225,000	2926, 2927	3/45	302B, 303B	
403C, 405C	FTB	225,000	2928, 2929	3, 4/45	304B, 305B	
406A, D, 408A, D	FTA	234,000	1756-1759	3/44		
406B, C, 408B, C	FTB	225,000	1763-1766	3/44		
410A, 410D	FTA	234,000	1760, 1761	5/44		
410B, 410C	FTB	225,000	1767, 1768	5/44		
412, 414, 416A, D	FTA	234,000	1938-1943	6/44		
412, 414, 416B, C	FTB	225,000	1952-1957	6/44		
418A, D 1st	FTA	234,000	1944, 1945	8/44		—, 460D
418B, C 1st	FTB	225,000	1958, 1959	8/44		—, 460C
418A, D 2nd	FTA	234,000	3492, 3494	10/45	252A, 300C 2nd	
418B, C 2nd	FTB	225,000	3498, 3499	10/45	252B, 254B	
420, 422, 424A, D	FTA	234,000	1946-1951	9, 10/44		
420, 422, 424B, C	FTB	225,000	1960-1965	9, 10/44		
426A, D, 428A, D	FTA	234,000	2930-2933	3/45		
426B, C, 428B, C	FTB	225,000	2934-2937	3/45		
430-436A, D even	F3A	233,000	4805-4812	8-9/48		
430-436B, C even	F3B	226,000	4813-4820	8-9/48		
438A, 438D	F3A	233,000	8014, 8015	10/48		
438B, 438C	F3B	226,000	8016, 8017	10/48		
440A, 440D	FA1	249,000	75995, 75996	8/48		
440B, 440C	FB1	249,000	76044, 76045	8/48		
442A, 442D	FA1	249,000	76838, 76839	4/49		
442B, 442C	FB1	249,000	76871, 76872	4/49		
444A, D, 446A, D	F7A	237,000	8511-8514	10/49		
444B, C, 446B, C	F7B	232,000	8515, 8518	10/49		
448A, 448D	F7A	237,000	9538, 9530	3/50		BN 660, 662
448B, 448C	F7B	232,000	9548, 9549	3/50		BN 661, 663
450A, D, 452A, D	F7A	237,000	9540, 9543	3/50		BN —, —, 664, 666
450B, C, 452B, C	F7B	232,000	9550-9553	3/50		BN —, —, —, 665
454A, D, 456A, D	F7A	237,000	9544-9547	3/50		BN 668, 70, —, 74
454B, C, 456B, C	F7B	232,000	9554-9557	3/50		BN 669, 71, 73, 75
458A, 458D	F3A	233,000	4821, 4822	10/48	306A, 306C	BN 676, 678
458B, 458C	F3B, F7B	225; 231,000	4825, 16098	10/48, 4/52	306B, —	BN —, 677
460A, 460D	F7A	248,000	17276, 1945	8/52, 8/44	—, 4180 1st	BN 672, 680
460B, 460C	F7B	246,000	17277, 1959	8/52, 8/44	—, 418C 1st	380B, 381B 2nd
462A-468A even	EMD F7A	246,000	17851-17854	1-2/53		BN —, 684, 88, 92
462B, 464B	EMD F7B	246,000	17859, 17860	1/53		382B, 384B
466B, 468B	F7B	246,000	17861, 17862	1, 2/53		BN 687, 691
462C, 464C	F7B	246,000	17863, 17864	1/53		383B, 385B
466C, 468C	F7B	246,000	17865, 17866	2/53		BN 689, 693
462D-468D even	F7A	246,000	17855-17858	1-2/53		BN 682, 86, 90, 94
470A, D-472A, D	F3A	231,000	4826-4829	10/48	264A, B, 265A, B	BN —, 696, —, —
470B, C, 472B, C	F9B	245,000	19334-19337	2/54		BN 845, —, 47, 49

554

ROAD NUMBER	BLD. & MODEL	WEIGHT	BLD. NUMBER	DATE BLT.	FORMER NUMBER	LATER NUMBER
474A, 474D	F7A	246,000	10081, 10082	4/49	272A, 272B	BN 698, 700
474B, 474C	F9B	245,000	19338, 19339	2/54		BN 851, 853
500, 501	E7A	319,000	2428, 2431	4/45	500A, 501B 3rd	BN 9901, 9902
502, 503	E7A	319,000	2429, 2430	4/45	500B 3rd; 501A	BN 9903, 9904
500A, 501A	E7A	319,000	2428, 2430	4/45		500, 503
502A-504A	E7A	326,000	2432, 34, 36	6/45		504, 506, 508
500B, 501B 1st	E7A	319,000	2429, 2431	4/45		500C, 501C
502B-504B 1st	E7A	326,000	2433, 35, 37	6/45		502C-504C
500C, 501C	E7A	319,000	2429, 2431	4/45	500B, 501B 1st	500B, 501B 3rd
502C-504C	E7A	326,000	2433, 35, 37	6/45	502B-504B 1st	502B-504B 3rd
500B-504B 2nd	E7B	250,000	9558-9562	6/50		359B-363B
500B, 501B 3rd	E7A	319,000	2429, 2431	4/45	500C, 501C	502, 501
502B, 504B 3rd	E7A	326,000	2433, 35, 37	6/45	502C-504C	505, 507, 509
504, 506, 508	E7A	326,000	2432, 34, 36	6/45	502A-504A	BN -, 9906, —
505, 507, 509	E7A	326,000	2433, 35, 37	6/45	502B-504B 3rd	BN 9905, —, 07
510-512	E7A	330,000	4338-4340	8/47	510A-512A	BN 9908-9910
510A-512A	E7A	330,000	4338-4340	8/47		510-512
550-564	SD7	344,000	16099-16113	4-10/52		BN 6000-6014
565-572	SD7	344,000	17896-17903	3-4/53		BN 6015-6022
573-578	SD9	343,000	19340-19345	2/54		BN 6100-6105
579-583	SD9	345,000	21247-21251	5/56		BN 6106-6110
584-589	SD9	346,000	22486-22491	1/57		BN 6111-6116
590-599	SD9	346,000	24092-24101	4/58		BN 6117-6126
600-605	GP7	247,000	11049-11054	11/50		BN 1500-1505
606-622	GP7	247,000	11032-11048	9, 10/50		BN 1506-1522
623-652	GP7	247,000	13336-13365	4-6/51		BN 1523-1552
653-655	GP7	247,000	17867-17869	3/53		BN 1553-1555
656-660	GP9	246,000	19364-19368	4/54		BN 1808-1812
661-674	GP9	246,000	19346-19359	3-4/54		BN 1813-1826
675	GP9	246,000	19360	4/54		(BN 1827)
676-678	GP9	246,000	19361-19363	4/54		BN 1828-1830
679, 680	GP9	246,000	19369, 19370	5/54		BN 1831, 1832
681-687	GP9	246,000	21254-21260	4/56		BN 1833-1839
688-699	GP9	246,000	22468-22479	4/57		BN 1761-1772
700-703	GP9	253,000	20843-20846	12/55		BN 1773-1776
704-709	GP9	252,000	21083-21088	4/56		BN 1777-1782
710, 711	GP9	252,000	21252, 21253	4/56		BN 1783, 1784
712	GP9	252,000	22480	4/57		BN 1785
713-722	GP9	252,000	22788-22797	4,6/57		BN 1786-1795
723, 724	GP9	252,000	24085, 24086	10, 11/57		BN 1796, 1797
725	GP9	252,000	24087	12/57		(BN 1798)
726, 727	GP9	252,000	24088, 24089	1, 2/58		BN 1799, 1800
728-732	GP9	252,000	24102-24106	4/58		BN 1801-1805
733-734	GP9M	252,000	25468, 25467	8/59		BN 1806, 1807
900-903	GP9M	240,000	24081-24084	2/58		BN 1350-1353
904-908	GP9M	240,000	25062-25066	3/59		BN 1354-1358
909-911	GP9M	240,000	25068-25070	4/59		BN 1359-1361
912, 913	GP9M	240,000	25060, 25061	2/59		BN 1362-1363
914, 915	GP9M	240,000	23067, 25071	4/59		BN 1364, 1365
2000-2011	GP20	255,000	25561-25572	4/60		BN 2000-2011
2012-2017	GP20	255,000	25700-25705	4, 5/60		BN 2012-2017
2018-2024	GP20	255,000	26286-26292	11/60		BN 2018-2024
2025-2034	GP20	255,000	26294-26303	12/60		BN 2025-2034
2035	GP20	255,000	26293	12/60		BN 2035
2500-2506	GE U25B	268,000	34962-34968	4/64		BN 5400-5406
2507, 2508	GE U25B	268,000	34984, 34985	4/64		BN 5407, 5408
2509-2523	GE U25B	268,000	35566-35580	4, 5/65		BN 5409-5423
2524-2529	U28B	274,000	35987-35992	6/66		BN 5460-5465
2530-2538	U33C	387,000	36776-36784	5-7/68		BN 5700-5708
2539-2544	U33C	384,000	37026-37031	4/69		BN 5709-5714
3000-3016	EMD GP30	261,000	28261-28277	4-5/63		BN 2200-2216
3017-3025	EMD GP35	260,000	28433-28441	3/64		BN 2500-2508
3026-3040	EMD GP35	260,000	30114-30128	7/65		BN 2509-2523
5100	AGEIR boxcab	212,000	66949/10078	9/26		
5101 1st	AGEIR NW	261,000	647	1/38		5300
5102 1st	AGEIR NW1	255,000	777	1/38		5301
5101, 02 2nd	AGEIR SW1	203,000	859, 860	2/39		75, 76
5103-5105	AGEIR SW1	203,000	1380-1382	9/41		77, 79
5200, 5201	GE 44 ton	89,000	12910, 12911	9/40		50, 51
5300	EMD NW	261,000	647	1/38	5101 1st	100
5301	EMD NW1	255,000	777	1/38	5102 1st	101
5302-5309	EMD NW2	251,000	861-868	2-5/39		102-109
5310, 5311	NW2	251,000	883, 884	5/39		110, 111
5312-5323	NW2	251,000	939-950	6-8/39		112-123
5324-5331	NW2	251,000	1370-1377	7-8/41		124-131
5332, 5333	BALD. VO1000	240,000	64211, 64212	10/41		132, 133
5334-5336	EMD NW2	251,000	1711-1713	8, 9/42		134-136
5337, 5338	BALD. VO1000	241,000	69785, 70109	11, 12/43		137, 138
5400, 5401	EMD NW3	214,000	869, 870	11/39		175, 176
5402-5404	EMD NW3	214,000	890-892	9/40, 4, 12/41		177-179
5405, 5406	EMD NW3	214,000	1719, 1720	3/42		180, 181
5600A, B	EMD FTA, FTB	233,000	1385, 1387	10/41		200A, B
5700A, B, 5701A, B	EMD FTA, FTB	233,000	1221A, B, 1222A, B	5, 6/40		250A, B, 251A, B
5900A, C	FTA	233,000	1383, 1384	10/41		300A, C 1st
5900B	FTB	233,000	1386	10/41		300B

BIBLIOGRAPHY

McDougall, J. L., *Canadian Pacific, A Brief History,* Montreal, McGill University, 1968.

Clark, Norman H., *Mill Town,* Seattle, University of Washington Press, 1970.

Martin, Charles F., *Locomotives of the Empire Builder,* Chicago, Norman House, 1972.

Hutchinson, Dr. Carey C., *Electrical Installation in Cascade Tunnel* New York, American Institute of Electrical Engineers, 1909.

Hult, Ruby L., *Northwest Disaster,* Portland, Binfords & Mort, 1960.

Abdill, George B., *This was Railroading,* Seattle, Superior Publishing Co., 1958.

Berton, Pierre, *The National Dream Vol. I,* Toronto/Montreal, McClelland and Stewart Ltd., 1971.

Berton, Pierre, *The Last Spike, Vol. II,* Toronto/Montreal, McClelland and Stewart, Ltd., 1971.

Robinson, Donald H., *Through the Years in Glacier National Park,* West Glacier, Montana, Glacier Natural History Association, 1960.

Monaghan, Jay, *The Book of the American West,* New York, Bonanza Books, 1963.

Riley, W. C., *The Great Northwest Illustrated 1890-91,* St. Paul, Brown Treacy & Co., 1898.

Orm, Robert & Case, *Victoria, The Story of The Cascades,* New York, Doubleday & Co., Inc., 1946.

Cook, Fred S., *The Fabulous Cascades,* Yakima, Washington, Franklin Press, 1963.

Freeman, Otis Dr. & Upton, Ronald H., *Washington State Resources,* Seattle, Washington State Resources Committee, 1957.

Blassingame, Wyatt, *American Expansion,* New York, Franklin Watts, Inc., 1965.

Wagner, Hol. F., *BN Motive Power Annual 1971,* Denver, Motive Power Services, 1971.

Haskell, Daniel C., *On Reconnaissance for the Great Northern, Letters of C.F.B. Haskell,* New York, New York Public Library, 1948.

Morrison, Samuel Eliot & Commanger Henry Steele, *Growth of the American Republic 1865 to 1937,* New York, Oxford University Press, 1940.

Sanford, Barrie, *McCulloch's Wonder,* West Vancouver, Canada, Whitecap Books Ltd., 1977.

Hearn, George & Wilkie, David, *The Cordwood Limited,* Victoria, Canada, British Columbia Railway Historical Assn., 1967.

Siemens, Alfred H. Ph.D., *Lower Fraser Valley,* Vancouver, Canada, Tomtalus Research Ltd., 1968.

Best, Gerald M., *Ships & Narrow Gauge Rails,* Berkeley, California, Howell-North, 1964.

Sale, Roger, *Seattle Past to Present,* Seattle, University of Washington Press, 1976.

Fahey, John, *Inland Empire,* Seattle, University of Washington Press, 1965.

Martin, Albro, *James J. Hill,* New York, Oxford Press, 1976.

Dorin, Patrick C., *The Lake Superior Iron Ore Railroads,* Seattle, Superior Publishing Company, 1968.

Attleck, E. L., *Sternwheelers Sandbars & Switchbacks,* Vancouver, Canada, The Alexander Nicolls Press, 1973.

Binns, Archie, *Northwest Gateway,* Portland, Binfords & Mort, 1941.

Bagley, C.B., *History of Seattle Vol. I & II,* Chicago, S.J. Clarke Publishing Co., 1916.

Locomotive Cyclopedia 1941, Milwaukee, Wisconsin, Kalmbach Publishing Co., 1971.

Brown, Dee, *Hear That Lonesome Whistle Blow,* New York, Holt Rinehart Winston, 1977.

Westcott, Linn H., *Steam Locomotives Cyclopedia Vol I,* Milwaukee, Wisconsin, Kalmbach Publishing Co., 1960.

Morgan, David P., *Steam's Finest Hour,* Milwaukee, Wisconsin, Kalmbach Publishing Co., 1959.

Farrington, Kip S., Jr., *Railroading From The Rear End,* New York, Howard McCann, Inc., 1946.

Dubin, Arthur D., *Some Classic Trains,* Milwaukee, Wisconsin, Kalmbach Publishing Co., 1964.

Farrell, Jack W., Pearsall, Mike, *The Northerns,* Edmonds, Washington, Pacific Fast Mail, 1975.

Knapke, William F., *The Railroad Caboose,* San Marino, California, Golden West Books, 1968.

Wood, Charles R. *Lines West,* Seattle, Superior Publishing Company, 1967.

Wood, Charles R., *The Northern Pacific,* Seattle, Superior Publishing Company, 1968.

Wood, Charles R. & Dorothy M., *Spokane Portland & Seattle,* Seattle, Superior Publishing Company, 1974.

ARTICLES & PAMPHLETS

The Great Canadian Railway Bluff, Montreal, Canadian Railway Historical Assn., May, 1977

Michell, Bruce, *By River, Trail & Rail, A Brief History of The First Century of Transportation in North Central Washington, 1181 to 1911,* Wenatchee Daily World, September, 1968.

Budd, Ralph, *Railway Routes Across the Rocky Mountains,* Civil Engineering, Feb., March & April, 1940.

Jones, W. B., *Silk Trains,* The Cascadian, April, 1961.

Blanchard, Leslie, F., *Electric Railroading on the Great Northern,* Puget Sound Railroader, September, 1959.

Mears, Col. Frederick M.A.M., SOC. C.E., *Conquering The Cascades,* Railway & Marine News, Seattle, 1929.

McLaughlin, D. W., *How Great Northern Conquered the Cascades,* Trains, Kalmbach Publishing Co., November, December, 1961.

Stevens, John Frank, Hidy, Ralph W. & Muriel E., Minnesota History, St. Paul, Minnesota Historical Society, Winter, 1969.

Air Brake and Train Handling Rules, St. Paul, Minnesota, Burlington Northern, 1972.

Examination for Promotion of Firemen to Engineers—Electrified Zone, GN Railway, 1951.

Locomotive Data, The Baldwin Locomotive Works, Philadelphia, 1921.

History of Great Northern Railway, Shipper & Carrier, New York, The Evans Brown Co., Inc., February, 1925.

Great Northern Railway Company et al, Interstate Commerce Commission Reports, Validation Docket No. 327, U.S. G.P.O. 1927, Washington.

General Electric Locomotive 1-C + C-1 Instructions, GE 1-1897, G.E. Company, 1929, Schenectady.

Westinghouse Electric Locomotive, Engineman's Instruction Book, GN Railway, 1927.

List of Equipment, GN Railway, 1942, 1950, 1965.

Consolidated Code of Operation Rules & General Insturctions, GN Railway, 1945, 1967.

Statistics of Railways in the United States 1902, Interstate Commerce Commission. U.S. G.P.O. 1903, Washington, D.C.

GN Timetables 1893, 1913, 1916, 1930, 1941, 1947, 1950, 1964, 1967, 1970.

GN Locomotive Diagrams, St. Paul, Minnesota, 1930, 1941, 1952.

Fraternal Order of Empire Builders, Reference Sheets, various numbers, 1976, 1977, 1978.

GN Railway Assignment of Locos 1936, 1940, 1942, 1949, 1954.

GN Annual Reports 1956, 1957, 1964.

Burlington Northern News, various issues.

Baldwin Locomotives, Pacific Railway Journal, Summer, 1956.

Great Northern Goat, 1926 through 1967, St. Paul.

Railway Age Gazette & Railway Age, July 31, 1914, Dec. 14, 1917, Oct. 13, 1893, Jan. 6, 1894, April 17, 1914, May 31, 1924, April 17, 1947, Dec. 1914, Feb. 20, 1932, Nov. 14, 1931, Jan. 13, 1911, Aug., 1927, Nov. 11, 1904.

Engineering News, June 4, 1914.

NEWSPAPERS AND MAGAZINES

Seattle Times
Seattle Post Intelligencer
Havre Daily News
Hungry Horse News
Minneapolis Star Bulletin
Tacoma News Tribune
Wenatchee Daily World
Spokesman Review, Spokane
Everett Herald

Portland Oregonian
Vancouver Sun
Vancouver Province
Vancouver Times
Railroad
Railfan
Railroad Model Craftsman
Model Railroader
Trains

INDEX TO THE TEXT

A. Guthrie & Company **138, 139**
Alaska Limited **292**
Alaska-Yukon-Pacific Exposition **293-294**
ALCO F12 **377**; E-2 and H-1 **378**; Z-6 **383**; Century Series **471**
American Car & Foundry **293, 304**
American Standard 4-4-0 class B **376**
Apgar **77, 80, 81**
Apgar, Milo P. **77**
Assiniboine Line **74**
Atlantic 4-4-2 class K-1 **378, 379**
Baldwin Locomotive Works **378, 380, 381**
Barney & Smith **293**
Beckler, E. H. **74, 76, 131, 133, 252**
Bellingham Bay Railroad and Navigation **257**
Belpaire boiler **377**
Belton **77-78**
Bennett, Nelson **257-258**
Berne **138, 139**
Big Bend **131**
Blackfeet **75, 77, 83**
Bonners Ferry **130**
Brooks Locomotive Works **376, 377, 378**
Budd - Dome cars and coaches **304**
Budd, John M. **301, 484**
Burke, Thomas **255, 256, 257**
Butler, William C. **254**
Butte Division **383**
Canadian National **261**
Canadian Northern **258, 261**
Canadian Pacific Railway **258, 259-260**
Canfield, Senator Eugene **257**
Carver, Jonathan **14**
Cascades - Electrification **134, 137-138, 139-140, 298, 383**; Geology **132**; Locomotives **305, 383-384, 472, 140**
Cascade Tunnel 1900 **133-134**; photo **162**
Cascade Tunnel 1929 **138-139, 298**; Map **140-141**; Ventilation **140, 472**
Cascadian - Timetable **235**
Challenger 4-6-6-4 class Z **383**
Chicago, Burlington & Quincy Zephyr **299, 469-470**
Chumstick Line **139, 298**; Map **140-141**
Clough, David M. **253**
Coast Line **257-258**
Coast to Kootenay Line **259-260**

Colby, Charles L. **253**
Coleman, James M. **255**
Columbia & Puget Sound Railroad **255**
Columbia River **130-131-132**
Consolidation 2-8-0 class F **133, 377**
Coquihalla Pass **260**
Corbin, Daniel Chase **259, 260**
Coulee City **131**
Dakota Division **383**
Dearborn Line **74**
Demersville **75-76**
Denny, Arthur A. **254**
Doodlebugs - gas electrics **468**
Eastern Minnesota Railway **52**
Electric locomotives **140, 305, 383, 472**
Electro Motive Corporation (EMD) **468-469, 470, 471**
Empire Builder 1929 **295, 298-299**
Empire Builder 1947 - Car names and interior decor **303**; Color and design **302**; Consist and schedule **300**; Power and press debut **301**
Empire Builder 1951 - Color scheme **305**; Equipment **303-304**; Power **304-305**
E-7-A **301, 304-305, 469-470**
Essex **80**
Everett **252-254**
Everett Land Co. **253**
Fairhaven & Southern Railroad **252, 257**
Falls of St. Anthony **14, 15, 16**
Farley, Jesse P. **18-19, 20, 22**
Fast Mail **295**
Father Hennepin **14**
First Division of the St. Paul and Pacific - Charter **18**; Map **30**; Time card **28**
Fisher River **75**
Flathead River - Construction over **76, 78**; Flood **123**
Flathead Tunnel - Map **532**; Ventilation **472**
Flathead Valley **75**
Fort Snelling **14, 15**
Fraser River Toll Bridge **259**
FT road diesel **384, 468-469**
F-3, F-5, F-7 **305, 470**
G.E. (diesels) **468, 471**
General Purpose Locomotive - GP-7, GP-9 **470**; GP-30, GP-35 **470-471**
Glacier Park - Accomodations and road building **80-81**; Creation of

Park by Congress **79**; Geology **78-79, 84**; Going-to-the-Sun Highway **84**; Placement of bells **82-83**; Pres. Hoover Summer White House **83**; Renaming stations and hamlets **83**
Glacier Park Hotel Company **82, 84-85**
Glacier Park Limited **294, 298**
Going-to-the-Sun Highway **84**
Great Lakes **23-24, 24-25**
Great Northern Railway - Color schemes: Diesels **472, 473**; Empire Builder **302-303, 305**; Steam **384**
Great Northern Railway - Glacier Park: Construction of roads and accomodations **80**; Glacier Park Hotel Company **82, 84-85**; Proposal to serve **78**; Promotion **82-83**; Trains **83-84**
Great Northern Railway - King Street Station and Tunnel **257**; Lines in Minn. map **64**; Marias Pass **77**; Pacific Jct. **74**; Shops **384**; Vancouver BC Station and Grandview Cut **261**
Great Northern Steamship Co. **292-293**
Grinnell, George Bird **77**; photo **90**
Haskell, C. F. B. **74, 75, 76, 130-131**
Haskell Pass **75**
Hewitt, Henry **253**
Hill, James J. - Arrival in St. Paul **14**; Early employment **19**; Everett Land Co. **253**; Manitoba **23**; SP&P **21-22**; Seattle **256-257**; V.V.&E. **258**
Hill, Louis W. **80, 82, 84, 260-261**; photo **99**
Howe, Charles **77**
Hoyt, Colgate **253**
Hudson's Bay Co. **16**
Internationals **261, 302**
Kalispell **75-76, 79-80**
Kalispell Division **383, 384**
Kennedy, John S. **20, 21, 22**
Kettle River Valley Railway Company **260**
Kittson, Norman **19, 20**
Klamath Division **384**
Kootenai Falls **76**
Kootenai River **75-76**
Lake Chelan **281**
Lake McDonald **77, 78**
Lake Shore & Eastern Railway Company **255**

Leavenworth **132, 135, 137**
Lewis Overthrust **79, 84**
Lima Locomotive Works **378**
Litchfields **18, 21, 23**
Logan, Major William R. **80**
Louisiana Purchase **16**
MacKenzie, William **258**
Mallet 2-6-6-2 class L **378, 379, 380**
Mallet 2-6-8-0 class M **379, 380**
Mallet 2-8-8-0 class N **380-381**
Mallet 2-8-8-2 class R **382**
Marias Pass **74-75, 76**
Martin Creek **132, 139**; Map **196-197**
McDonald, Duncan **77**
Mastodon 4-8-0 class G **133, 376-377**
McGilvra, Judge **255**
Mesabi Iron Range **56, 377, 383**
Miike Maru **292**
Mikado 2-8-2 class O **379, 380**
Mill Creek **138**
Milwaukee Road Hiawatha **299**
Minneapolis **15**
Minneapolis and St. Cloud Railroad
  Company **24, 25**
Minnesota **15-16, 17**; Map of
  GN lines **64**
Mississippi River **14**
Mogul 2-6-0 class D **133, 376**
Montana Central Railway
  Company **24, 74**
Moses Coulee **132**
Mountain 4-8-2 class P **381-382, 384**
Nason Creek **131, 132**
National Park Service **81, 85**
New Westminster and Southern
  Railway **257-258, 259**
Northern 4-8-4 class S **382-383**
Northern Pacific - Canada **23**;
  Cascades **133**; Columbia River
  Gorge **132**; North Coast Limited
  293, 299; Puget Sound **254, 255,
  256**; SP&P **18-19, 23**;
  Yellowstone **78**
Northern Steamship Company
  24-25, 52
NW-3, NW-5 **470**
NYK Line **292-293**
O'Neill, James H. **135**
Oregonian **293**
Oriental Limited 1905 **292-293**;
  1924 **294, 295, 299, 303**
Pacific 4-6-2 class H **378**
Pacific Coast Railroad **257**
Pacific Junction **74, 76**

Pembina Branch **22, 23**
Pembina House **16**
Pend Oreille River **130**
Prairie 2-6-2 class J **378-379**
Portland **252**
Puget Sound **252**
Puget Sound Shore Railroad **255**
Pullman Co. **293, 294, 300, 302, 304**
Pyle, Ernie **83**
Radial stay boiler **382**
Ravaili **76**
Red River Valley Exploration and
  settlement **16**; Ox carts **16-17**
Renton **255**
Rockefeller, John D. **253**
Rogers Locomotive Works **376,
  377, 378**
Russell, Charles M. **77**
St. Paul—Pig's Eye Landing **15**
St. Paul and Pacific Railroad -
  Charter **18**; Dutch bondholders **20**;
  Extend-lines **22-23**; Foreclosure **23**;
  Partnership of Hill and associates
  20; Purchase **22**; Receivership **19**
St. Paul, Minneapolis and Manitoba -
  Formation **23**; Land sales and
  extension west **24**; Map **34-35; 376**
Santa Fe 2-10-2 class Q **381**
Scenic **134, 135, 136**
Schultz, James Willard **77, 83**
SD-7, SD-9 **470**
SD-45, F-45 cowl units **471**
SDP-40, SDP-45 **471**
Seattle **252, 254, 255, 256, 292, 294**
Seattle and Montana Railway
  257-258
Seattle & Walla Walla Railroad **255**
Silk Trains **294, 300, 381-382, 453**
Similkameen Valley **259-260**
Skykomish **134, 137-138, 305**
Skykomish River **132**
Smith, Donald A. **20, 22**
Snohomish River **132**
Snowsheds **136, 137**
Synder, George **78**
Soap Lake **131**
Sperry, Dr. Lyman B. **77, 78**
Spokane - Spokane Falls **130**
Spokane Coeur d'Alene & Palouse
  138, 276
Spokane Falls and Northern **130, 259**
Spokane International Railway **210**
Spokane, Portland & Seattle/Oregon
  Trunk **288, 293, 302, 303, 378,
  383, 471**

Spokane River **131**
Stephen, George **20, 21, 22**
Stevens, Isaac **254**
Stevens, John F. **74, 75, 131, 133,
  138, 258**; Photo **86**
Stevens Pass **131**
Stimson, Henry L. **77**
Strandrud Family Album **188**
Surrey Cut-off **24, 383**
Switchbacks **133, 136**; Photos
  152-153, 158-159
Switchers - diesel **468**
Tacoma **252, 254, 301**
Ten Wheelers 4-6-0 class E **377-378**
Tobacco River **75-76**
Tumwater Canyon **133, 139**
Twelve Wheelers (Mastodon)
  133, 376-377
Tye River **132**
Union Pacific City of Portland **299**
Vancouver, Victoria and Eastern
  Railway & Navigation Co. **258**
Vancouver, Westminster & Yukon
  Railway **259**
VanOrsdale, Lt. John T. **76-77**
Victoria and Sidney **259**
Victoria Terminal Railway & Ferry
  Company **259**
Villard, Henry **255**
Warren, James John **260**
Washington Great Northern
  Railway **130, 258**
Waterton Lakes Park **78**
Waterville **130-131**
Wellington **132, 133**
Wellington Disaster **134-136, 181-182**
Wenatchee **137, 305**
Wenatchee/Orville Branch **260, 280**
Wenatchee River **131-132, 139**
Western Star **304**
Weyerhaeuser, Frederich **253**
William Crooks **18**; Photo **31**
Windy Point **135, 137**
Winnipeg Limited **530-531**
World War II **300**

MOTIVE POWER PHOTOGRAPHS

STEAM:
0-4-0 No. 192 **39**

0-6-0 No. 32 **188**; No. 71 **421**; No. 6 **421**; No. 1 **422**; No. 16 **422**; No. 98 **423**; No. 30 **423**

0-8-0 No. 837 **68**; No. 829 **424**; No. 850 **424**; No. 896 **424**

2-6-0 No. 204 **52**; No. 351 **391**; No. 453 **391**; No. 419 **391**

2-8-0 No. 511 **394, 395**; No. 1130 **396**; No. 1138 **396**; No. 1195 **396**; No. 1192 **397**; No. 1326 **397**; No. 1327 **397**

2-6-8-0 No. 2000 **430, 59** No. 1978 **56**; No. 1951 **431**; No. 1972 **431**; No. 1973 **433**; No. 1984 **433**

2-8-8-0 No. 2013 **59**; No. 2020 **444**; No. 2019 **447**; No. 2002 **447**; No. 2009 **447**

2-6-2 No. 1531 **416**

2-8-2 No. 3100 **59**; No. 3077 **289**; No. 3108 **435**; No. 3086 **435**; No. 3002 **435**; No. 3104 **436**; No. 3035 **436**; No. 3149 **436**; No. 3205 **439**; No. 3201 **439**; No. 3207 **439**; No. 3306 **440**; No. 3254 **440**; No. 3368 **440**; No. 3355 **441**; No. 3393 **442**; No. 3399 **442**; No. 3391 **442**

2-10-2 No. 1754 **448**; No. 2182 **448** No. 2179 **448**; No. 2118 **450**; No. 2115 **450**

2-6-6-2 No. 1909 **174, 175, 426, 427, 428, 430**; No. 1964 **177**

2-8-8-2 No. 2032 **462**; No. 2031 **463**

4-4-0 No. 1 **29, 31**; No. 127 **51**; No. 101 **52**; No. 113 **71**; No. 207 **385**; No. 103 **385**; No. 204 **386**; No. 125 **386**; No. 185 **386**; No. 290 **386**; No. 192 **386**; No. 226 **388**

4-4-2 No. 1705 **322, 420**; No. 1702 **420**

4-6-0 No. 903 **399**; No. 907 **399**; No. 904 **399**; No. 926 **401**; No. 936 **401**; No. 925 **401**; No. 965 **403**; No. 954 **403**; No. 1070 **403**; No. 1055 **404**; No. 1054 **404**; No. 1053 **404**; No. 910 **406**; No. 911 **406**; No. 948 **406**; No. 970 **407**; No. 971 **407**; No. 1001 **407**; No. 1010 **408**; No. 1076 **409**; No. 1089 **409**; No. 1082 **409**

4-8-0 No. 609 **392**; No. 768 **392**; No. 722 **392, 393**

4-6-2 No. 1443 **412, 306**; No. 1423 **339**; No. 1404 **411**; No. 1413 **411**; No. 1408 **411**; No. 1450 **414**; No. 1490 **414**; No. 1364 **415**; No. 1361 **415**; No. 1379 **418**; No. 1375 **419**

4-8-2 No. 2505 **320**; No. 2517 **324, 453**; No. 2515 **336**; No. 2510 **343**; No. 2501 **344**; No. 2521 **454**; No. 2519 **455**; No. 2524 **457**

4-8-4 No. 2551 **459**; No. 2555 **459**; No. 2576 **460**; No. 2585 **461**; No. 2581 **337, 461**; No. 2588 **113, 343**

4-6-6-4 No. 4000 **465**;

GE No. 2 (steam-turbine-electric) **474**

Electrics:
Spokane Coeur d'Alene & Palouse Passenger Motors—No. 20 **276, 279**; No. 43 **278**; No. 60 **279**; Freight Motors—No. 606 **277**; No. 502 **278**; No. 503 **278**

B-B (1909 Motors) **165, 166**; Class Y **215, 217, 225, 228, 237-243, 245** Class Z **222, 229, 234, 236**; Class W **242, 245**

Diesels
Early types: No. 5100 Ingersoll Rand **474**; No. 5300 GMC **476**; No. 5332 Baldwin VO-1000 **477**; SW-8 **477**; SW-4 **483**; FT **475**; F-3, F-7, F-9, P-3, P-5, P-7 **480, 490, 492, 493, 498, 510, 519, 526**; F-3 **479**; F-7 **485, 493**; FA **503**; NW-5 **480**; NW-3 **482**; RS-1 **483**; RS-3 **495**; RS-4 **500**; ALCO S-2 **486**; E-7 **494, 496, 497, 530**; SD-7 **508**; SD-9 **508**; GP-7 **504, 508**; GP-9 **504, 507**; GP-30 **510**; GP-35 **516**; GP-20 **529**; SD-45 **512, 513**; SD-40 **538**; SDP-40 **515, 527**; U-25B **516**; U-28B **517**; U-33C **529, 536**

Gas-Electrics
No. 2532 **479**; No. 2300 **479**

RDC
No. 2350 **518**